M000286214

Yes, you may feel unqualified, undereducated, under-gifted, or even unworthy. Yet ... those are excellent qualifications for God to do a mighty work. This story is a perfect example! It demonstrates how amazing things can happen as a result of sincere faith and obedience.

Charles R. Swindoll
Evangelical Christian pastor, author, educator and radio preacher

When God has a job that needs to be done, how does He go about getting it accomplished? From one end of the world to the other, God called a single divorced mother to trust Him and follow. What a journey! Who would believe it? From California to Kenya, Darla Calhoun said yes…and she went. This is a wonderful love story of a Mama's heart for one little street boy after another. Equipped with a huge God-given gift of compassion, this amazing ministry exploded from caring for a few lost boys to the point where now we know that through Agape Children's Ministry, the population of street children in Kisimu, Kenya has been significantly reduced.

Dr. David Seifert
Pastor Emeritus, Shelter Cove Community Church

Agape's Children is a wonderful story of how God calls Darla Calhoun to begin a journey of changing the lives of hundreds of street boys in Kenya, Africa. These forgotten and abandoned children discover trust, hope, and security through the Agape Ministry. It's a remarkable insight into the life of a missionary.

Bob Phillips, Ph.D.
Licensed family counselor and author of over 130 books
Former Executive Director for Hume Lake Christian Camps and co-founder of the Pointman Leadership Institute

Witnessing Kisumu's street children compassionately care for an abandoned puppy stirred and challenged the author to provide such children with similar care. You too will be stirred and challenged as you read the gripping stories of boys who, without hope or purpose, have had their lives turned around by the transforming power of compassion. You will gain valuable insights into the foundation and pillars of Agape, a biblical ministry model that all are called to emulate.

Phyllis Kilbourn, Ph.D.
Founder, Crisis Care Training International

After having lived a fair number of years, I have a small and very exclusive hall of heroes. Darla Calhoun may be at the head of this exemplary group. There are so many people who can see that something needs to be done, but precious few who have the courage to actually say, "Lord, send me." Thousands of children owe the quality of their existence to Darla's humble obedience. I have never seen any indication that she was looking for praise or applause as she reached out to throngs of street children in Africa to feed, house, educate, and, when possible, reunite them with their families. Darla doesn't think in those terms. She thinks simply, "What would be best for the children?" Then she does it! I've met well-known people who are worthy of note, but none of them quite like Darla. Come and read one story after another that will make you smile, make you believe, and break your heart in a good way.

Gary Richmond
Best-selling author and speaker
Director of Gary Richmond Ministries

I am so blessed because of your missionary work in Kenya ... you forsook so much to come and serve in Kenya and become a vessel that God would use to turn around not only the lives of street children, but also families hundreds of miles away from Kisumu. You will never know the impact and the reach until we are able to see the bigger picture in heaven!

Nicholas Nzivo
Former employee of Agape

AGAPE'S
CHILDREN

To Brayden —

Blessings to you!

Darla Calhoun

II Cor. 9:15

AGAPE'S
CHILDREN

Freed from the Streets

DARLA CALHOUN

with DONNA SUNDBLAD

Visit Darla's website: www.agapechildren.org

Agape's Children – Darla Calhoun

Copyright © 2016

First edition published 2016

All rights reserved. No part of this book may be reproduced, stored in a retrieval system, or transmitted in any form or by any means – electronic, mechanical, photocopying, recording, or otherwise, without written permission from the publisher.

Scriptures taken from the Holy Bible, New International Version®, NIV®. Copyright © 1973, 1978, 1984, 2011 by Biblica, Inc.™ Used by permission of Zondervan. All rights reserved worldwide. www.zondervan.com The "NIV" and "New International Version" are trademarks registered in the United States Patent and Trademark Office by Biblica, Inc.™

Cover Design: Natalia Hawthorne, BookCoverLabs.com

eBook Icon: Icons Vector/Shutterstock

Editors: Heather Thomas and Ruth Zetek

Printed in the United States of America

Aneko Press – *Our Readers Matter*™

www.anekopress.com

Aneko Press, Life Sentence Publishing, and our logos are trademarks of

Life Sentence Publishing, Inc.
203 E. Birch Street
P.O. Box 652
Abbotsford, WI 54405

BIOGRAPHY & AUTOBIOGRAPHY / Religious

Paperback ISBN: 978-1-62245-321-4

eBook ISBN: 978-1-62245-322-1

10 9 8 7 6 5 4 3 2 1

Available where books are sold

Share this book on Facebook:

I dedicate this to Paul Calhoun, my life partner and best friend, without whose persistent encouragement this book would never have made it to press, and also to the children throughout the world who still wait to be freed from the streets.

The stories in this book are true, though in most cases, the names of the children have been changed for their privacy and protection.

Contents

Foreword

God's Preparation for My Missionary Journey

As I walked down the sidewalk, two street boys summoned me. "Mama, Mama, come quick. Mwangi is asleep, and we can't wake him up!"

A few steps away, a young teenage boy lay motionless under a mango tree. Concern etched the boys' young faces. I knelt down beside his lifeless form and touched his cold forehead. A shudder rippled through my body. *No pulse. No sign of breath. This child is dead!*

The street boys explained that Mwangi had suffered from stomach pain earlier.

"Maybe he ate some bad food," they said.

In addition to my horror, anger welled up inside me. *How could one so young suffer and die alone? How could children be so ignored and abandoned? How could people walk past them with deaf ears and blind eyes? Why wasn't someone dealing with this issue? Why didn't they care?* It all seemed so wrong.

Those questions were suddenly replaced by God's voice. He asked *me* to be the one to *do something.* The Lord used all the experiences of my life to prepare me for this very moment.

During World War II, my father served as a marine in the Solomon

Islands. I was two years old when he came home on leave just before Christmas. He brought me a wooden pull toy with a little black boy in a red striped shirt who stood on top of a yellow wagon. As the wheels rotated, the little black boy moved up and down along with some colorful flowers. Apparently, that was my favorite toy, because I still have it.

In 1950, my grandmother took me shopping. We spotted a beautiful baby doll on a shelf at the five-and-dime department store. In her pretty yellow organza dress with brown polka dots, this little doll also happened to be black, and I still have her. The Lord prepared me to work in Africa even at that tender age.

A highlight of my adult life includes time I traveled with the African Children's Choir when my boys were grown. When the choir first arrived from war-torn Uganda, they were understandably ill at ease in our culture and they carried a lot of baggage.

They had very few earthly possessions, but plenty of emotional baggage. They lived through the horrific experience of civil war in their home country. However, during the sixteen months we spent together, I watched God transform their lives. I looked forward to the start of each day. Every morning I received twenty-six good-morning hugs. Those children were precious to me, and I truly grieved when our tour ended.

I believe all my experiences were foundation stones for the work God called me to do with Kenyan street children. Amy Grant's beautiful rendition of "Through My Father's Eyes" took on special meaning when I met those ragged, dirty little boys. Their hands, often infected with scabies, reached out for some simple human contact. In reality, they were shunned like lepers. But God granted me the grace to see past their outward appearance and accept them just as they were.

On one occasion, I packed up some authentic street-boy clothes to bring home in order to show others the reality of their desperate condition. An older Agape boy named Evans stared at me with wide-eyed alarm when he saw me put the clothes in a plastic bag.

He leaned in and in a confidential tone asked, "Mama, aren't you afraid of the little animals?"

That caught me by surprise, until I realized he meant the lice. Street-boy clothes are commonly infested with tiny *visitas*, which the children also referred to as lice.

I reassured Evans. "I've carefully sprayed them with Doom" – a fitting name for the local insect and mosquito repellent. Then I brought them home and put the clothes in an empty freezer just to make sure the visitors were goners.

I had a lot to learn when I first moved to Kenya. I tried my best to pick up the tribal language called *Dholuo*, so I could go out to the village and be understood. One of the first times I tried out my vocabulary, I walked down a dirt path and came to a village school. I encountered children dressed in their school uniforms as they played on the playground. I approached the sea of purple-and-white gingham shirts with a sense of excitement mingled with nerves.

A few children near the fence saw me and called out, "Muzungu, muzungu!" (White person, white person) I smiled and waved.

The commotion brought others running to see the oddity. A handful of them screamed with fear. Some had never seen a white person before.

I tried my best to calm them by saying the words "An Dala."

The Kenyans find it difficult to pronounce "R" and "L" together because they don't use that combination of letters in their language. So I had become used to people calling me Dala instead of Darla. At that point, I thought I was simply saying, "I'm Darla."

A teacher hurried out to see what caused the uproar.

I repeated my intro, "An Dala."

She replied in English, "Yes, yes, you are welcome, but what is your name?"

It took me a moment to put the pieces together. Then it dawned on me. She thought I was saying, "I'm home," because the word for home is *dala*. So there I was, scaring those village school children to death. And on top of that, I was announcing, "I'm home!" How embarrassing.

This book tells the story of what happened after I'd been in Kenya long enough to adjust to my new environment a little bit. I hope you are blessed by reading what the Lord accomplished over the last twenty-four years of ongoing ministry. I also hope these stories will stir you to do what you can for at-risk children in your own neighborhoods. Perhaps, as the Lord lays it on your heart, you might even consider supporting Agape Children's Ministry as we branch out into other cities to share God's love with more and more needy street children.

Acknowledgements

Heartfelt thanks go to all of the churches, organizations, groups, foundations, and individuals who have so generously and faithfully supported Agape with their prayers and their finances for all these years. The stories in this book could only happen because they were willing to respond to God's prompting in their hearts to give to Agape. The Lord has used and continues to use their contributions to accomplish His purposes in the lives of thousands of street children in Kenya. Though their names are held in confidentiality, God knows them well.

However, I must acknowledge the Rotary Club International, Dr. David Gallagher, and the Local Kisumu Rotary Club for the enormous blessing they have been in providing funds for our Agape campus. We would still be struggling if it weren't for their provision of many of our basic needs. Agape would never have been able to even take the first baby steps without the foresight and faith that the Lions Club Kisumu and the Lions Club/Hayer Family demonstrated by building the first buildings on campus. In addition, Team with a Mission brought a team with all the tools and supplies necessary to build our second dorm. A number of other teams that helped complete the construction were indispensable. We are forever grateful.

Several people encouraged me to write this book, with my husband Paul leading the charge. We normally juggle a busy schedule, and Paul made sure I set aside enough time to write. When papers were scattered all over the table he organized the stories and created a timeline of events.

Perhaps you can tell that writing a book wasn't something I aspired to do. I admit it was never on my bucket list, though I can't say the idea never crossed my mind. But that's all it was … an unrealized idea, until Jeremiah Zeiset, the Director of Acquisitions for Aneko Press contacted our Modesto office saying he'd seen our website and read some of our newsletters. He said, "Surely, there must be a book here." That started the ball rolling, and with his kind advice and counsel, the book you are holding materialized.

I first met my co-author in Calhoun, Georgia. That seemed appropriate enough. While in the process of making my travel arrangements, I received a phone call from the LaQuinta Motel asking for my room preference. That had never happened before! The woman calling introduced herself as Darla from Calhoun and wanted to meet me, Darla Calhoun, when I arrived. Was this mere coincidence? I don't think so. The Lord used such subtle confirmations to lead me during those tentative first steps. I believe them to be what Squire Rushnell calls a "God Wink."

Special thanks to my co-author, Donna Sundblad and her family for their warm hospitality. I am grateful to have had Donna's expert advice regarding the rules of writing, and so appreciated her patience when I changed whole paragraphs. In addition, I had her undaunted support for nearly a year.

The next step was editing and proofreading. It was exciting to get to that point, but I'm sure this can be a tedious task at best. Heather Thomas the editor, and Ruth Zetek the proofreader did it joyfully and thoroughly, for which we can all be very thankful.

Angie Holcomb added the finishing touches as the layout and eBook formatter. Good books don't just happen. As you can see, it took "a village" to bring this one together. Angie has done an amazing job. I know this because I saw the manuscript before and after she worked on it.

Kudos to Natalia Hawthorne for her masterful job creating the cover. I appreciate how she chose to use the colors of the Kenyan flag. That means a lot to the people for whom this book is written. Then she found the photo of this precious little Kenyan boy who won our hearts at first glance.

All of these people are incredibly talented, but what is really special is their hearts. They love the Lord and the work they do in making His glory known through books. Blessings to you all!

Introduction

Being confident of this, that he who began a good work in you will carry it on to completion until the day of Christ Jesus. (Philippians 1:6)

In the early '90s, Darla worked as a camp nurse in the infirmary at Hume Lake Christian Camps during the summer.

Dr. Mark Harmeling, an orthopedist who volunteered there asked, "What do you plan to do with the rest of your life?"

His question caught her off guard. She had to admit she didn't have a good answer.

"Have you heard of Mission: Moving Mountains?" he asked.

She hadn't.

"They are holding a fundraising event. Would you consider attending as the guest of my wife and myself?"

She agreed. She accompanied them with an expectation to learn and hear about the organization. It turned out to be more of an interview. Because she'd been to Uganda and worked with African children, they wanted to know if she might be interested in filling in as a team member doing community development in Kisumu, Kenya. With her experience as a nurse, her role would be to teach preventative healthcare in a village environment.

For Darla, that interview can be compared to a step of faith onto a skateboard straight to Kenya. People at Hume Lake really supported her as she pursued the opportunity. Within about nine months' time, the Lord provided the outgoing expenses for her trip from a variety of sources.

Before she fully committed, however, she had a serious talk with her boys. "I really need to know the truth. How do you feel about my being gone for three to five years?"

She had to ask herself the same question. Mission: Moving Mountains wanted a commitment of up to five years with a visit home allowed only after three years. Two of her boys already lived on their own.

Her youngest, Lance, said, "Mom, you've been here for us all these years. Now, if those people need you, and God wants you to go, you need to go. I really mean it. And we'll be proud of you."

Darla says Lance's answer made her love him even more – if that were possible. With her children's blessing, she agreed to go.

Upon arriving in Kenya, she was given six months to learn the language of the Luo people. She followed the advice from language helpers and tried to use her new vocabulary words in town. When she talked to the street children, they laughed.

She says, "We became friends and that's how it started."

The children ran to greet her every time she went to town.

Later, a friend said to her, "Darla, if you're not careful, you're going to have an organization here."

At that point, she hadn't even given the idea a thought.

Within the pages of this book, Darla shares her personal story to show how God is the real founder of Agape. "I just had a part to play and will always count it a tremendous privilege to be part of such a wonderful ministry."

Today she is thankful for each person God brought to Agape. She is also thankful for all the people who prayed for and supported Agape over the years. This includes the boys, staff, missionaries, administrators, and financial supporters.

It's the Lord who kept this ministry growing, through people who cared enough to pray and show their support through time and finances.

She gives God all the glory for Agape and admits, "It's evident Agape is His ministry and every aspect is in His hands. I'm so blessed to be a part of what God is doing in Kenya."

No other ministry in Kenya does exactly what Agape does. It's the most amazing group of adults – Kenyans and missionaries – who go way beyond what most people would do. Agape isn't a children's home, but rather a place of safety and care with the goal of reintegrating as many children as possible back with their family members. At the time of the writing of this book, Agape has helped more than two thousand children. They've had a 70-percent success rate of boys and 80-percent of girls remaining home after three years of being reintegrated with their families. This is made possible because of so many follow-up visits. For example, in 2015 our staff made 10,500 visits. Quite amazing!

This leads to the question of why Kenya? The short answer is that God orchestrated events to place her there. Darla just smiles and says, "I thought I was going to Kenya to teach preventative healthcare in a rural village as part of a team needing a nurse. But God had other plans."

> *"For my thoughts are not your thoughts, neither are your ways my ways," declares the* LORD. *"As the heavens are higher than the earth, so are my ways higher than your ways."* (Isaiah 55:8-9)

"As I met with street boys and saw firsthand how they were chased around town like little stray dogs, I did some deep soul searching. I knew God didn't intend for children to live that way. It broke my heart to watch."

At one point, Darla prayed, "Lord, if you'd just help me get a few boys off the street, I'd be the happiest missionary you've ever had."

While it seems like a clear-cut choice on this end of things, to change direction once she was already in Kenya was a very difficult decision to make. Friends and relatives prayed for Darla. Some even wondered if she'd had too much African sun to even think of going out on her own. But God made it clear. He wanted her to reach out to neglected and abandoned children. They needed to know they had a heavenly Father who loved and cared for them. Darla saw them as an unreached people group. But not everyone did.

During a luncheon with the former president of her mission, a surprising exchange occurred. This gentleman sat across the table and pointed his finger at her as he exclaimed, "Someday, you'll ask my forgiveness for this. We are very disappointed in you leaving this mission after all the preparation we've made."

"I'm so sorry you feel that way," she humbly replied. "But I can't ask your forgiveness for something the Lord is asking me to do." That difficult moment demonstrates some of the struggle she endured in getting Agape started.

She says, "I could only take the risk if I knew God was in my corner – or should I say that I was in *God's* corner, following His will. In Scripture, I read, *No branch standing by itself can bear fruit* (John 15:4 Darla's paraphrase). I read this over and over, and I'm grateful not to be alone."

God always honors our obedience. Whether you pray for Agape, support us financially, or help in some other way, everyone associated with Agape thanks you. In fact, we also pray for you. The prayers of these boys and girls are fervent and sincere and must make the angels rejoice. Please know we appreciate your sacrifice of time and energy. Thank you and may the Lord richly bless you for blessing Agape.

– Donna Sundblad, Coauthor

CHAPTER 1

He Knows My Name

"For I know the plans I have for you," declares the LORD. (Jeremiah 29:11a)

After months of planning for the big move to Kenya, I was happy to be settled into my new home in Kisumu. It was May of 1992. To say my move involved a big adjustment would be an understatement. Along with getting used to my new surroundings, I experienced full-blown culture shock. I'd definitely have preferred to skip this part. As I watched the colorful sunset over Lake Victoria, my emotions surfaced. I thought of my family and friends back home and wished I could share the beautiful sight with them. I felt so lonely. In other words, I was home-sick. If I'd had a phone handy and it didn't cost four dollars per minute to call the U.S., several phones in America would have been jingling.

The trip to Kenya itself was a bit grueling. It took eleven hours to reach London from Los Angeles, then a six-hour layover, followed by another eight hours to reach the capital city of Nairobi. My traveling companion and I were tired puppies by that point, and with the eleven-hour time difference, my body rebelled. That first night, we bedded down in a guesthouse for a short night's rest. Early the following morning, they served a satisfying breakfast with some strong coffee. That was exactly what I needed.

Then our host family met us in a flurry of excitement. Finally, we climbed into the Isuzu Trooper, and with four other adults and two children, we headed for Kisumu. On that leg of the trip, I discovered what an incredible ability missionaries have to utilize the space they have available. In addition to the passengers, they fit luggage in, on, and around the vehicle. In all, they transported eight heavy footlockers standing on end, tied together, and on top of the Trooper. With all the other baggage inside, we still had room for our feet and made the five-hour trip in good spirits.

On the way, we stopped at an unusual Mexican restaurant called Gringos. My taste buds were challenged to adjust. The seasonings were different than anything I'd ever tasted. Plus, of course, the culture was different. For instance, I asked for sour cream and they brought me a little dish of exactly that – spoiled curdled milk – not what I had in mind. Ugh!

The lush, green, African countryside surprised me somewhat. I imagined things more dry and brown, but we arrived during the rainy season. The landscape enjoyed plenty of rain that time of year. Impressive thundershowers moved in over the lake most nights as the sun went down. Everything seemed to grow bigger than at home. The leaves were huge and the flowers delightfully fragrant. They reminded me of God's mighty hand in creation. I marveled at cows and zebras as they grazed together in patches of green grass edged by bright red dirt.

I drank in all the new and unusual sights. In the distance, I spotted a salmon-pink hue at the edge of a lake. As the distance closed, it turned out to be a flock of flamingoes on the shore of Lake Nakuru. I even did a double take at what I first thought was a black and white bird in a tree. It was a monkey.

The wheels of the Isuzu Trooper droned on. I drifted off into a haze as my mind wandered.

My friend suddenly startled me from my reverie. "Look up ahead!"

Pine branches scattered in our lane created a roadblock. It wasn't the least bit windy and it seemed odd to even *see* pine branches in Africa. I wondered at the strange obstruction. It turned out that branches in the road were commonly used to warn vehicles of somebody stalled on the road ahead. Ironically, the size of some of those branches could be more of a hazard than a stalled vehicle.

On three other occasions, spiked bars in the road marked police checks. But as muzungus, we were waved on each time. We just pulled around to miss the menacing spikes and continued on our way. With such commonplace adventures, I could hardly wait to start driving there.

The scenery and terrain changed drastically several times during our trip. In the beginning, we were greeted by flat-topped acacias, which Kenyans refer to as umbrella trees. My favorites, however, were the spectacular Jacaranda trees that lined the streets. In full flower, they dropped clusters of purple flowers everywhere. We traveled through the forest highlands, then journeyed through the dry savanna of the Rift Valley, which resembled the Grand Canyon, and climbed over Mau Summit near the expansive, green, quilt-like tea plantations. Finally, we descended to the plains and onto the rice fields. It was dark when we reach Kisumu. We emerged from our vehicle exhausted and truly ready for a good night's sleep.

May 23, 1992

My container of belongings arrived and, along with it, stacks of boxes that needed to be unpacked. In the meantime, I cautiously explored the town. I became more familiar with new sights and faces, open markets, and how to use Kenya shillings to buy curtains and a mosquito net. I learned the difference between adaptors, converters, and transformers. Adaptors allowed an American plug to fit into the three-pronged outlet in Kenyan walls. A converter changed the local 220V power to 110V for small appliances like hair dryers and curling irons. A transformer converted power for large appliances like washing machines and kitchen equipment.

I thought I had it all figured out until one Sunday morning. I sat on the floor in front of a portable dressing mirror framed in ornate trim to curl my hair. Suddenly, my curling iron started smoking. I pulled it away and found a lock of my hair still attached. Yikes! A sulfurous odor filled the room as I leaned in for a closer look in the mirror. How did *that* happen?

That very moment, a man walked by the door and inquired about the "funny smell." That's when I realized I'd mistaken the adaptor for a converter. I was so embarrassed that I wanted to shrink into a tiny little cobweb. Instead, there I was with my frizzy, singed hair, on my way to church in Africa.

When we got home, I enjoyed some quiet time unpacking. At least that was something I knew how to do. In the distance, lively African music drifted from a local hotel. It reminded me of Latin music with the drums, heavy bass, and rhythmic stringed instruments. It kept me company as I pondered the new direction my life had taken. My next adventure would be to tackle the tribal language called *Dholuo*. It means the "language of the Luo people." I had six months to learn it, and *that* would be a challenge.

CHAPTER 2

He Knows My Every Thought

During my first months of life in Kisumu, I slept in a room with my language helper. From the time I spent with the children in the choir, I learned Africans don't like to sleep in a room by themselves. So instead of staying in my room, I slept on a twin bed to keep Joyce company.

Dogs barked all night and made it hard for me to fall asleep. They untied the dogs each night to serve as watchdogs. In addition to this, when someone passed away, the people wailed and beat on drums from midnight to dawn. If they didn't do this, they believed ancestral spirits would come to haunt them.

As morning light leaked into my room, it was common to hear voices, roosters, dogs still barking, and motorcycles roar down the street. I'm not a morning person, and that cacophony also included big trucks with air horns.

Giants in the Land

We all have "giants" to face in life. They come in all shapes and sizes. Usually, they are based on fear. Some people possess a fear of public speaking or flying over an ocean. When I first went to Kenya, my giant was learning how to drive a stick shift on the "wrong" side of the road.

You may smile at that thought, but I actually fought back tears when I slipped the key into the ignition and let out the clutch. Driving in Kisumu was a necessity, but that challenge became the Goliath of my life. It terrified me to think of getting into an accident and hurting someone, and I begged God to protect us all. It bothered me so much, that it was a good thing I came to Kenya with a one-way ticket. The whole experience used up all my courage for the day and left me exhausted. My fear of risk-taking could easily have kept me from working with street children.

I soon realized one of the giants that street boys struggle with is trust. Many of those children were hurt so badly and let down by adults so many times, they erected an emotional wall and decided never to trust again. They wear a certain look in their eyes that tells you to keep your distance. Their basic needs aren't being met, yet they build emotional barriers to protect themselves from further pain. It's hard to imagine what goes on in a child's mind when someone tells him about the love of a Father he can't see and a Jesus he's never met. Little by little, the boys soften under the steadfast love they are shown and so desperately need. It might be through a smile and a gentle touch, a meal of rice and beans, a soccer game, or just a feeling of acceptance. Gradually, they relax and listen to what you have to say. Maybe they can dare to trust again … just this once.

Agape Children's Ministry began in such a simple way. I took a risk and so did the kids. But God's plan was so much bigger than we ever imagined. Today, some of the boys who first came to a Sunday afternoon meeting are graduates of high school, work a steady job, and are heads of their own families. Now, we have a younger generation of boys who are on their way to the same success. Sometimes we travel a bumpy road, but it's hard to express the immense joy we feel when these young men stay on course and make wise choices.

Amid all the changes in culture, sounds, and smells, the thing that made me laugh the most was just being with the kids and trying to get the language right. I loved to hear the street children laugh and have a good time. What a blessing to see the difference just a little love and acceptance made in their lives.

> *I know your deeds. See, I have placed before you an open door*
> *that no one can shut. I know that you have little strength,*
> *yet you have kept my word and have not denied my name*
> (Revelation 3:8).

CHAPTER 3

He Sees Each Tear that Falls

"KXU, Mama KXU!" the street boys called out.

I felt so out of my element those first days. As I drove down the street, I glanced right and left to see whom they were talking to, but didn't see anyone else. Not only did I not know whom they were talking to, but I also had no idea what they meant. As a newcomer in Kenya, I felt a bit self-conscious. I gave a halfhearted wave just to be friendly and drove on.

As I mentioned earlier, I arrived in Kenya in May of 1992 to work with a mission team doing community development. As a registered nurse, my intent was to teach preventative health care to the Luo tribe in the Nyanza Province. Our home base, in the port city of Kisumu, sat on the shore of the beautiful two-hundred-mile-wide Lake Victoria.

Some days I enjoyed my language studies as I worked with a language helper in a condo that overlooked the lake. However, my teammates and I were encouraged to leave our vacation-like setting and get out among the people. They said, "Go into town regularly to practice your vocabulary words."

I accepted the challenge to move beyond my comfort zone and learned how to drive a stick shift. As I said, it was more than just learning to use a manual transmission. It involved driving on the wrong side of the car *and* the wrong side of the road. And nightmare of nightmares, I had to navigate Kisumu's roundabouts. The roundabouts joined several busy roads and the unspoken rule was that the biggest vehicle wins.

As if that wasn't enough of a challenge, daunting potholes the size of hippo ponds pockmarked the roads. To make matters even worse, shock-damaging speed bumps referred to as "sleeping policemen" turned the already bumpy roads into an obstacle course. Now, as you imagine all this, also picture countless bicyclists weaving in and out of traffic as they carried passengers perched side-saddle behind them on padded seats.

Driving truly stressed me. To add to that stress, other traffic included poor ragged men who trudged up and down hills pulling large wooden carts loaded with sacks of maize flour or heavy cardboard boxes. My heart raced each time a cart sped downhill slightly faster than the man's ability to run. I feared for his safety. All I could do was hope and pray he stopped before a truck sped through the intersection.

The traumatic road conditions affected me before I even climbed into the car.

Streets of Kisumu

When I mustered enough nerve to drive around, the post office was usually my first stop. I always hoped for news from home, like a ten-year-old away at summer camp.

The first time I needed to buy stamps, it became clear that in Kisumu, different rules applied for that too. The post office reminded me of something from an old British movie, with dark wooden ledges and wrought-iron cages that separated the clerks from their patrons. The bars left just enough room to slide a letter or stamps under the opening. I took my place in line at a counter labeled "STAMPS," or so I thought. The line moved slowly. Finally, I reached the window, stepped toward the clerk, and opened my mouth to speak. I didn't utter a single syllable before a man elbowed his way in front me.

He slid coins beneath the grate and received his stamps. I blinked in disbelief. His rudeness stunned me. What really shocked me was that others continued to cut in front of me in the same way. Quietly waiting my turn got me nowhere. Finally, I mustered the courage to be a little more aggressive. I wished I knew enough Dholuo to say, "Hey, I was here first!" What came out instead was a timid, "Excuse me, please."

After some time, I learned to navigate the post office just like I did the streets. One day, I parked at an angle in front of the post office. I used my newfound knowledge to get my stamps. I clasped them in hand triumphantly and I walked out to my car. At this angle my eye caught the license plate on my car: KXU 685. The mystery of the street boys calling out "KXU!" was solved. It finally made sense. I let out a chuckle.

Our language helper explained how, in the Kenyan culture, a woman is known by the name of her firstborn son, such as "Mama David." Since the street boys knew nothing about me except that I drove a vehicle, my new identity became mama of the vehicle, "Mama KXU."

CHAPTER 4

And Hears Me When I Call

He has made everything beautiful in its time.
(Ecclesiastes 3:11)

M ajestic osprey and a variety of other birds nested in the trees and foliage around Lake Victoria. For me, the refreshing lake breeze felt like a touch from God, and the glorious sunsets reminded me of the greatness of my Creator. At times, I even heard the hippos "barking" in the lake. I drank in the natural beauty of colorful bougainvillea, the stunning orange and crimson colors of the flame tree, and the beautiful lavender flowers of the Jacaranda trees. It reminded me that God was near. *For since the creation of the world God's invisible qualities—his eternal power and divine nature—have been clearly seen, being understood from what has been made, so that people are without excuse* (Romans 1:20).

In contrast, I saw women carrying loads of branches on their heads, babies on their backs, and toddlers at their side. They carried firewood for the day with hopes their children wouldn't fall into the cook fire. Sadly, that's a rather common occurrence.

Women commonly carried loads on their heads. Once, on my way to one of the community development projects, a lady walked downhill toward me as I climbed a narrow red-dirt path. The woman balanced a rather large rock on her head that she would use to help protect the water spring for drinking water. When we met on the path, she stood slightly above me on the incline and reached out her hand to greet me.

In my head I cried, *Hold your head up!* I'm not sure if my face reflected my concern, but as I accepted her greeting, all I could think about is how that rock could slip from her head and tumble in my direction. Thankfully, the rock stayed on her head. After she greeted me, she managed to amble down the path with the rock still perfectly balanced.

The Kenyan men and women were hardworking and used what they had available, which wasn't much. I admired their resourcefulness. For example, they made large open-weave baskets, used for storing potatoes and other such things, and sold them at the market. They only had a bicycle to transport them to market. So they turned the basket upside down over their head and body while pedaling the bike. They peeked through the open weave to see where they were going. It was a funny-looking sight, but ingenious.

The women performed most of the labor for their families, but all the people learned to make-do with what they had.

Woman's work

Just the Basics

Little did I realize the lessons I would learn in my own day-to-day activities as my American mindset came in contact with the Kenyan way. The only thing that kept me going some days was the beauty of nature. Nothing was easy or straightforward those first few months, not even something as basic as a phone call. Kenya had red telephone booths, like you see in London, but most of the phones didn't actually work. Often, if they did, to make a call required some quirky trick known only to the locals. Once, I tried several times to make a call by following the directions exactly. I dropped in the right coins, and nothing happened.

Finally, a young lady took pity on me, and said in her Kenyan-British accent, "You have to punch the star key."

She reached past me and pushed the button several times in rapid succession. My call went through.

I felt like a three-year-old in a fifty-year-old body. I didn't know how to do anything here, and inwardly it annoyed me. Even shopping challenged me. I didn't know which shops to buy from or which brands to buy. On top of that, I didn't even know the cultural routine expected when I entered a store. I was required to check my purse in exchange for a frayed cardboard number. They stored checked bags in a little open cubicle until checkout. I did that once, but it seemed too risky. The next time, I only carried a small wallet, which they allowed me to keep while I shopped.

Language continued to present a problem too. Even though English is actually Kenya's national language, nothing sounded the same. For example, when I asked for green beans, the clerk directed me to a bin of tiny hard-shelled balls.

"What are these?" I asked.

"You wanted green grams," the worker said indignantly, ignoring my surprise.

Guess I didn't say that right. Neither did I know cookies were called *biscuits* and orange punch was called *squash*. You can imagine my surprise when someone politely asked if I would like a snack of squash and biscuits. When you go to a foreign country, it really helps to pack a good sense of humor.

Opening a bank account was a task I thought I could manage on my own, but in 1992, I had to bring a Kenyan resident to vouch for me. The bank officials called me a "legal alien." Isaiah, my new Kenyan friend, and I were escorted though a black swinging gate at the rear of the bank. We walked past several small offices until we arrived at a spacious office with a great big desk. They cordially served milk tea while the manager finished his official paperwork. I admit it all felt quite "alien." Finally, he looked up and asked a whole list of questions. As I answered, the manager often glanced at Isaiah to see if he would back me up. When he reached the bottom of the form, the manager announced that I would be notified by mail when the account was ready. I was stunned. *Not today?*

That was only my *first* banking lesson in Kenya. Cashing a check could take up to forty-five minutes. Forms were filled out in triplicate and, since they still used carbon paper in the '90s, little sheets of shiny blue paper littered the floor.

When I returned to the bank in the morning, I waited.

I learned the proper way to greet the clerk was to say, "Oyawore." (The sun has come up.)

I had to follow that with "Entie." (You are here.)

He verified that by saying, "Antiei." (I am here.)

With that confirmed, I said, "Idthi nade?" (How are you?)

Then he responded, "Ber ahania." (Very fine.)

With all that said, I could finally announce, "I'd like to cash a check."

When the clerk looked up at me and said, "So, you want to cash a check?" I replied, "Yes, I want to cash a check." In my most virtuous, patient way, I tried to keep smiling.

With that settled, he proceeded to give my check a prolonged examination and walked to a back room to have it approved. That discussion took more than a few minutes too. Needless to say, I learned to budget extra time on banking day.

Shopping also took extra time. I finally learned my way around and knew to buy cleaning products at the store, fruit and vegetables from a neighborhood kiosk, meat from a butcher shop, and live chickens at our gate.

One time, a man bicycled up to our gate with live chickens tied and hung upside down on his handlebars. My housekeeper told me they were good hens, and we should buy one. I agreed, gave her the shillings, and went to town for other supplies.

I worked up an appetite while out and looked forward to dinner. I stepped through the door and expected the savory aroma of roasted chicken. Instead, I found a note saying we were low on propane gas for the stove.

That was frustrating, but I decided on a cheese sandwich and started to put the groceries away. I reached down to put the sugar away, and my hand brushed warm feathers. I jumped back. *The hen!* My housekeeper was unable to cook the chicken, so she kept the hen's feet tied and put her in a box on the pantry floor before she left. Only, I didn't know that.

The frightened hen clucked desperately. The poor thing; she couldn't be ignored. I untied her and gave her a drink of water and some corn flakes. After a little time, I named her Helen. We ate breakfast together the next morning before I took her to work with me. Helen lived a good long life and laid many brown eggs for us. Maybe that was her way of saying thank-you.

It took a year to get a phone installed. Someone was obviously waiting for a bribe. During the yearlong process, I visited the telephone company. When I looked out the window, I couldn't believe the massive knot of tangled wires going in every direction. It actually caused me to wonder how *anyone* had a working phone. Even after I finally had a phone, I had to pay close attention to my bill, because it wasn't uncommon for people in the phone company's office to keep a line open after you completed your call and charge their personal international phone calls to your number. That was my first personal encounter with corruption in Kenya.

Once, I went to the telephone office around 10:30 a.m. after cleaning the house, doing the dishes by hand, and filling the washing machine with a hose.

The receptionist said, "Oh, you should have come in the morning hours."

Several times, the lunch hour, which ran from one to two o'clock, caught me off guard. Almost everything in town shut down, and I was just hitting my stride. What a frustrating waste of time for an American.

My African friends said, "Mama, you act like this is your last day on earth. Just take it easy. The sun will come up tomorrow."

CHAPTER 5

Growing Pains

The generous will themselves be blessed, for they share their food with the poor. (Proverbs 22:9)

During my first visits to town, I felt so white, so conspicuous, and so out of place. After a while, I grew used to my new surroundings. People were friendly and I gradually learned my way around. However, I *never* got used to the sight of ragged and dirty little children propped up next to a building or asleep on the sidewalk.

I talked with my teammates and the team leader.

I asked, "Couldn't we figure out how to do some community development in the urban area? Those children are another unreached people group."

The mission leaders agreed something needed to be done, but were concerned it would blunt the focus of their particular mission, which was designed to work in rural areas.

Their answer disheartened me. I constantly thought about the street kids. I spoke with a missionary I respected very much back home. He thought I should stay with the mission I had committed to.

"After all," he said, "you can work with the children in the village."

I prayed, "Lord, I can go out in the village and work with the children. They don't have much, but they do have caring families. The street children have no one. If I can cut my heart out and put it on a shelf, I can continue to serve in this mission in the villages. Lord, if you want me to continue where I'm serving, then why have you given me a burden for street children?" *Am I now trying to win the approval of human beings, or of God?* (Galatians 1:10a).

I cried myself to sleep that night. It was true, I'd made a commitment. The mission was an authority in my life. Yet my growing relationships with the children made it a real struggle. They needed to know they had a heavenly Father who loved and cared for them. No one seemed to be telling them that. Their families were unable or unwilling to provide for their basic needs. So they survived in the streets the best they could. The city officials made it clear that they weren't wanted in town. It was a no-win situation.

I wrestled with the enormity of it all. I asked God why I had the privilege of being born into a Christian family in America. I accepted Christ at the age of eight in a neighborhood Bible school. "Lord, why, when I had these advantages, was I sent to Kenya? And why, seeing these faces in front of me, am I not able to do a thing to help them? Some of the mothers of these boys died from HIV/AIDS through no fault of their own. What if I was one of those mothers? Wouldn't I want someone to come and help my children, take care of them, and show them a better way to live? And why, dear Lord, do you let these children roam the streets?"

According to UN sources, there are more than 150 million street children in the world today. "These children are chased from home by violence, drug and alcohol abuse, the death of a parent, family breakdown, war, natural disaster, or simply socio-economic collapse. Many destitute children are forced to eke out a living on the streets, scavenging, begging, hawking in the slums and polluted cities of the developing world."[1] At that time, I also learned how three-fourths of the current prison population of Sao Paulo, Brazil, was made up of former street children. I asked myself, *What would keep Kisumu from having similar statistics?*

The pleasant weather in Kisumu made living on the streets feasible

---

1   http://www.unesco.org/new/en/social-and-human-sciences/themes/
fight-against-discrimination/education-of-children-in-need/street-children/

for the kids. However, the government officials and citizens of Kisumu considered the street kids a menace. They carried disease and resorted to petty crimes just to survive. In Nairobi, hardened street thugs carried hypodermic needles. They threatened to stab people and infect them with AIDS if they didn't give them money. Children became thieves because they needed to eat. The street boys survived by their wits. They manipulated people. People complained that they were little wild animals. Yet how would I react if I were forced to live in the streets? These were children whose brains weren't even fully developed and who had lost their trust in adults. They had no resources, schooling, medical care, or even shelter.

One of the boys we rescued smelled like burnt rubber because he'd been sleeping under a truck next to a warm tire. For street children, it wasn't just a matter of finding a place to sleep, but a safe place.

It's said that a person can't move forward with both feet firmly planted on the ground. I knew God couldn't direct me if I wasn't willing to be moved. I pled with Him, "What is it you want me to do? Everyone seems to have an idea, but what do you want?"

The Not-So-Good Samaritan

But a Samaritan, as he traveled, came where the man was; and when he saw him, he took pity on him. He went to him and bandaged his wounds, pouring on oil and wine. Then he put the man on his own donkey, brought him to an inn and took care of him. (Luke 10:33-34)

While I pondered my future in Africa, the Lord made something clear to me the very next Sunday. I attended our little church as usual. It was an intracultural experience in itself. Founded by Baptist missionaries ten years earlier, on a good day, the congregation numbered about seventy-five people. Those assembled were approximately one-third Africans, one-third East Indians (commonly referred to as *Asians*), and one-third missionaries from Europe, the United States, and Canada.

We gathered in a small cement-block building with a high ceiling formed by a tin roof. The rafters provided a perfect roost for bats, and occasionally a few bat droppings sprinkled our heads during the service. I wore a scarf.

Seating included a few white plastic chairs, but mostly wooden benches. I didn't mind the benches unless I held a sleeping child or the sermon went on too long. If I sat too long on the hard wooden benches, it encouraged spasms along my back, and I'd get squirmy like the teenagers.

That particular morning, the chairman of the church board, Mr. Steve Macwan, spoke. He announced his topic, the Good Samaritan. I groaned inwardly, because it reminded me of an experience I had when I first arrived in Kisumu. It made me feel like a total failure as a Good Samaritan. Now, I really wasn't in the mood to feel like more of a flop as a missionary, and wondered why he chose *that* particular topic.

My Good Samaritan failure remained clearly etched in my memory. My teammate had dropped me off in town alone. He had other errands to run and said, "You should become more familiar with where things are located."

I climbed out of the vehicle and suddenly felt conspicuous again.

"I'll pick you up in about twenty minutes," he said.

"Twenty minutes! What I am going to do with all that time?"

Amusement danced in his eyes. "You'll be fine."

I wasn't so sure as I watched him drive away.

I squared my shoulders and tried to look like I was there for a reason. I walked into a couple of shops and looked around. Then I bought some ginger biscuits. When the lady quoted the price, I gathered my coins and held out my hand.

"Take what you want," I said.

Even as I said it, my brain registered disbelief. I had no idea whether she took what was needed or more, because I wasn't familiar enough with the currency. I had so much to learn.

I ducked out of the shop and explored a side street. *Maybe there won't be so many people there.* I turned the corner and discovered a grungy-looking boy lying in the middle of the sidewalk. He looked unconscious. As a nurse, I wondered if he was in a coma or had a head injury. *Or could he possibly be drunk or just in a deep sleep?*

At that time, I knew very little about street kids. I hadn't learned about how they often stayed awake all night and then fell asleep exhausted under the influence of sniffing glue. That day, I just felt useless and frustrated. I didn't know enough of the language to ask what was wrong. I didn't have a clue as to where the nearest hospital was located, and I only had a few shillings in my pocket.

The locals casually walked by. They stepped over him like it was normal, sort of like I'd do to avoid stepping on chewing gum. I watched for a few minutes and prayed for the boy. Then I made my way around him, because it somehow seemed a little better than stepping over him. But I knew the story of the Good Samaritan and should have stopped to help the boy. What I had done didn't set well, and it never has.

So, when Mr. Macwan preached on the Good Samaritan, it dredged up all those memories. The Lord used the message to communicate directly to me. I wish I could remember all the good sermons I've heard in my life, but this one stuck. Twenty-two years later, I can still tell you the main points:

What qualities did the Good Samaritan have?

A. He was willing to take risks.

B. He was willing to make sacrifices for others.

C. He was willing to be misunderstood.

I thought about what was required to work with street boys and could check off each thing on this list. Was I willing?

In his closing remarks, Mr. Macwan said, "If you have the opportunity, the desire, and the knowledge or ability to do something in ministry, you'd better have a good reason not to do it. This is how God leads us."

He quoted Ephesians 2:10. *For we are God's handiwork, created in Christ Jesus to do good works, which God prepared in advance for us to do.*

By the end of the message, I knew it was meant for me. Tears spilled down my cheeks. I didn't want to cry but couldn't help it. Talk about awkward. People avoided me. Crying in public is not the Kenyan way. But none of that really mattered, because God confirmed what He sent me there to do.

If that wasn't enough, when I reached my rented flat, the watchman greeted me with a message. Dan Severson wanted me to call him. Dan was a Canadian man whom I'd known from the African Children's Choir. He had made a stopover visit in Kisumu a few weeks prior, and we had discussed the situation of having three hundred kids roaming the street until dawn. I made the one-mile trek down the dirt path to the nearest phone.

When Dan answered, he got right to the point. "Darla, if you decide to open a school or a home for those boys, my brother and I would like to give you your first thousand dollars. It would be in honor of our mother, Marjorie Severson, who always wanted to be a missionary."

The still small voice from the Lord touched my heart again. *What is left to understand?* Seed money was a huge confirmation. I was on the right track. It all humbled me spiritually in a deep way, and I rejoiced in the blessings of that day. That night before bed I prayed, "Lord, if you really do let me work with the street children, I'll be the happiest missionary you've ever had."

CHAPTER 6

God's Amazing Grace

It was Saturday morning. I caught up on the letters I owed to family and friends. My adjusting to being so far from home continued. On top of that, I still wasn't used to being divorced. After twenty years of marriage and having three wonderful sons, it was a difficult period in my life.

I landed far from the life I had pictured for myself. As a fourteen-year-old teenager, I committed my life to the Lord and told Him I would go wherever He wanted. Everyone knew I wanted to be a missionary nurse. Yet marriage and a family changed those plans. I worked in the hospital as a maternity nurse, and my family became my mission field and first priority.

The idea of overseas service had cooled on the back burner of my life where dreams met priorities. I thought missions work could wait for later, or maybe my family was enough to fulfill that desire. Then came the earthquake that rocked my world. Divorce. Though it wasn't my choice, I suffered from guilt that maybe I had been an inadequate wife. I tried to be a good one, but I felt like a complete failure and a terrible role model. I was sure I couldn't qualify to be a missionary.

Thankfully, God didn't see things that way. I'm now confident our worth to the Lord is not conditional. He demonstrated this truth when He allowed me to go into the mission field six years later; the first divorcee that Mission: Moving Mountains ("M:MM") ever sent. I'm humbly thankful for His amazing grace.

The Desires of Your Heart

Take delight in the Lord, and he will give you the desires of your heart. (Psalm 37:4)

Africa was a naturally beautiful place to live, but the seasonal heat took some getting used to. In fact, I didn't ever really get used to it. I just learned to accept my makeup running off my face. The same held true with the red dirt; it stained anything it touched.

Meals challenged my comfort zone too. Basically, we only ate what we could cook or peel. We used bleach water to kill parasites on our lettuce, which sometimes left our salad tasting a little bleachy, but that was preferable to parasites. And we only drank filtered water.

Those types of things I adjusted to, but they paled in comparison to the poverty and dire circumstances of the homeless children who lived in the street. Perhaps things weren't comfortable or convenient, but I was where God wanted me. And that's exactly where I wanted to be. I learned early on that I wanted to be in God's will and do what He was blessing, rather than asking God to bless what I was already doing on my own.

Amid all those changes and cultural differences, God encouraged my spirit. He continually knew what we needed, and I often marveled at how those needs were met.

For instance, I missed my dog, and most people don't keep pets in Kenya. All those barking and howling dogs at night weren't pets – they were watchdogs. When I even mentioned a dog as a pet, it garnered some strange looks. But God knew the desire of my heart and filled that spot in His special way.

Simba

Kenya teemed with dogs. Most of them were related, and they all looked alike. The dogs remained caged all day to make them more aggressive. When the night watchman arrived, they started to howl. After the dogs escalated into a frenzy, they were released to help the guards patrol the compound. Snarling sounds from deep within their throats sounded like they were ready to eat any intruder alive.

Fortunately, for pet-loving me, a teenage boy who lived on the other side of the hedge owned a dog with six-week-old puppies. One day, Elvin squeezed through an opening in the hedge with a little puppy tucked under his arm. It was his gift to me. Thrilled doesn't begin to describe how excited I felt. By this time, I lived alone in a house with plenty of room, and it comforted me to have a bouncy little puppy greet me when I came home. We were good company for each other. Because of her golden-tan-colored coat, I named her Simba – the Swahili word for "lion."

I missed my three grown sons and really got homesick. It took me six weeks to even *start* to feel like I belonged in Kenya, even though I knew God wanted me there. We didn't have cell phones back then, and I wanted to call my son on his birthday. To make that happen, I walked to a hotel where they gave me a code to make an international call. I listened to the phone ring with anticipation. David's voice came on the line. We greeted each other and then "click." We lost the connection.

I tried over and over again to reconnect. Instead of talking to my son on his birthday, I stood in the lobby with tears of frustration painting wet tracks down my face as I clutched the dead phone in my hand.

The time difference of eleven hours between America and Africa made it difficult too. I taped pictures of my sons on the wall from when they were little. When I felt lonely, I stared at the photos.

But even amid those frustrations, I knew God sent me there for a purpose. So Simba and I faced the challenges together. God used her to help dispel some of the loneliness and frustration I felt.

With each passing day, my concern for the street boys grew. Each time I saw them dressed in their ragged, dirty clothes begging for shillings, it filled me with a mixture of sadness and anger. That wasn't how God intended children to live. Everything about it was so wrong. The Bible says in Matthew 18:5 that *whoever welcomes one such child in my name welcomes me.* Jesus also said, *for the kingdom of heaven belongs to such as these* (Matthew 19:14).

Soon, I longed to bring a few of those boys home with me to give them a meal, a warm shower, and a change of clothes. However, our mission leader warned that if I ever told even one street boy where I lived, I might wake up one morning with my whole front yard full of street boys.

Our mission was to teach community development in the rural area. The leaders explained that it would blunt their focus to set up a project in an urban community. Perhaps someday they would consider doing that, but right now they advised me to stay on track with my work in the village.

A struggle brewed within me. I curled up with Simba on my bed and prayed that someone would come and help those poor little *street urchins*, as the newspaper called them. My heart ached for them, and their faces appeared in my mind as I fought to go to sleep at night.

CHAPTER 7

Garrett Goes to Jail

Being a newcomer, I was a curiosity to those kids who had nothing to do but roam the streets. I soon realized that they could be playing and having fun, but as soon as they spotted an opportunity to beg, they put on their sad faces and came running.

I had raised three boys of my own, and their friends hung out at our place most of the time. So I was used to boys. I was *not* used to little kids being despised by townspeople. The hard truth was that they were just part of the environment, and people got used to avoiding them.

Guards stood out in front of businesses with their threatening batons to keep them away from the customers. "Nenda zako!" (Go away!)

Once I became fully aware of the street-boy problem, I discovered another organization that sheltered and fed street children. But the boys stayed for only a short time there and later returned to the streets. That puzzled me.

When I talked about my concern for those forgotten children, friends suggested I might be thinking with my emotions instead of being more rational. *Are they right?* I wondered. I stayed home for three days and really prayed about it. I begged God for clear direction. This passage in James haunted me. *Suppose a brother or a sister is without clothes and daily food. If one of you says to them, "Go in peace; keep warm and well fed," but does nothing about their physical needs, what good is it?* (James 2:15-16)

At the end of those three days, I needed to check my mail and go into town. My language helper, Joyce, went along with me, and I was grateful for her company. As we drove, I secretly but fervently prayed. I asked God to make sure I didn't see any street children this time. I was pretty sure He would understand and grant my request.

We arrived at the post office. To my dismay, a little boy named Garrett, who looked like a nine-year-old, leaned against the post office wall near the big brass door. He quickly jumped up when he saw my car and smiled. I had nothing to give him. I waved and asked Joyce to talk to him while I checked for mail. *Maybe she would take care of things, and he would leave before I came out.* That just didn't happen.

The two of them were still talking when I walked out.

Joyce looked at me and said, "He spent all of his shillings to buy his 'new' green shirt and those baggy white pants, because … he wants to go home with you today."

My heart sank. *What should I do?* We talked some more and promised to come back for him the next day and take him to the shelter. I needed to check first and make sure they had room. We bought him some peanuts, gave him a hug, and headed for home.

That night a big storm rolled in across the lake. It was monsoon season. Heavy rain battered the windows and seeped in through the casings to the point it puddled on the floor. I ran around to each room and tightly closed all the windows. I used every towel I owned to sop up the mess. It was a spectacular storm with frequent sheet lighting that brightened the room, quickly followed by roaring thunder.

When things calmed down and I was ready for bed, my thoughts turned to the events of the day. I shuddered to think about that lonely little boy trying to find a place to keep dry.

Out of frustration, I asked myself, *Why did I come all the way from America and leave my family behind for this? What have I ever done to deserve being an American anyway? What has this little guy ever done to deserve living in the streets? Why can't I do more to help him? Dear God, I just don't understand.*

I cried. Finally, light but restless sleep claimed me.

The next morning, I learned it was okay to take Garrett to the shelter.

Joyce and I went back to find him. I planned to visit him there every day and make sure he was doing well. When we arrived in town, Garret was nowhere in sight. We looked and looked. A couple days later, I asked our friend Lebaus to try to find him. He searched everywhere he could think of and later went to the authorities. Through his connections, Lebaus learned a boy fitting Garrett's description had been picked up for stealing wood carvings. He'd been sent to a jail in Nairobi.

Such a young boy – in jail. That experience made me more determined than ever to do what I could to help the children. *Maybe I can do both ministries*, I thought.

I prayed daily for Garrett and asked God to protect him from harm. He used this little boy to stir my heart and give me a deep conviction to reach out to those kids. I never saw Garrett again.

Three Stones and a Pan

In spite of the poverty, the area where I lived in Kisumu was beautiful. That's what kept me going. The mornings awoke bright and beautiful. Bougainvillea blossoming like wildflowers and colorful birds added to God's artistic palette. On one of those glorious mornings, I attended a Child Evangelism Fellowship conference. Our team leader and his wife came by at 8:30 a.m. and called me out of the meeting. Another storm cloud rolled in, but not the weather kind; it was the personal kind.

Missionary friends had a message for me. Apparently, someone told the president of our mission organization that I planned to resign. I hadn't gotten that far in my thinking, but I had to admit I wondered what I should do.

By that time, I had several little friends in town. When they saw me park, they ran from the alley and across the street. They wanted to "watch my car" to protect it. For this favor, I usually bought an extra loaf of bread, some peanuts, a few bananas, or bars of soap so they could bathe in the lake. In fact, one little guy actually tried to bite the soap the first time I bought it for him. He thought it was something to eat. Our interaction caused me to practice my Dholuo and they were able to learn more English. Things seemed to be going well. I laughed when a local businessman told me my car could never be stolen in Kisumu because my best friends were the thugs.

The message I received that morning originated from our East Africa director who lived in Uganda. He wanted to see me right away. I went home and quickly packed a bag. I felt the dread of a child called to the principal's office and wondered what he wanted. A precious, third-generation missionary named Andrea Probst offered to drive me all the way to Jinja, Uganda, for the meeting.

She reminded me: "God is in control, and He does all things well."

I nodded, but swallowed hard.

When we reached the director's home, he greeted me and we engaged in small talk over cups of tea. Then he and his wife hit me with the more difficult questions. I replied with honesty. It became clear that he and his wife believed the street children distracted me from the mission's goal of community development. I wholeheartedly believed in community development, but I also felt like street children were an unreached people group.

I said, "They are so vulnerable and need to know they have a Savior who loves and cares for them."

They agreed, but the director said, "The thing is, I don't feel you're being honest with your donors if your heart isn't fully in the rural community work which you were sent here to do."

I had nothing more to say. By the end of the day, I was kindly asked to resign. They explained my funds could continue to come through the organization for a few months, but I needed to look for another way to channel my support. I sat in front of a typewriter in tropical Uganda as I tried to keep my wits about me and compose a coherent letter of resignation.

The next evening when Andrea and I returned to Kisumu, it hit me like a ton of bricks. I asked myself, *What have you done?*

I talked to another veteran missionary friend and he said, "Well, Darla, most people try the very difficult before they tackle the impossible."

Another lady said, "When you jump off a cliff, it's customary to know where you're going to land."

Such encouragement.

When I shared the news with my language helper, she supported me. It dawned on me that because I bought my stove, refrigerator, mattress, and car with money I raised for outgoing expenses, the executive board could legally require me to return all those items to the mission.

When I voiced my concern about that, my young friend said softly, "But Auntie, I don't have any of those things. All you really need here are three stones and a pan."

I thought to myself, *That may be what it comes down to, but it will have to be okay.* As a matter of fact, the *sufria* (big pan, held over a fire by three stones) my friend referred to was much more than any street child owned. They had nothing but the clothes on their backs. Honestly, I didn't know how I would deal with that level of poverty. Sniffing glue (a common habit among street boys) started to make sense.

> *Then you will call, and the LORD will answer; you will cry for help, and he will say: Here am I.* (Isaiah 58:9)

The Three-Legged Puppy

It was a cool, breezy evening in Nairobi. UNICEF invited me and our provincial children's officer to tour their existing projects for street children in the large capital city. We hoped to learn from the experience of others. We instantly connected with our host, an elderly priest named Father Groel. His compassion for the street kids poured out of him. They all knew him.

In the evening, we drove around to see some of the boys' campsites. I climbed into the vehicle without any idea of what to expect. It turned out to be a moving experience God used as a building block for the Agape ministry.

We stopped at a summit on the outskirts of town and spotted a pillar of black smoke as our van approached the "camp." We stepped from the van and acrid smoke assaulted my nostrils. The campfire burned in the center of an old worn-out tire.

We filed out of the van and about a dozen dirty, smelly street boys ran to greet us wearing big smiles. The boys gathered around the familiar vehicle.

One boy caught my arm and said, "This way, Mama."

Each of the boys seemed eager to escort us. The face of the boy who held my arm lit up with a smile I'll never forget. I leaned down and instinctively hugged him. My hospitable companion happily accepted the physical contact.

He took me over to the warm-but-offensive tire fire. A long rectangular box served as a bench. I sat, and after a few words of introduction and explanation by Father Groel, we were on our own to make conversation with the kids. I didn't really know what to say. To my relief, one of the boys asked if we wanted to see their dog.

I nodded and glanced around but saw no signs of an animal. Not even a whimper or bark. Then, to my amazement, I learned we were sitting on the doghouse. The boys built the box out of scrap material and even put a door on the end of it. My young friend crouched and reached inside. The rest of us waited expectantly.

Out came a cute, roly-poly puppy, but something was wrong. It only had three legs. The story of the three-legged puppy came to us in Swahili. One of the boys told the tale of the stray mother dog he saw give birth. The poor thing was starving and became cannibalistic toward the puppies. She bit the leg off the puppy, and the street boy who befriended me rescued it. The other boys in the group saved their shillings and shared cartons of milk with the puppy. They played with and loved the poor maimed puppy until it thrived.

I was struck by how much love those neglected children had to share. I blinked back tears. Those boys showed more love to a three-legged dog than most adults showed to them.

It reminded me of a quote from an Indian chief. He said, "Children don't question the wrongs of adults ... they suffer them."

We received our good-night hugs and requests to come back and boarded the van. I smelled like a smoldering tire, and I didn't really care.

We returned to warm showers and comfortable beds that night, but I couldn't sleep. Thoughts of those boys raced through my mind. We left them out in the cold, damp air to breathe the stench of smoldering rubber in the middle of a busy city. In contrast, I lay beneath a nice warm blanket, sheltered and protected. It made no sense. "Why God?" I asked. "Please don't let me forget what I saw tonight. Please God."

Defend the weak and the fatherless; ... Rescue the weak and the needy. (Psalm 82:3-4)

CHAPTER 8

Lebaus Onyango

So many providential events and rescues took place during those fragile early days as we tried to obey God's leading. One of the most significant things He did early on was to bring Lebaus to us.

I met Lebaus Onyango in 1992 at the Fellowship Bible Church of Kisumu. He was in his early twenties, friendly, and responsive when I stood up in church to ask if anyone had a desire to help start a Sunday afternoon meeting for street boys. I longed for those young boys to know a heavenly Father who loved them and would not forsake them. I needed help, because I had no way to get that message across with my limited language skills.

How could I convey the idea of a heavenly Father to boys whose own fathers abandoned, neglected, and abused them? What would the word *father* even mean to them? Would they just tune out when we talked about God? How could we reach those emotionally scarred, premature adults with the love and compassion of Christ? Had they gotten used to being treated like stray dogs? Would they trust us?

Not many people wanted to invest time or energy in street urchins, especially with a foreign white lady who didn't know what she was doing. No one stirred. It was one of those moments in time when the sweeping of the second hand made each second feel like a full minute. Then Lebaus stepped out. My heart rejoiced. He volunteered to help, and it didn't take long to realize he was gifted to work with street kids. He had the language skills, and he possessed an ability to connect with boys hungry for a father.

We wasted no time and started meeting with the boys. At the start of every meeting, Lebaus asked every boy to stand and say his name. Through that simple request, he affirmed every boy as a contributing member of the group, and it made all the difference. We sang songs. Then Lebaus told Bible stories in their native language, followed by imaginative applications to their situations or humorous skits.

I remember the first time I heard a group of street boys laugh. In the skit, Lebaus pretended to beg and interacted with a small boy whose unlaced shoes were about five times too big. The boys recognized their own behavior in the skit and thought it was hilarious. Though boisterous, their laughter sounded like music to me.

The skit emphasized how to show gratitude for what people gave to them. Lebaus had connected. And he also taught them to be thankful for the Lord's protection in keeping them alive. It amazed me how many boys answered his review questions the following week. It confirmed they were really listening.

As each meeting progressed, the boys turned to their concealed glue bottles less and less. We successfully captured the boys' imaginations. They had more energy for singing and gave us their full attention. We prayed together and shared our meager food supplies. Sometimes we shared a special treat like sodas, but usually just something simple like bread, hard-boiled eggs, or packets of milk.

Our time with the kids was bittersweet. It provided two and a half hours of escape from their harsh world. However, the painful part for us came at the end of the meeting. It broke our hearts as they grabbed their burlap or heavy plastic bags, walked barefoot over hills of garbage, and returned to the street.

Our afternoon meetings didn't change their lives very much. They just provided a nice intermission. Thankfully, Lebaus didn't let it end there. He took daily walks around town and spent time with the boys. That demonstration of care and friendship became the secret ingredient of our ministry. And I dare say, it produced the most polite street boys in Kenya.

Soon, Lebaus became regarded by the police department as the go-to person most intimately acquainted with the street boys. He knew their individual needs and background stories, or at least the ones they wanted him to hear. Those kids lived by their wits, so sometimes their stories weren't 100-percent accurate. But they were always heart wrenching.

The kids saw Lebaus as a father figure, which put him in a very unique situation with the police. They often called him first when a problem arose. In fact, it wasn't long before the police assigned Lebaus a small office at the police station, where he interviewed and interceded when a young boy landed in jail.

I still marvel at this brother in Christ. When he started with Agape he didn't have a wife or family yet. He had an average education and was still a young man himself. But he was the magnet who drew large numbers of street boys when we started the church in the park.

As our church meetings started, the boys sang praise choruses and hymns. Then Lebaus, with the help of some of our staff and visitors, shared the hope of the gospel. Afterward, he held a first aid clinic, where he cleaned and bound the wounds so common to street life.

I'm sure one of the greatest rewards for Lebaus is to see older boys follow in his footsteps. Some senior boys have become big brothers to the younger ones. The boys are eager to share their testimonies and reach out to younger children who still live in the streets. Instead of being enslaved to a life of crime and degradation, these young men found hope and purpose for their lives. Now, not only are they following Lebaus's example, but they are also walking in the footsteps of Jesus.

Follow my example, as I follow the example of Christ.
(1 Corinthians 11:1)

CHAPTER 9

Understanding Street Kids

Speak up and judge fairly; defend the rights of the poor and needy. (Proverbs 31:9)

I t's helpful to understand some of the reasons these boys live on the streets. In the Luo tribe, which many in Kisumu belong to, if a woman gets pregnant before marriage and gives birth to a son, then later finds a man to marry, the child becomes a problem. This is because the man doesn't want to give his inheritance to another man's child.

Superstition also plays a role. As recently as the '90s, they believed that if a man took on the responsibility of raising another's son, he wouldn't be able to father a son of his own.

Many times the boy is sent to a grandmother. She may grow enough food on her *shamba* (small plot) to share, but not enough to pay for school fees. As a result, the children are often sent to the streets to earn money or they become bored and go on their own. Very few boys who go to the streets actually make enough money to bring any home. It's often stolen from them, or they are forced to give it to pimps in exchange for protection.

Another common scenario is that men in rural areas often have more than one wife. If the mother of one child dies and another woman has to take over, a stepchild is frequently treated harshly. Then the unwanted kid ends up *in* or *on* the street. For clarification, if a child comes to the street during the day and goes home at night, it is said he lives *on* the street. However, if a child spends all of his time there, we say he lives *in* the street.

Some of the kids are orphans, most often due to HIV/AIDS, but the majority of the street children we've encountered do have some family. We've taken them as far as Tanzania and Uganda to reunite them with family.

First Encounter

Whoever is kind to the poor lends to the LORD.
(Proverbs 19:17a)

Before I resigned from M:MM, I talked about doing something for the street boys with our mission team. They understood the need and gave me permission to do anything I wanted in my own free time, which was Sunday afternoons. I talked to a business lady named Mama Sophie about where I could possibly hold a meeting with some of the boys. We seldom ever saw a girl on the street at that time. Since Mama Sophie closed her shop on Sundays, she kindly offered her compound as a meeting place.

Once I had the place lined up, I approached people in our church for help. I needed assistance with the language and controlling any unruly kids who might disrupt a meeting.

Then I had one more issue to address. Most of the boys stayed high by sniffing cobbler's glue. They used it to cope with life on the street. It was cheap and easy for the boys to get. Several cobblers along the side of the road were willing to make a few extra shillings even if they sold to children. This led to tragic results because the glue contained a chemical which could cause permanent brain damage.

The kids said, "When we sniff the glue we aren't so hungry, and it makes us feel warmer at night."

It also made them braver during the day so they could run faster and fight harder when chased by police or older boys. They tended to stay in groups or form gangs, which offered them some sense of belonging.

I'm still amazed at the courageous ways they looked out for each other. One ruse, for example, included a hungry boy who stole some food from a vendor.

If the vendor called out, the thief yelled, "Look, there he goes!"

Another boy nearby ran as fast as he could to create a diversion. Of course, if caught, the runner had nothing to hide.

He just said, "I ran because I was afraid of being chased for no reason."

Each time I went into town, more boys ran to greet me. Of course, they were always hungry. So when I went to the grocery store, I usually bought an extra loaf of bread or some bananas. At first, chaos exploded when I tried to share it. They thrust their grubby little hands out and just grabbed for it.

Even when they managed to snatch a piece, they complained, "Mama, I didn't get," when in fact, they hid the bread in their other hand behind their back.

To prevent those shenanigans, I asked them to sit on the curb.

"Just let me see one hand," I instructed.

They shoved one eager hand out for me to fill with bread and tucked the other behind their back. They actually seemed to like the drill. I can only imagine what a sight it was to people who watched from across the street.

Our very first meeting with street boys was February 21, 1993, just nine months after I arrived in Kenya. I put the word out to a few of the younger boys that we would meet at 3:00 p.m. at Mama Sophie's place. Twenty boys showed up, including several teenagers. Lebaus, who you met in the previous chapter, helped lead the meeting and did a fabulous job.

I didn't feel well that day and wanted to keep the meeting short, but the boys didn't want to leave. Somehow, they learned that my good friends Dr. Mark and Miriam Harmeling were due to fly in that evening. They wanted to stay and greet them. To have people come from America was very exciting.

Since we had no supplies, we drew pictures in the dirt with sticks to pass the time. I walked around admiring and discussing their artwork. I wish you could have seen the smiles. Then Lebaus led them in some familiar African songs. Between songs, he asked the boys to stand and introduce themselves. This was very significant, because they were seldom given positive recognition for anything. Here, someone actually cared who they were.

Lebaus used humor to teach them how to appreciate what people gave them and to say thank-you. Laughter didn't happen very often in their glue stupor, but most of them sobered up by that time. The mind-numbing effect of glue lasted twenty or thirty minutes, and the boys usually panicked if someone tried to take their glue bottles away. But this day, they hid their bottles in their clothing to keep them close by, but they weren't sniffing it. Their laughter floated through the air like the sound of happy music. Fun distracted them from the glue. We thanked the Lord for our white bread and Blue Band margarine sandwiches and small packets of juice. It felt like a real party, and we all had a great time.

CHAPTER 10

Meeting the Mayor

I answered a knock at my door to find a stranger there with a note bearing the name "Ms. Peter Dallas." I smiled. My name at the time was Darla Peters. As I explained earlier, the Kenyans don't put the letters "R" and "L" together, so it was difficult for them to say *Darla*. But *Peter* was a common name, so my second new identity became Peter Dalla (pronounced Peeta Dala). At the time, the popular TV series *Dallas* was familiar to the Kenyans, and as all things worked together, the name Peter Dallas evolved.

I stared at the envelope in my hand. *Who could it be from?* To my surprise, the return address was from Mayor Oile's office. *It must be some kind of mistake.* I had never met the mayor and wondered, *How could he possibly know me?*

The stranger just stood there. I tried to return the note and explain that it must be some kind of mistake.

But the messenger refused. "No, I am definitely at the right place."

I opened the letter, and it left me even more perplexed. The mayor wanted me to come to his office for a meeting. I moved around in a slight state of shock, as I gathered my things and got ready to go. I didn't think I had broken any laws, at least I hoped not. And I certainly hadn't done anything for officials to find noteworthy.

When I arrived, Mayor Oile greeted me warmly and said, "We are holding a 'Clean Up Kisumu Campaign' this weekend, and I want your help with it."

I stood there stunned. *Why on earth am I here?*

He said, "I've heard you are friendly with the street boys."

He had my interest.

"I want you to organize them to do some work in town."

Oh brother, I thought. *He can't be serious!* But he was.

To my surprise, the boys not only cooperated but also really rose to the occasion. The campaign provided a great opportunity for the boys to contribute to Kisumu and be recognized for something positive.

The mayor also proposed a Sunday afternoon soccer match between the street boys and the town council. Everyone worked hard on Saturday, and the councilmen and two councilwomen showed up at the stadium on Sunday. About one hundred boys showed up to see what would happen next.

The councilmen and women were great sports and everyone seemed to have a great time. The street boys were on their best behavior. They weren't rowdy in any way and didn't fight among themselves. I doubt that number of street boys had ever gathered in one place, at the same time, before this event. God definitely did something special for us that day.

After the game, we headed to a small community social hall outside a slum area called Kaloleni Estates. Our support team from the Fellowship Bible Church was all set up to serve rice and beans to the group as we had been doing for weeks. Of course, the mayor's presence made it an incredibly special event. We took several photos of Mayor Oile serving plates of food to the street boys.

Everyone seemed pleased except for the town clerk. He looked a little frustrated when he invited me outside. *Now what?* I wondered.

It didn't take long to find out. We were no sooner out the door when he blurted, "How did an event of this magnitude escape my notice?"

Once again, without knowing, I failed to follow diplomatic procedures. Under normal circumstances, the town clerk kept the mayor apprised of important events scheduled to take place in town. He should have been the first to know we had the ability to feed this many people on one day's notice.

I tried to look appropriately penitent and told him, "I'm sorry for the blunder." But to be honest, I was quite proud of our team's impressive accomplishment.

The following day, an article appeared in the national newspaper with the mayor's photo. It read, "His Lordship, Mr. Oile, helped feed eighty-six street boys on Sunday." The picture showed him giving plates of food to the boys. The article also mentioned how I had held a press conference from my "Kaloleni Estate office." It all sounded quite important. In reality, I talked to a lone reporter on a dirt path outside a well-worn social hall in a rundown area of town. After the newspaper made it sound so prestigious, I spared my mother those little details when I sent her the clippings.

> *For I was hungry and you gave me something to eat, I was*
> *thirsty and you gave me something to drink.*
> (Matthew 25:35)

CHAPTER 11

Lost Sheep Without a Shepherd

The meetings provided an excellent opportunity for outreach. One young man was born in a park gazebo on a rainy night to a street girl who was all alone. At the age of three, Moses' mom told him she was going to buy bananas. She never returned. Moses grew up on the streets and became a familiar beggar in Kisumu. When we held our first meetings for street children in 1993, he attended. His face showed little expression.

Someone said, "Don't worry, Mama, he isn't normal, but he won't hurt you."

Later, we had him tested and found out it was only a speech impediment.

I'll tell you more about Moses later, but I want you to remember that each of these boys has a story of how they came to live in the street. None of them wanted to be there. I saw them like lost sheep. *When he saw the crowds, he had compassion on them, because they were harassed and helpless, like sheep without a shepherd* (Matthew 9:36).

They had no one to care for them and no one to share the love of God with them. As the Lord tugged on my heart to reach out to those neglected, hopeless boys, I knew without a doubt I was doing what God wanted me to do. We held meetings every Sunday afternoon. It was one little baby step, but God blessed it.

Learning As We Go

Even small children are known by their actions, so is their conduct really pure and upright? (Proverbs 20:11)

Each Sunday afternoon, more boys showed up at the meetings. One or two at a time, they walked into our gathering with their plastic mesh or burlap bags. The bags contained their treasures of cardboard, charcoal, or pieces of soap they'd plucked from the trash heap. They also still had their glue bottles hidden in long stretched-out sleeves or behind their backs. We asked them not to use the glue during the meeting, but we didn't take it from them.

Months later, one of our missionaries hung a wooden cross up on a tree. During his talk, he encouraged the boys to trust God to provide for their needs. He explained the effects of the glue on their bodies. At the end of the meeting, he encouraged them to commit their lives to the Lord and tie their bottles or cans to the cross. It was a heartrending sight to see how many glue containers hung on that cross for weeks to come.

One particular Sunday, our East Indian friends arranged to provide a meal of rice and beans for the boys. They brought plastic plates for the food. By this time, I knew a little more about street boys. I performed a little role-play before the meal was served. I took a plate and pretended to be eating from it. Then I looked around and placed it behind my back under my shirt. I let them see what I had done, and they all laughed.

Then I said, "What will we do next time we have food if there are no plates? How will we eat?"

They got the message and returned all the plates.

A similar thing happened with Coke bottles. In order to buy crates of Coke for nearly eighty kids, I had to make a scary drive down to the hectic industrial section of town. A deposit was required for each bottle. It added up quickly. When it came time to collect the bottles, I asked an older boy, known to be a thief, to collect them for me. He accepted his assignment with pride and made sure each and every cubicle of the crate held a bottle. Trust was being built, and it gave a deep sense of satisfaction to all involved.

CHAPTER 12

Let Us Take Bread Together

And if anyone gives even a cup of cold water to one of these little ones who is my disciple, truly I tell you, that person will certainly not lose their reward. (Matthew 10:42)

It amazed us how the boys behaved when given a meal. After we asked God's blessing on the food, we lined them up by the water faucet to wash their hands. Then we handed each one a plastic plate with a generous helping of rice and beans. To them, a plate of hot food was like a steak dinner. But all this was a process. It took time to develop trust with them, and they learned to wait patiently for their plates without fearing we'd run out of food. If that happened, it could have instigated a riot and possibly shut down our program. I understood that about the street boys.

It always touched my heart when I walked by the boys seated on the ground and heard them say, "Mama, take some." They willingly held their plates up to share their precious food with me. I looked into their entreating eyes, and at first, I was taken aback. In all honesty, I considered the risk of getting sick if I shared the food they'd been eating with their fingers. Then I thought about the joy it would bring if I accepted their kindness, and the harm it might cause if they felt rejected again. Plus, we asked for God's blessing on the food, and I meant every word of it.

All those thoughts ran through my mind in a millisecond. I knew it pleased God when I knelt down and accepted a small bite from the untouched side of the plates they held up. Never once did I suffer illness from this, and joy filled every intimate moment of our shared meals together.

This demonstrated just one way I learned to put my faith into action. I'm not saying this choice would be right for everyone, but it was the right thing for me.

I've also learned that no matter how poor people are, there's always joy in sharing with friends. That proved to be true once again when Lebaus and I visited the street boys in the park. We took along loaves of bread and gave each boy three slices.

Before gobbling it down, the boy who sat next to me asked, "Mama, where's yours?"

His question surprised me. I had plenty of food at home. They had nothing but the three slices of plain bread we gave them. Yet they unselfishly wanted me to join them in their "feast." Those boys, when shown a little love, wanted to return it.

I'm not naive enough to believe all street children behave this way. Some have been in the streets long enough to become dangerous. But God used us to build trust with those boys over the months we visited them in town. We became friends. I cherish those memories and can still hear their voices calling out to me.

CHAPTER 13

Trouble in Town Hall

'Not by might nor by power, but by my Spirit,' says the LORD
Almighty. (Zechariah 4:6)

O ur Sunday afternoon meetings continued to grow. We still held
soccer games, but we had a big kids' team in one section of the
field and a little kids' team in another. It became apparent we had to
do something more to accommodate our growth. The boys stayed as
long we'd let them. When the time came to leave, they picked up their
meager belongings and headed back to the streets.

I had a talk with the deputy mayor. He had gradually become my
friend. I didn't take our friendship for granted because it definitely
didn't start out that way. After we held the Clean-Up Campaign, the
mayor's office summoned me again. This time I was more relaxed. I
approached the meeting thinking we might enjoy some tea and talk
about the results of our efforts. But instead of a comfortable chat among
friends, it turned out to be a very awkward meeting.

I stepped into a room lined with important-looking men, including
the deputy mayor and the town clerk, plus a couple of female secretar-
ies. They stared at me with stoic, somber faces. As I looked from one to
the next, not one of them smiled. I whispered a prayer. "Lord, I don't
know what I'm doing here, but please help me."

The meeting started with polite formalities but gradually turned into a grilling session. The questions started.

"Would you introduce yourself and share what you are doing in Kenya?"

I briefly talked about my family and why I came to Kisumu. I also spoke about my work with the street boys and how I wished I could do more to help them.

The mayor spoke to me in a stern tone. "And what makes you think you can solve a problem that has defeated the government?"

Gulp!

He pressed further. "What experience do you have to qualify you for such an undertaking?"

In my mind, I had no problem answering. *I raised three boys. I was a Labor-Delivery, Nursery Nurse. I traveled with the African Children's Choir. I enjoyed kids and wanted them to know Jesus.*

In reality, I said something like, "I know the government will solve the problem. I only want to do what I can for a few boys I've met here in Kisumu. I think they have potential and I don't want to see them end up in a life of crime." I licked my dry lips and continued. "I'm used to being around boys, since my sons always invited their friends to our house. And now it's just something that comes naturally. I am a Christian and want to share the blessings God has given me." I hoped they'd accept my truthful reply.

Instead, they eyed me suspiciously and asked, "Why are you taking so many pictures? What are you going to do with all the money the photos bring? Will you be lining your own pockets?"

They didn't let up. I felt like I stood before a firing squad as they continued to shoot accusations.

"Why did you come here when you are divorced? What are you looking for?"

They asked questions faster than I could think. By that point, I just wanted to get out of there, but gradually the questions subsided and their faces softened. That kindled a hope that they decided I wasn't going to be a threat to the government after all. I know the Lord was there with me. The result wasn't by my power or strength. He's the one who changes hearts and that's what He did in that meeting.

From that day forward, I had a much better relationship with people in the town hall. The mayor even gave me the phone number of his personal sergeant at arms. Maybe I should have been worried about that.

CHAPTER 14

Give or Take

I was told that when you approach a street child, instead of asking their name, tell them yours. There's a subtle psychological transaction that takes place. In essence, you're giving something rather than taking their name.

Often, people forget those children had nothing. This includes no guidance from adults who showed they cared.

One time, a persistent boy followed me down the street with his hand outstretched. It was a bit annoying, and that day I had nothing to give him but some gum.

When I placed a piece of gum in his hand, he scowled and turned on his sad face. "Mama, hungry ... hungry. Shilling ...."

"The money is gone," I said and showed him my empty pocket.

He continued to give me the sad face as if it would make money appear. To teach him a lesson, I casually took the gum from his outstretched hand. His sad look transformed to shock. As we walked along together, I explained to him that it's good to say *Asante* (thank-you) when someone gives you something. People like respect and will be more generous the next time. I gave him his gum back, and he sheepishly responded with a smile.

Once, a guard threatened to put me in jail because I talked to a street boy outside a large grocery store. The guards were equipped with batons or a weapon called an *arunga*, which could be used to take down a lion single-handedly. They were paid to keep street children away. But by the time I had my run-in with the guard, I had dealt with street children on a regular basis. For me, those children represented a mission field instead of a nuisance. This particular twelve-year-old boy named Jonathan spoke English and had attended three years of school. English is the national language, but there are forty-seven tribal languages spoken in Kenya. Swahili is considered the language of trade.

The two of us were chatting when the guard came along and said, "Mama, don't talk to that one."

"He's not bothering me," I said. "We're having a nice talk. It's okay."

The guard scowled. "You don't understand. These are not good children. I could have you put in the cells," he threatened.

I thought, *Jail! For talking?*

He took a step closer to me.

My mother-bear instinct took over. I stuffed the boy behind my back to protect him, and said, "Okay you can take me, but I need to talk to this boy first."

God watched out for me that day. Somehow, I convinced the guard to leave me alone. When the others with me that day walked out of the store, we boarded the van. Jonathan followed me with his hand extended. After what we had just been through, and because I wanted to make Jonathan feel better, I gave him fifty shillings (about seventy-five cents). He already told me that he wanted to buy a clean shirt, because the president's motorcade was scheduled to come through town. This dear boy simply wanted to fit in with the rest of the crowd as they lined the streets and waved to the president. I'm sure the guard must have thought he was protecting me and doing his job, but the experience was traumatic all the way around.

Two years later, Jonathan spotted me. He called out, "Mama Dala, rememba me?" He pinched the fabric of his shirt between his thumb and index finger and said, "See my shirt?"

At first, I didn't recognize him because he'd grown so much.

He persisted. "Mama, rememba me? You bought me this shirt."

I was stunned. Two years later, he wore the same shirt and wanted to thank me for it. I'm convinced most street kids are not bad people.

CHAPTER 15

Birth of Our Project

*And my God will meet all your needs according to the riches
of his glory in Christ Jesus.* (Philippians 4:19)

Deputy Mayor Onyango Radier informed us that he would take it
upon himself to find a public piece of land where we could continue to work with the boys. He also offered to go to the town council
and present a proposal. Before any of this could take place, however,
I needed a registration certificate that identified us as a Self-Help
Community Project.

He told me, "You need to go to the Social Services building."

Like everything else in Kisumu, that sounded far easier than it
proved to be. Social Services scheduled a series of meetings. At the
time, Mr. Charles Anyang Kondiek served as the director of Social
Services and Housing, and he was called into one of our meetings. He
greeted us with a warm, exuberant handshake and welcoming smile.
His manner relaxed me a little, because he seemed genuinely happy to
make my acquaintance.

Known around town as Mr. Anyang, the street boys recognized his
little red motor scooter wherever he went. They knew him well. I loos-
ened up a little and asked my questions about the wisdom of taking a
few boys off the street.

I asked, "Do you think they would stay if they had food and a safe place to sleep? Do you know of any houses with a big backyard for rent? Do I have to have a board of directors to qualify for registration? What kind of forms will I need and where do I send them? Is there a fee involved?"

If there was one thing I wasn't short on, it was questions. And he was the man with most of the answers.

To start with, we needed a local board. The number of good Christian men I knew limited my choices. I chose a bright young man who'd grown up as a sponsored child of World Vision. Another man served as the pastor of the church I attended. Then there was my language helper's husband. The fourth board member was the pastor of a local Nazarene church. We met to choose a name for our project. Agape Children's Ministry seemed like the best fit. In Greek, *agape* means the highest form of God's love. It is unconditional and has no racial, political, or social boundaries. It described just the kind of love we wanted to show those children. We also discussed the direction we wanted this little project to go. We talked about staffing needs, a budget, and other people we could contact for assistance.

A short time later, I received a phone call from a real estate agent. "I've heard about what you want to do, and I've found the perfect house with a large compound. You'd better come see it quickly before it's gone."

Curiosity set me into motion. Since it was the lunch hour, I stopped to pick up Mr. Macwan, who was not only the speaker who convicted me with his Good Samaritan sermon, but also a very successful businessman.

CHAPTER 16

A Skeleton Staff

And my God will meet all your needs according to the riches of his glory in Christ Jesus. (Philippians 4:19)

The agent was right. The property suited our needs perfectly. The freshly painted house came with a sitting room, kitchen, and two large bedrooms. It even had a flush toilet. Mr. Macwan agreed the price was reasonable, and we found a way to pay the first month's rent. It was a step of faith. I trusted God to keep me healthy and hold my car together so I could dip into my available funds. I believed God meant what He said about supplying all our needs according to His glorious riches in Christ Jesus.

The compound came with a guard stationed at the gate. His name was Gordon and he wore a Muslim cap. The neighbors told us he had been a faithful guard, and we kept him on. Then Lebaus volunteered to be a houseparent. And a lady who could live in the servant's quarters with her two small children was recommended as our cook.

To complete our skeleton staff, I hired Peter. He sold mosquito nets and other trinkets by the grocery store. After greeting him in Dholuo on a regular basis, and occasionally buying things from him, I learned he had grown up in the streets. As a young teenager, his uncle rescued him and sent him to school. He professed to be a believer and said he wanted to pass on what his uncle had done for him. He became the night houseparent. We were one step closer to our registration.

Of course, we had no furniture, and without curtains, the rooms were bright and sunny. But we had a roof to keep the boys dry, windows with screens to protect them from mosquitos, a porch to sit on, and a big backyard for them to play in. The boys would be safe with no one to hassle them at night. These things alone were major factors, and I started to learn what was most important to street children. For them, shelter held more value than food.

They said, "If we have food but no place to keep it, the food will be stolen."

Once they had shelter, food came second.

CHAPTER 17

Our First Boys

But Jesus called the children to him and said, "Let the little children come to me, and do not hinder them, for the kingdom of God belongs to such as these." (Luke 18:16)

M r. Anyang became my personal hero. One day he arrived beaming as if someone had plugged him in. In his hand he held a certificate. It read: *AGAPE CHILDREN'S MINISTRY, Self-Help Community Project, Kisumu, Kenya.* I really felt like jumping up and down, but I contained myself. We were so excited. It took several weeks to process the document, and without Mr. Anyang's help we would probably still be trying to get it. But there it was in our hands. It gave us the right to take in our first boys.

We decided to start with five and see what happened. We sincerely hoped they'd be able to leave the glue habit if their basic needs were met, but we really didn't know what to expect regarding behavior issues or withdrawals. We walked by faith.

In anticipation, our staff prayed about who the first five boys should be. We had built a good relationship with many of the boys through the weekly soccer games. Even so, we came to a unanimous agreement. We invited Jacob, Evans, Kalil, Tim, and Rafiq.

What a joyful day as we witnessed God's divine answer to prayer.

Lebaus and Peter quickly went into town and found the boys. They talked about it for a while, and the boys came one at a time.

Lebaus brings street boy to Agape

It must have been scary for them too, since they had no idea what to expect. Would there be too many rules? Would we take away all their freedom? How could they survive without glue? What would their friends in town say about them?

Jacob was a kindhearted boy, though undernourished and dirty. But after a good bath, a haircut, and some clean clothes, he looked much better. After some time, we discovered he was a talented artist. At first, he just sat on the porch with the others and played gambling games with kernels of corn. The games were a common pastime for street boys, and we decided not to take that away from them. They needed to feel comfortable with us, and it would take time to build their trust. Gradually, his interest in art consumed his free time.

I met Evans in the marketplace. He was a handsome eleven-year-old in spite of burn scars on the left side of his face and chest. He fell into a cook fire at the age of two. Evans was very polite and never became aggressive or demanding. I later found out he was one of the few boys who actually saved some of his shillings and took them back to his destitute mother.

Kalil, an absolutely adorable child, wore a wide grin. It revealed perfectly straight teeth with dimples in both cheeks. His joyful nature was evident. He made others smile as he walked around swinging the long, dirty sleeves of his shirt, which was about two sizes too big. Kalil faithfully attended our first meetings in town, and I always looked forward to seeing him. He loved to sing and did so with all his heart when the glue wore off.

In contrast, Tim looked miserable. He needed to be out of that street environment. His unresolved anger left him moody at times, and sometimes even he didn't understand why. He was a good fighter but an even better soccer player. That's how we eventually reached him and gained his trust.

Rafiq was young and precious. He ended up on the streets after his mother died. We eventually learned he had a stepmother who sold used clothing in the market. But many times in the Luo culture a stepchild is not accepted. This lady had other children and struggled to keep her household together. With no money for school fees, she sent Rafiq out to make his own way.

The boys had their differences at times. Fights flared up over the simplest things. It could be as simple as two boys who both wanted to carry the soccer ball out to the backyard and fought before they even got there. If a boy kicked the ball out of bounds, it led to a lot of yelling and name calling. We got really good at conflict resolution. One time, I talked to one boy who had trouble communicating with the others and often put them on the defensive. So I advised him to try "making a sandwich" with his words. Here's an example.

Begin with something to give the benefit of the doubt:

"Hey Jon, what happened to my soap? You didn't use it all on purpose, did you?"

Then fill it by tackling the issue:

"Now I don't have any. You need to ask me before you just take my stuff."

Put the top on with something positive to help you stay friends:

"It's okay this time because we're friends. You'll remember to ask me next time."

A couple days later, I walked by and overhead the same boy as he talked to a friend. He looked rather annoyed. I gave him a motherly reminder look. He picked up the cue and said to me, "Don't worry, Mama. I've made the sandwich and it's ready to be eaten!"

That really happened, and it still makes me laugh.

When they eventually settled into a routine and the fighting subsided, we took in another boy.

First days of Agape

CHAPTER 18

Sammy's Rescue

Even as a street boy, Sammy proved to be unique. I met him in 1992, when everything about Kisumu was still new and strange to me. In my early months, as I learned the language, Sammy approached me to beg for shillings. At the time, he was a young teenager. To my great relief, he actually understood what I said to him.

"Eh Mama, you speak Dholuo!" He flashed a big smile. "Me, I want to learn Englees."

That's how our friendship began.

He'd attended school to the second grade and knew a little English. So we had fun with that. One time he actually reached up and pulled my ear closer to him so I could hear the correct pronunciation of a word. That made me laugh.

The times I encountered Sammy in town, I noticed a kind of big-brother leadership quality he displayed with the other street boys. He was also the only one who understood if I happened to be in a hurry. One day, I met a group of kids as I tried to pick up groceries before the shops closed. It drove me crazy that the stores closed for the lunch hour. When I explained this to Sammy, he spread out his arms and made a barricade to keep the others behind him.

As I entered the shop, I heard him exclaim, "Give her time!"

Even though Sammy was a born leader, he lived a very sad life filled with trauma. His alcoholic father often beat his sons when he came home drunk. Sammy shared that sometimes his little brother's head would "get real big" (swollen). Being the eldest, his mother told him he would be better off in the street. His family lived in Nakuru. He pretended to belong to other passengers who boarded the *matatus* (large African taxis) and made his way to Nairobi. Unfortunately, when he reached Nairobi, he got into serious trouble with a boy who jumped him. A witness vouched for Sammy and said he acted in self-defense. Nevertheless, Sammy was sent to a harsh life in the remand center (juvenile hall). Eventually, they transferred him to Kisumu and then released him. By this time, he'd developed a glue habit to numb his pain and loneliness.

Sammy attended our Sunday afternoon meetings faithfully. Even though he was often high from glue fumes and sometimes couldn't stay awake, he made it a priority to be there. My heart ached to see a boy with such promise voluntarily damage his mind with cobbler's glue. But it was the only way he knew how to cope with life.

We watched Sammy for a while.

Christian counselor and teacher Jack Ngoblia shared his worries with me. "Sammy is on his way to becoming a teenage schizophrenic."

That nearly broke my heart. I saw such wonderful qualities in Sammy. I even had a video clip of him sobered up at one of our meetings. We had sodas as a special treat that day. A boy who sat next to Sammy accidentally tipped his bottle over and spilled the rest of the soda. Sammy immediately picked up his friend's bottle and poured his own orange Fanta into the empty bottle. Amazing. What a touching and generous act of kindness for a street boy. To this day, Sammy is a generous and compassionate young man.

In 1993, I invited him to Agape. Each opportunity like this elated me. What a blessing and honor to offer a roof and some good food to a few desperate kids. In this case, I remember it as one of my best days in Kisumu. I just couldn't get into town fast enough.

My friend and I found Sammy behind a group of shops by a little campfire, getting settled in for the night. He stared at us glassy-eyed from sniffing glue. My language helper spoke his language and explained how we had a house for him to stay in. Sammy looked happy about coming with us and headed toward the car.

I said, "But Sammy, what will you do with the glue? You know we can't take it with us."

He looked at me and at the glue can in his hand. Slowly, he surveyed the area. With a grand sweep of his arm, he threw the can into the street. I'll never forget the sound of that glue can as it bounced across the pavement.

When it stopped clanging, he said, "Let's go."

We arrived at Agape just in time for dinner. Since we had no tables or chairs, the other four boys sat on the floor. They had just been served steaming bowls of rice and beans and were diving in.

When they saw us, they shouted, "Sammy's here! Sammy's here!"

Sammy waved and smiled at his friends.

"Before joining the group," I said to him, "go wash your hands."

He hurried to wash his hands and joined his friends. We had plenty of food for one more person, and the cook carried out a plastic bowl with a generous portion. Sammy sat down on the concrete floor and bowed his head. Without any prompting, he prayed an earnest prayer, thanking God for this place and for the food.

It's difficult to express the emotions we felt during those days as the boys bonded with each other. Their rough behavior fell away and they learned that God's way is the best way.

Unfortunately, due to his frequent use of glue, Sammy suffered some permanent damage. Academic studies frustrated him, but he *loved* to play soccer. He organized countless games at Agape, which provided an effective form of therapy for all involved.

We realized Sammy needed a vocational skill. So we paid close attention to his traits and natural abilities. Sammy liked animals and proved to be a responsible caretaker for them. He also had a way with people and liked to save the shillings he earned. We thought about setting up some kind of business. Then we learned that a new houseparent had worked for a large chicken ranch in Nairobi and still had connections there. We knew we had found our answer.

Sammy became the first young man at Agape to be specially trained to raise poultry. He took to his new venture with great enthusiasm and it encouraged all of us to see it. While he was still at Agape, the sounds of his business filled the compound. Roosters crowed, hens clucked, and the chicks thrived under his care. But eventually, the occupation became a bit too much for him to manage on his own.

Later, when I went back to visit, I found Sammy in a water cart business. He's strong and willing to work hard. So it's the perfect job for him. He faithfully delivers water jugs to his clients and plans to buy a second cart soon to expand his business.

CHAPTER 19

A Surprising Visit

One evening, while our local pastor visited, I answered a knock at the door. Two Indian gentlemen stood on the porch. I hesitated with a somewhat puzzled look on my face. They quickly introduced themselves.

"We are brothers," they said.

The younger man worked at the local stationery store. I had recently visited the store in search of a scrapbook. It turned out that no one understood what a scrapbook was. I explained that I needed the book to keep newspaper articles in about the street boys. It would help describe and validate the needs they had and the lives they lived.

The man proved to be especially inquisitive and helpful. It turned out that his brother, Naresh Patel, was the chairman-elect of the Lions Club. Naresh was looking for a good community project for his term of office. When his brother reported our meeting, he decided to visit in order to determine if they could be of some assistance.

We had a nice time together. Before the visit ended, Mr. Patel offered to build a dining shed for the street boys. Of course, the prospect thrilled me. There was just one problem. We had no land on which to build a dining shed or any other kind of shed, for that matter.

The next day, I went to see the deputy mayor. Mr. Patel kindly took time from work to help me explain the situation. We needed a place to put a dining shed.

The deputy mayor said, "There is a piece of public land just outside town that could be a possibility. It would take time to meet with the other city officials and we would have to acquire the proper building permits."

I happily offered to pursue any leads he suggested. In effect, I visited the town hall so many times in the next few months that some people thought I had an office there. I visited the planning commission, various council members, the architect, the land office, and the Children's Department. They all had to give their approval.

I even made eight overnight trips to Nairobi to acquire a piece of paper that gave us a ninety-nine-year lease. I wondered if the Lions Club chairman's term of office would run out before we received permission to build. I learned some important things firsthand through that process, however. Sometimes my paperwork would get "lost." Sometimes it sat under a big stack of other folders … waiting. The waiting was for a "cup of tea"; in other words, a bribe. I had no extra money in those days and didn't want to get that cycle going, even if I called it a fee. So I waited. Perhaps a little Irish stubbornness came into play, but the day finally arrived when we had everything we needed. I clearly remember the day I walked into that big office for the last time. The man in charge gruffly asked if I had learned any Swahili.

I smiled and said, "Well, you have taught me a couple words." He looked quizzical, so I added, "Ngoje kidogo." (Wait a little while.)

Everyone in the office had a good laugh as he handed me the document I spent so many hours waiting for.

Wait for the Lord; *be strong and take heart and wait for the* Lord. (Psalm 27:14)

CHAPTER 20

Supportive Friends

The Lions Club liked to do things in a big way. The opening of our home and later our dining shed turned into formal events with the cutting of a large ribbon across the entrance. The occasion included several encouraging speeches, music from the boys, and a large array of cakes and sweets for both celebrations. Everyone got a soda, which, even today, remains a treat for any special occasion.

The Lions Club donated bamboo mats and blankets for the kids to sleep on. Up until that time, we had very little to work with. For instance, we had plastic cups and plates, but no utensils for the boys. They were used to eating with their fingers. When I purchased forks and spoons, they often went missing when they were sold to passersby through our back fence.

An artist visiting Kenya from Israel heard about us. She kindly offered to bring sheets and paints so the boys could decorate their own curtains. This was a major event, which gave the boys a sense of ownership of their new home. Those colorful sheets lasted several years and were always attached to tender memories of fun and accomplishment.

A businessman in town offered to make a blackboard. He painted charcoal on a large framed board. I could afford some pieces of chalk, and one of our houseparents was a former teacher. We could now have school. Every morning we moved the mats from the bedroom into our "sitting room." We propped the blackboard against a ledge and created an instant classroom.

Some of the boys had attended school for a couple of years, but others had never set foot in a classroom. Our teacher reviewed the alphabet and basic numbers. Then English vocabulary words and greetings were added. Each day when I arrived, the boys eagerly shared what they'd learned. Fortunately, I had brought some crayons, coloring books, and a few pairs of scissors. We tore a page out of the coloring book for each student and gave each one about three crayons to work with. Then we taught them how to use the scissors. Everything was very basic but so satisfying when it was mastered. The kids loved learning. For entertainment, in addition to soccer, they sang and danced to music from a boom box. We became one big happy family.

CHAPTER 21

A Timely Rescue for Zack

I am frequently asked how it's possible for so many young children to be abandoned to the street. There are as many answers as there are children. Zack was born into an all-around bad situation. His unemployed, unwed mother lived in a slum area. A defeated lifestyle led her to increased frustration and anger. Occasionally, she deserted the children and left them in the care of an elderly neighbor who took pity on them. The mother gradually became more violent and frequently chased the children from the house when she had male friends visit.

Her behavior forced Zack to seek refuge with the kind neighbor lady. However, she had no money for school fees, and he grew bored with idleness. Looking for adventure, Zack searched for a better way of life in various towns. Finally, he met some boys who befriended him and gave him a sense of belonging. At the age of nine, he became a wandering street boy. He lived by his wits and his fists. After four years in the streets, he became one of the best street fighters in Kisumu.

When he attended some of our first Sunday meetings, he looked like a typical street boy. We learned he made a living by collecting and selling bits of waste paper and charcoal. He spent the money he earned on food and glue. The effects of the glue made him feel warmer when he curled up to sleep on shop verandas or in treetop hammocks woven from plastic sacks.

We preferred to rescue younger boys who had not been hardened for so long in the street. But we took a chance on Zack. At thirteen, we brought him to Agape. We received information that his mother could sometimes be found in the bus station. One Sunday, as the boys rode home from church in a matatu, Zack spotted his mother and called out to her. Peter the houseparent halted the matatu and jumped out with Zack at his side. They thought Zack's mother would be happy to see him and they eagerly approached her.

To their complete disappointment, she coldly looked at Zack, and said, "You're not my son."

Can you imagine how this rejection affects a child? For several days after the encounter, Zack stayed moody and downcast. He cried easily and became difficult to handle. He often ended up in the center of a confrontation with the other boys. The situation made him a real prayer challenge for our staff.

He had difficulties in school, and his English skills were poor. As a result, he struggled in several classes. His school was a long walk from our center, and he looked for opportunities to voice his discontent.

Once, he pointed to his leg, and said, "Mama, when I get to school, the leg is broke."

Another time, it rained, and his sweater was wet when he arrived. His teacher slapped a ruler on the back of his hand.

We learned that the local public schools weren't the answer for former street boys. Sometimes the boys were older than their classmates and that further complicated the situation. They felt like they didn't belong, and it created an ongoing sense of failure. So, with the help of other missionaries, we started a literacy school. The boys could be encouraged in their studies and experience God's love in a consistent way.

We knew God had plans for this boy. Through our efforts, Zack grew in the knowledge that Jesus loved him. It transformed his life. A year later, through our home visitation program, Zack and his mother were reunited. They met in their village home for the first time in five years and began to reconstruct their relationship. His mother saw his new nature and was proud of the change. Zack returned to Agape for the next school term a much happier boy.

Sadly, after a brief illness, his mother died. Now an orphan, Zack's only known relatives were two younger brothers and a blind, ailing grandmother. But he continued to go to school and made good progress. One day, he came back to Agape and flashed his disarming smile.

He announced, "The teacher asked me who my mother is, so I told her my mother is Auntie Darla."

After eleven years, Zack graduated from Agape and supported his own family. The road has been a journey with many potholes along the way. Often, when he came to visit me he needed money.

On one summer visit, he said he didn't want to ask for any more money. He had gotten his driver's license and was earning a little money. "You will see, Mama. Next time I will buy *you* a soda."

I forgot about the conversation. When Zack arrived the next time, he wore a broad smile.

After our initial greetings, he exclaimed, "Mama, I came to keep my promise."

He stuffed his hand into his pocket for shillings and told me about his successful new job as a driver. When the sodas arrived, he popped the caps off ceremoniously and handed a bottle to me. It symbolized his maturity and responsibility. Now he had earnings to share.

"Zack, this is the best soda I've ever tasted," I said. And I meant it.

CHAPTER 22

Born and Bred in a Park

The title of this story is actually a caption from one of Kenya's national newspapers called *The Standard*, dated Wednesday, August 8, 1990. It's the story of one of our older boys known at that time simply as Kalulu (Swahili for "clown"). Later, we learned his real name was Moses Angote. This is the same Moses I mentioned in chapter 9. However, everyone in town knew him as Kalulu. He was always around somewhere. The street was his home.

When he told the reporter about his life, Moses said, "One day I was sleeping beside a path at the Jamhuri Park after begging the whole day for money to buy food. Then suddenly a powerful kick landed on my backside and a harsh voice said, 'Stand up quickly. You are the people destroying this town.' Then the man kicked the little tin can where I kept my coins and forced me into a car waiting nearby."

That's how Moses ended up in police custody at only five years old. Later, they set him free with a strict warning never to be seen in the streets again. Since that time, he had been arrested countless times, but released every time.

One might wonder why he didn't just go home, but Moses *was* at home. He was born in the park in Kisumu in 1977 during a heavy downpour. An old man who used to live in the park knew his mother and told Moses the story. He explained how his mother begged for food and money from the businessmen and women at the market. When she was pregnant, she grew thin and tired as her delivery time approached. It was raining heavily when she felt labor pains. She delivered Moses in a flimsy shelter built with plastic sheets in a gazebo, with no one to help her.

Moses doesn't recall the gazebo, of course, but he does remember the last time he saw his mother. He was just three years old.

His mother said, "I'm going to get some bananas."

She disappeared toward the marketplace and left him playing in the park. Some time passed, and he grew tired of playing and fell asleep. He hoped his mother would return soon.

Today, as he recalls the life-changing event, he says, "When I woke up, I felt more hungry and didn't know what to do. I decided to go to the market where some people from India gave me bananas and coins for lunch."

Sadness still fills Moses' face as he admits, "I have never seen my mother since."

The article was written when Moses was thirteen years old. I first met him in town in 1993, when he was sixteen. Moses came to our Sunday afternoon meetings. Even though the meetings were intended for the younger boys, Moses attended faithfully. Later, he stood on the sidelines at our soccer games. He hesitated to participate. After a few weeks, he became part of the team and clearly enjoyed himself. Finally, I observed some happiness in his eyes.

With Agape under way and the first few boys settled in, our staff discussed the possibility of including Kalulu. He was older than the others, very shy, and seldom spoke. This would present challenges. His shyness made it difficult to communicate with him, and was compounded by the fact that he knew no English. After a lot of discussion and prayer, we decided to try. I'll never forget the day he came to Agape.

Our houseparent Peter went into town to pick up the barefoot boy in his dirty, shabby clothes, and gave him a ride on his bicycle.

Peter told me later that he said to him, "Kalulu, you're going to like Agape."

Kalulu's slow and deliberate response was, "My name is Moses."

Peter said, "That's a great name, Moses. What's your second name?"

Moses placed his hand on his forehead and answered hesitantly, "Angote ... my name is Moses Angote."

No one had used his name for so long, he hardly remembered what his full name was.

I arrived at our rented house to greet Moses, and found him hiding behind the door all cleaned up with a fresh haircut. He wore a rolled-up, long-sleeved white shirt and gray trousers. Still barefooted, because he had never worn shoes, he shuffled his feet uncomfortably. As the days wore on, he fit right in with the rest of the boys.

Our houseparent and teacher, Collins, wrote letters on the blackboard while the kids sat on the floor. He asked them to repeat the sounds of the letters. It wasn't long before Moses took the pointer and stood at the blackboard naming the letters and saying the vowel sounds. I had to take a picture, because his face just beamed with his accomplishment. To this day, that photo is one of my treasures. Moses' ability to learn encouraged all of us very much.

It wasn't a smooth road for Moses. We tried carpentry training for a while. But selfish people took advantage of his lack of social skills. Four years later, however, Moses Angote became the first of our young men to become an Agape staff member.

From beggar to man with dignity

For the last eighteen years, he has worked as our gardener and maintenance man. It pleased him so much when he received his first paycheck that, when he walked around the corner of our building and thought no one was watching, he did a little dance. He kept a few shillings for pocket money and put the rest in his savings box, kept safely in the main office.

Moses saved enough to rent a small house and live on his own. He even hosted a group of visiting Agape students and served us tea and bread. What a special day that was for all of us. In fact, it was probably the most special day in Moses' life up to that point. We sang praise choruses in his home and thanked God for the miracles we witnessed in his life. It was quite a spectacle for the surrounding neighbors to see a whole group of muzungus parade into Moses' small house. While we were there, he proudly pointed out a single light bulb. It hung from a thick wire in the middle of his sitting room. Not all the homes in the area even had electricity. He was definitely living the good life.

Then one day I received word that his mother had been located in a village outside of town. Although she suffered from mental illness, she and Moses were reunited. He made sure she had food and received care. He did this while he put his younger sister through school. His progress was amazing to witness. God still does miracles and this is no doubt one of them.

My bi-annual trip to Kenya held more good news. Moses arrived at work with a lovely young lady named Grace at his side. She became Moses' wife. Because arranged marriages are still common in Kenya, Moses had asked Lebaus and other staff members to help him find a wife. This lovely Christian lady possessed a quiet strength and obviously loved Moses. It almost seems impossible to imagine that this lonely, abused little beggar could become a respected, hardworking family man.

And there's more. On my latest trip to Kenya, I felt a deep sense of elation when Moses came to Agape's twentieth anniversary party all dressed up in a suit. Grace accompanied him with their little boy named Paul Darla and a brand new baby boy. Moses is one of the most amazing transformations we've ever seen. And to think we struggled with our initial decision about whether or not to bring Moses to Agape.

Nicholas, Grace, baby Paul, Moses and Darla

Moses built a house in his mother's home area, which was quite an accomplishment. He still cares for her and is the father of three sons, Paul, Julius, and Steven.

Treat a man as he is and he will remain as he is. Treat a man as he could be and he will become what he should be.

CHAPTER 23

Water, Water Everywhere. But Not a Drop to Drink

Lake Victoria is two hundred miles across and the second-largest freshwater lake in the world. You might think a good water supply wouldn't be a problem in Kisumu, since it's located on the shore of this abundant source. But it is. We survived a span of three months with no running water at Agape. The intake plant proved unable to meet the needs of the rapidly growing population of Kisumu. It could have caused a long-term problem.

The fire chief came up with a plan to deliver a tank of water twice a week if we would pay half the cost. That seemed reasonable enough, but we didn't realize our limited capacity for water storage. The supply only lasted two days. God met that need through a generous Asian friend who donated a big new storage tank. The size of the tank required us to build a platform and have a new tap installed. Another small investment.

Two weeks later, the project was completed. The fire department pulled up with the water. I paused on my way to a meeting to watch. The hose hung over the tank and the water flowed ALL OVER THE GROUND. It turned out that the tank had about ten holes in it caused by improper welding. The holes created the effect of a giant shower. We ran for basins, cooking pans, and a neighbor's water drum in an effort to claim at least some of the precious commodity.

After more handcart deliveries, more expense, and more waiting, the holes were finally mended. Again, I sent a message to the fire department to let them know we were ready for the water.

The reply came, "The fire truck can't come. It has a punctured tire." The whole experience was a real test of a missionary's sense of humor.

The Agape board met and we came up with some options. The best one seemed to be to lay new pipes and connect with a more dependable line. Permission to do that held us up four more weeks. While we waited, we also considered investing in our own water cart and letting the boys haul the water in. But before we did that, the city came through. At last, the problem was solved.

CHAPTER 24

Washington Gains Wisdom

Washington came into the world as the seventh child in a family that was breaking apart. He never knew the security of a mother and father who were there for him and his siblings. In the early years of his life, his father killed their neighbor and ran away. He was eventually caught and thrown into prison where he died in 1992. From that time on, Washington's mother drank heavily. Not only did she drink, she also brewed and sold a local brew known as *chang'a*. Her little business was illegal and landed her in and out of jail. Her unstable life left no one to care for the children.

Washington's oldest sister, who was ten at the time, did the best she could. When Washington was seven, she took him to nursery school. Conditions at home were extremely difficult. The children struggled to get even a little food to eat. At the age of nine, Washington ran away to an aunt's house, but wasn't well received. His only option? The streets in Kisumu.

Washington described his first day on the streets as a nightmare, and he has the scars on his body to prove it. As a small boy of almost eleven, he had no one to protect him. So he tried to find shelter in the Kenol Petrol Station. Some older boys attacked him with a knife, severely wounding him, and stole the few decent clothes and shoes he had.

The next day, he moved to the city dumping grounds. There he met Kachock, a kinder, older boy who took him under his wing and showed him the ropes of how to survive. For six months, Washington stuck to him and learned all he could.

In August, he met three other boys. They hung out together, slept in nylon gunny sacks, and collected plastic to sell for money to buy glue. Glue became a big part of Washington's life. It comforted him from the cold and the misery of his condition, and it helped him not to think about his problems.

After a year in the streets, Washington and several other boys were chosen to come to Agape. From the combination of many years with no authority figure in his life and no real bond with his family, the feelings of rejection and trauma caught up with him. It left Washington restless. He didn't feel like he belonged anywhere and found it difficult to settle down. Shortly after he arrived in Agape, he entered a cycle of running to the streets, being brought back, running again, and being brought back. This happened four times over the period of a year. Each time, we reached out and lovingly brought him back and told him he belonged.

During his time at Agape, something very significant happened. Washington came to know Jesus. It happened through the memorization of Proverbs 5:1-2. *My son, pay attention to my wisdom, turn your ear to my words of insight, that you may maintain discretion and your lips may preserve knowledge.*

His Sunday school teacher explained who Jesus is and prayed with him to receive the gift of salvation. Washington told me Lebaus gave him a small Gideon New Testament in English that he loved to read. Lebaus spent time with the street boys in a group to sing and talk about the Lord. Washington joined an Agape choir that ministered on the streets and in churches. Through all those experiences, Washington grew and matured in his faith. In fact, he developed a strong desire to tell all of his siblings and relatives in the village that Jesus wanted to work in their lives as well.

Washington was the only one in his entire family to finish eighth grade. He diligently prayed for his family. As he looked back over all the Lord accomplished and the opportunities he had been given, he believed it was all for a purpose. He believed God wanted to use him to reach his family.

CHAPTER 25

God's Practical Advice

"Be still, and know that I am God." (Psalm 46:10)

God revealed Himself through His Word in many ways. It's where I often turned for comfort and strength as I faced challenges in Kisumu. Psalm 37 became one of my favorite psalms because it reminded me to "fret not" (Psalm 37:1). I needed that practical reminder over and over again, especially when we tried to get some property for Agape and had no money.

Psalm 37 offered loads of other reminders too. As I waited my turn in the town hall, I pondered verse 4: *Take delight in the LORD, and he will give you the desires of your heart.* In verse 9 it says, *those who hope in the Lord will inherit the land. Inherit* was the operative word there, because I didn't need money for that.

Verse 7 reminded me to rest in the Lord. Occasionally, I got so tired physically and mentally that I felt like a goldfish in a shark tank. People in Kenya had so many dire problems. Elderly widows struggled to eke out a living, people needed jobs, children begged for school fees, hawkers desperately tried to sell their wares, and patients were forced to stay in the hospital until their bills were paid. Money seemed like the solution to every problem. I understood their needs, but locals couldn't believe I didn't have money. They believed that every American was rich. After all, we had machines for everything from brushing our teeth to mowing the grass. I did what I could even if all I could do was listen. It's amazing what a smile and a friendly word will do for a person's outlook. Of course, that worked both ways. Proverbs 12:25 says, *Anxiety weighs down the heart, but a kind word cheers it up.* Remember that!

CHAPTER 26

An Ordinary Street Boy

"Whoever welcomes one of these little children in my name welcomes me." (Mark 9:37a)

Some stories I've heard about street boys and why they live in the streets were absolutely appalling. Fortunately, it turns out many of those stories weren't true. Street boys survive by their wits, and their ability to tell good stories becomes an art form. They won't tell the truth about their names or where they're from if they're afraid the police will send them back. They learn to manipulate a person's emotions to get what they need to survive.

I've seen little boys wear two pairs of pants. The worn-out pair on top covered the holes in the pair underneath. Their dirty, ragged shirts drooped over one shoulder because they were so stretched out around the neck. I never understood how they did that. Perhaps they pulled their arms inside the shirt to stay warm at night and stretched it out in the process. Sometimes they smelled like oil and rubber if they slept under parked trucks. Most often, they'd go barefoot or wear rubber flip-flops. If a child owned shoes, they were often mismatched and didn't begin to fit. But at least they provided some protection from bits of glass, stray nails, and animal droppings.

To find food, the boys searched behind hotels and restaurants to find discarded scraps. Once, I took a picture of two boys as they shared a breakfast of cold french fries and a spoiled tomato. They warmed water in an old tin can on top of a tiny charcoal fire in an attempt to have something hot to drink.

On any given day, boys rummaged through the trash heaps in search of something to salvage. A discarded bag of leftover food was a real treasure. Sometimes they'd be exhausted enough to take a nap right on top of the trash heap.

When hotel employees emptied the trash, boys nearby made a bee-line for pieces of soap or tubes of toothpaste with a little left inside. They ate wormy cabbage, old dried fish, or whatever else they found. And yes, some of the boys become sick with salmonella-induced food poisoning. Sometimes it was deadly.

Life in the streets is a harsh and dangerous existence. Agape has been called upon several times to hold funeral services for young boys who fell victim to their environment.

CHAPTER 27

George Bush

O ur smallest boy, George Bush, leaned against my legs as we watched a soccer game. The two campus dogs curled up on the ground beside us. I didn't take any of it for granted. Those boys were rescued from the street. They now lived safe and healthy lives, including little George Bush. God gathered us into a big family, which made all the hassles worthwhile.

I've always had a heart for animals. I get so concerned and sad when I see a strange dog wandering aimlessly around the neighborhood. The frantic movements and look of fear in a dog's eyes makes me do everything I can to calm the animal down.

Now, imagine a small boy with that same frantic fear in his eyes. We found the little guy near a busy bus stop. He was clearly lost. The other street boys tried to help him but without success.

They said, "Mama, please take him. He cries all the time, and he's too heavy to carry around."

What should we do? I wondered. *What if someone is worried sick and looking for him?* We talked to one of the officials and other Kenyans around the bus stop. They said they'd keep an eye on him for a few days.

When we checked back on him, the street boys reported that he was sick. "He started coughing," they said.

That did it for me. We had to take him. Even if someone accused Agape of kidnapping him. If left alone, his life was at stake.

The little guy stared at me with unsure eyes as we took him in a vehicle to a strange compound. We tried to reassure him with a bowl of warm rice and beans. He took his bowl and quickly disappeared. It broke our hearts to find him crouched in the corner behind the hallway door. He scooped the food into his mouth with his fingers as fast as he could, fearful someone would take the bowl away. Even after he had lived with us for a while, we found food stuffed under his mattress and in the closet. He was obviously still in survival mode.

When we asked him about his name, he replied, "Agush."

Our houseparent explained, "It's probably a tribal nickname."

That's all we had to work with. Agush didn't know any other name. So it was difficult to discern what tribe he was from. He didn't know how old he was but he still had all his baby teeth. He was the size of a four- or five-year-old but acted more like a three-year-old. When I held him on my lap, for example, he reached up and twisted my hair while he fell asleep. Our cook had a small baby, and Agush knew how to hold him. That told us he might not have been the youngest in his family.

We reported him to the Children's Department and circulated his picture at the large agricultural fair. After a month or so, it appeared he was truly on his own. Had someone just left him at the bus park to find his own way? The older boys treated him like their little brother. They gave him rides in the water cart and played games with him. They also called him Bush, as in bush baby, which he seemed to like.

After some time, we put him in nursery school. Lebaus took him to get registered.

"What's his name?" the lady in charge asked.

"Bush," Lebaus replied.

"And what of his second name?"

Lebaus thought for a moment and said, "'George' would be nice." And so it was.

Later, when the deputy mayor came to visit, he said, "I hear you have a celebrity here."

Little George Bush remained quite shy. When he met someone new, he backed up, grabbed both of my hands, and crossed them over his body. He held on tight and smiled sweetly. He was the baby of the family. But, loveable as he was, he pinched, bit, and spit faster than any of the other fifteen boys on campus. We worked to correct those undesirable behaviors with consistent, loving discipline.

George Bush (left) and friend

Bush grew strong and fit. Before long, he even tried to carry his bigger brothers around. He loved to sing and learn Bible verses. Then one day, he prayed to receive the gift of Jesus' sacrifice on the cross for his sins.

Things went very well for a couple of years. But it was on the soccer field where Bush really came into his own. He quickly developed skills that made him a sought-after teammate.

One of his young friends said, "Bush is a dangerous man on the soccer field."

As Bush got older, another part of his personality surfaced. He would do as we asked only if *he* thought it was a good idea. If not, he resisted with all his might. At school, his behavior became a growing problem. For example, he would leave and hide if he didn't want to study. We wondered what on earth brought on this type of behavior.

At my wit's end with the situation, I talked to counselors and learned more about attachment disorder. It's a syndrome caused when a child never learns to bond with a loving adult. He feels like he's responsible for himself and doesn't really care what adults tell him to do. Even though loving "aunties" and "uncles" took care of him, it wasn't the same as the tender, nurturing love given to a baby from the beginning. We tried many different approaches. We even had him live with a stable Christian family. He did well there for a while, then, sadly, he started to stay out late at night and get into fights. He always blamed someone else for the encounters and couldn't seem to take responsibility for his own actions.

One day, Bush blamed our administrator for a run-in he had with a policeman.

I said, "Bush, no matter how flat a *chapati* [flat, pancake-like bread] may be, there are always two sides. Now what did you say to the policeman to make him arrest you?"

It grieved our entire staff to see him get in trouble around town. We all prayed for him daily. Our experience with Bush taught us how important a child's experience with a mother or caregiver is at an early age. Sometimes so much damage was done before a child arrived at Agape, we just couldn't fix it or make it all go away.

As a teenager, Bush often turned up in a certain nightclub outside of town. He seemed to feel comfortable there with the music, dancing, and general atmosphere. That caused me to wonder if it was a familiar place to him. Was his mother a prostitute? Did he just get in the way? Did someone purposely drop him off at the bus stop thinking he would find a sympathetic family to care for him? In spite of all our efforts and those of the Kisumu Children's Department, no one ever found the village he came from.

As a young adult, Bush contracted TB and was taken to the hospital. Our staff and his friends visited him often. However, Bush refused to take his medicine and seemed to have lost his will to live. He was tired of getting into trouble, and had no close relatives. But he knew about heaven and longed to be there. Those who loved him prayed with him on many occasions. We believe the Lord rescued him from this worldly turmoil when He took him to his real and final home. What a blessed thought to picture Bush radiantly happy in heaven with the Lord. I look forward to seeing him again. I wonder if he will still give me a backward hug.

As the boys became more rehabilitated, we wondered how we could relate more effectively to the Christian community of Kisumu. This presented a challenge. I reflected on reasons Americans are reluctant to become closely involved with people on the street. I realized that Kenyan Christians might be reluctant to expose their own children to our former street boys. They thought the kids might steal from them or be a bad influence on their families. In fact, even simple requests were met with apprehension. We asked a church to let us show *The Jesus Film* to street boys. It took a while for them to agree. Then, as we prepared to show the film, they removed anything that could be stolen. There wasn't a hymnbook or pencil in sight. They even roped off the part of the building we used, to keep us quarantined. We filled our designated area and enjoyed the movie.

The evening ended on a light note when all the kids laughed as Jesus said, "Kwaheri" ("Good-bye" in Swahili).

It had a different ring to it.

It became our challenge to prove the boys had been transformed by the love of Christ. They weren't perfect, but they were teachable. What they needed most at that point was to experience models of Christian parenting in functional homes. Some of the boys had no place to go during school holidays. We placed the children in volunteer families for the short period. The most success we ever had was when our devoted staff members took the children into their own homes.

It took a long time to find such reliable and caring staff. So many people told me in the beginning they "just loved to work with street children." Unfortunately, that could have been translated into "I just want a job with a lot of money from an American." It didn't take long to weed out those employees, but it was always a traumatic event to have to fire someone. Sometimes confrontations with our native-born employees erupted. If we learned a child was beaten or deprived of a meal, we held a meeting.

I was told, "Mama, you're just trying to make little Americans out of these children. We were caned and it worked for us. That's the African way."

I replied, "If these children needed one more beating, we could have left them in the street. *Agape* means the highest form of God's love, and that's the kind of love we're going to show these kids. Appropriate discipline, but no more beatings."

Eventually, we looked to a well-run Christian college for the answer. Several of our long-term employees came from that college and these days we have very little turnover.

CHAPTER 28

Rite of Passage

We always intended to integrate the boys back into their own communities and make them feel like they belonged. We preferred the boys be able to visit relatives in the rural villages.

However, in the early days of our ministry, that plan sometimes backfired. The custom of the Luhya people was to have their boys go through a rite of passage at the age of fifteen, which included circumcision. Witchcraft was clearly a part of the ritual practice. Levi reached fifteen and asked to go home to take part in the ceremony. He wanted to be seen as a man in the sub-tribe of Tiriki.

Levi was a new Christian. He loved to sing and be the first to quote a memory verse during our devotional times. He was a great kid. His funny antics endeared him to everyone and made him very popular with the staff as well as the other boys. At the time he wanted to take part in the ceremony back home, he'd been at Agape about four years. He was becoming a young man, and because we weren't his legal guardians, we couldn't legally refuse his request.

Diane and Colby, our administrators at the time, prayed earnestly for wisdom. We had no vehicle to take him home and no reintegration team to make the trip with him. Our only choice was to let him go. We hoped and prayed that his newfound faith was strong enough to handle the pressure.

A few weeks later, Levi reappeared at the gate. Everyone was excited to see him again. Things went along fine for a while, but then some of the boys reported their things were going missing. No one admitted to borrowing anything, much less stealing it. Then one day, Lebaus found a pair of stolen tennis shoes hidden on the windowsill behind the bathroom curtain. He waited to see what would happen. Out of curiosity, he kept his eye on Levi.

When Levi asked for a gate pass to go out, Lebaus followed him to the open market. Sadly, Lebaus caught Levi red-handed as he handed over those same tennis shoes to someone ready to buy them. Through that intervention, we learned what was behind Levi's behavior change.

Levi confessed to Lebaus that when he arrived back at his village, the villagers prepared the boys to go through the rite of passage. The witch doctor made an intoxicating brew from a snake head, special herbs, and other nasty things. He forced all the boys to drink it, including Levi. After the circumcision, the witch doctor told Levi that he would now have super-human powers as a thief. This was to be his new life.

Levi believed the witch doctor. Even with counseling and second chances, the stealing at Agape continued. Finally, we had no alternative but to ask him to leave. It broke the staff's heart to watch him escorted through the gate for the last time.

This all took place while I was in California. I grieved for several weeks. My heavy heart pleaded with God to forgive us for failing Levi.

Lebaus reminded me, "We must leave Levi in the Lord's care. Levi made his decision. God will watch over him. Remember, his life isn't over yet."

I found his words consoling.

Several years later, I heard Levi went to Nairobi where he joined the Undugu Society of Kenya. That's where Father Groel worked. It brought me wonderful relief to hear the news. Levi is all grown up now and works in Nairobi. Lebaus was right, and God is faithful. I pray that Levi will continue to make good choices for his life.

Because of that experience, we took steps to make sure all the boys at Agape who didn't have a stable home to go to became wards of Agape. That also allowed them to receive medical treatment and immunizations as needed. The legal benefit was that we could no longer be accused of kidnapping boys off the street. Parents and family members were made aware of their location and were invited to come and visit anytime. We didn't require advance notice, because we *wanted* visitors to find us involved in our day-to-day routine. If relatives wanted to take the boys back home, we visited to make sure it was a safe environment and that the boys could go to school. We didn't want to see any of the boys used as laborers or mistreated the way they had been before. We went through the legal process to become guardians for all the children in our care. It even enabled us to take the boys for circumcision at the Kima Mission Hospital in the Vihiga district.

Whenever possible, we reunited the boys with their families. The transition from life at Agape to life in the family's home required discernment on our part. We asked the family member in charge to hold a simple conversation with the child. If it was an easy and loving conversation, we knew chances were good for a positive reconciliation. However, in some cases, the boy continually looked down at the ground and refused to make eye contact with the adult. If a child clearly displayed such negative body language, our houseparent brought him back to Agape. We knew we had more work to do.

Occasionally, the relative didn't have enough money for school fees or a school uniform. We worked those situations out with the principal of the school and sent money as needed. Sometimes the family had no food in the home. In one such case, all the children had to eat were small unripe avocados from their tree. It's hard to fully comprehend what that kind of poverty does to a family.

Currently, our reintegration team consists of totally devoted Christian nationals who are completely devoted to the well-being of the children.

CHAPTER 29

Patience Takes On a New Definition

Life in Kenya has its challenging moments for those accustomed to the fast pace of American life. The Kenyans dryly refer to us as people who have wristwatches, but refer to Kenyans as those who have the time. Truly, Kenyans celebrate relationships, and we tend to flurry around accomplishing things. Their emphasis comes at the expense of efficiency, however.

Vic Thiessen is one example of God's favor bestowed on Agape. In my absence, Vic, a friend from the African Children's Choir, became the project coordinator. He learned about Kenyan time firsthand. I relate the following narrative in his words to help make my point.

Running Out of Dog Food and Patience

There is no canned dog food in Kisumu. The dogs here get mash, which is cooked each day. Lucky dogs. Last Friday we ran out of dog food. I drove to where I had been told there was a nearby feed mill. Nothing I saw looked like one to me, so I drove to a feed mill farther away. However, they didn't have any dog food.

"The dog food is finished," they said. "We haven't had any for a month now."

"Do you think you will ever have any more?" I asked.

"We might not."

I moved on to a third feed mill. I asked the security guard if they had dog food.

He pointed to an office. "Go there."

I headed into the office and asked, "Do you have any dog food?"

The man at the counter said, "Have you paid?"

I said, "No, I've come here to buy dog food."

He said, "Go to the sales office across from Kisumu Motors."

I took in a breath and let it out slowly. "I was just there."

With a tone of authority he said, "You go with this man; he's going there."

I proceeded out the door with one of the workers who said he would lead me. He added, "But first I must load a few small bags onto my truck."

To my surprise, a line of men brought huge bags of feed in our direction. They stopped to count, brought more bags, and counted again. Feeling discouraged, I just left.

I went to a door directly across from Kisumu Motors and asked if it was the mill.

"No, it's three doors down."

I walked farther and asked again.

This time the guard pointed to a stairway. "Yes, you go up there."

"Where is your sign?"

He shrugged. "We don't have one."

I found my way to a reception window and said, "I'd like to buy dog food."

The man nodded in the direction of a large office occupied by an elderly Asian man. "You go in there."

The older Asian man asked if I wanted a twenty-kilogram or a seventy-kilogram bag. I went for the one I could carry and paid five hundred shillings (about ten dollars).

Then he said, "You go back out there for your computer copy."

Yet another man took my receipt and put it on a pile.

I stiffened, and said slowly, "I came to get my dog food."

He said, "You wait."

I waited to see if the man at the computer would start preparing my receipt. After a while he did, but very slowly. Ten minutes later, I asked if there was a problem. The first man said that unfortunately, the second man started a big job just before I came in, and he had to finish it. I told him my dog was getting hungry.

He said, "You wait two minutes."

After ten more minutes, the computer ran out of paper and had to be reloaded. I stood up again, and this time the man started working on my receipt. He handed me a long computer printout, and I drove back to the mill. Still another man took the paper and disappeared. When he came back, I had to tell him who I was, who I work for, and my license plate number. Then I signed the logbook once and my receipts three times.

After all that, he said, "You go out there."

Hooray! My dog food was waiting to be loaded, but first I had to sign that I actually received the dog food. All told, it took about twenty men to get one bag of dog food.

That's why we say everyone should bring a sense of humor to the mission field. I don't like frustrations any more than anyone else, but it's good to remember that God never wastes a trial.

CHAPTER 30

Life on Sunset Lane

I had a lovely apartment, or *flat* as they termed it, in Kisumu, situated in an international community. Flats were constructed on an incline and on two levels. People from Holland, Germany, India, Japan, and America lived there. I lived between the Tootleboom family from Holland and the Patels from India. The complex employed a guard at the gate who spent most of his time in the guardhouse. Families of the housekeepers lived behind the guardhouse. With all those interconnected relationships there was always some sort of activity going on.

A bamboo shade covered a portion of the fenced parking lot. People often sat on the cement walls in front of their flats in the evenings. I, on the other hand, ran upstairs to my window overlooking the lake and watched the sunset. The glorious colors highlighted the artistry of God's signature on the close of each day. Sometimes the clouds rolled in over the lake ahead of an evening storm. They painted an even more spectacular picture with plenty of lightning and thunder. Storms were a thrill to watch as long as you had a roof over your head. I often thought of the street children trying to find shelter under trees or doorways of abandoned buildings. It was just an accepted part of their young lives.

One night, I came home and went upstairs as usual. I sat down on the bed and took off my shoes. As I did, I heard a distinct swishing sound coming from my bathroom. I couldn't imagine what it could be.

At first, I thought a snake might have somehow made its way up the sewer pipe. That didn't seem feasible. When I mustered enough nerve to go take a look, I heard the sound again. This time I saw ripples in the water of the toilet bowl.

I wasn't just hearing things. I laughed to myself, thinking how ridiculous this was as I sat on the edge of the bathtub. I waited. Nothing happened. Eventually, I turned out the light and left the room. A few minutes later, there it was again. I flipped on the light and ran over to the toilet. There, to my complete astonishment, was a frog going head-first back into the bowl. *No one is ever going to believe this,* I thought. *This is crazy.* I tried to stay calm and rational. But I knew I couldn't just leave him there.

How did a frog ever manage to get up here in the first place? In my limited knowledge of the care and feeding of frogs, I knew they liked lily pads. The only problem was I didn't happen to have one at the moment, so I cut one out of cardboard. Amazingly, the frog jumped onto it, but he didn't stay long. After several unsuccessful tries to flip him out of the bowl, I gave up. He moved too quickly for me.

My only recourse was obvious. I called the guard. Theo didn't speak much English, and trying to explain why I needed him to come upstairs to my bathroom was a little tricky.

When he understood the situation, I pleaded with him, "Please go in there and don't come out without the frog!"

I sat on the bed and thought about how no one at home would ever believe this. The guard eventually walked out with the frog in a towel and a suppressed grin on his face. I thanked him profusely. About ten minutes later, loud laughter drifted over from the servants' quarters. I can only imagine the story he told them.

Another month or so passed before the next incident. This time it happened at 3:00 a.m., and I was sound asleep.

Loud, repeated banging rattled the door, accompanied by an African voice calling, "Mama!"

I recognized Theo's voice and threw on my robe, fearing the worst. I raced downstairs and talked to him through the locked door. "Theo, what's happened?"

"There was a thief who ran away."

I opened the door to hear the rest of the story. Theo explained how he saw a man try to steal the battery out of my car, but he chased the thief away before the battery was disconnected.

Unfortunately, the thief cut through the wire fence in order to reach my car. And since it was my car he tried to rob, I would be responsible for the damage. I understood what Theo said, though it made no sense to my American brain.

I finally said, "We can talk about it in the morning," and closed the door.

From the other side of the door, he said, "The police will come and want to talk to you."

I stopped midway up the stairs and called over my shoulder. "It will wait until tomorrow." I walked back into my room and climbed into bed.

As I look back now, I wonder if he was so insistent on me paying for the damages so it wouldn't be taken out of his paycheck. I have no idea what happened, but at least Theo didn't lose his job over it. And of course, I took my car into the garage to have it checked out. It's amazing what desperate people will do to make some money.

Everyone in those flats had a housekeeper. Nationals viewed it as selfish or greedy if a foreigner didn't offer a job to a local. Jobs were so scarce. I decided to make the best of it. I was introduced to Sarah and hired her. I loved that girl and called her "Sweet Sarah." She took her job so seriously that she cleaned things before they were even dirty. Usually, that didn't matter, but the material I purchased for some curtains was guaranteed to shrink, wrinkle, and fade when washed. The guarantee held true.

One day, Sarah busily cleaned the top of the valences on the back windows by the purple bougainvillea. There, on the top of the valence and inside the house lay a poisonous green mamba snake. Apparently, the window was left slightly open and the snake slithered in from the bougainvillea vines. Determined to handle the problem, she reached for the big red can of insect repellent called Doom. When she told me she sprayed the snake with that, I gulped and wondered if it went away coughing or laughing. But we never saw it again.

In addition to toads and snakes, I also had a kitten and monkeys visit my flat. My flat had a glass patio door. It led to the back porch where the washing machine sat in a corner. It sat outside because I used the garden hose to fill it. The washer came from the States and the timer didn't work with Kenyan electricity. So I watched the timer and moved the dial from cycle to cycle. It was still easier than doing all the wash by hand, but it took most of the morning. Then the hose emptied the water into the backyard garden. (I wondered why the tomatoes tasted soapy.)

A decorative iron gate stretched across the patio door as a security measure. One Sunday afternoon, the door was open and a tiny kitten wandered into my house. I closed the door to play with her for a while. Suddenly, a family of five monkeys came swinging through the trees and jumped onto the security door. It looked like a mom, dad, a couple of teenagers, and a baby.

The largest adult jumped onto the washing machine and played with the dial. It twirled it around and around. I figured no one would ever believe this and I snapped a picture. Later, I showed friends the picture and told them I taught the monkey to do the wash.

In the meantime, the other monkeys looked into the house. My little kitty friend hid behind a chair leg and hissed bravely as they stared at her. I tried to stay still so they wouldn't run away. They were curious and peered into the room. I got the definite feeling they were the spectators looking in *my* cage. They stayed about twenty minutes, made some monkey noises, and turned to leave. However, the baby monkey didn't want to go. A moment later, the mid-sized monkey grabbed its little ear and pulled it away. I wish someone had been able to share this experience with me. Africa can be a delightful place.

CHAPTER 31

Battles and Blessings

With more and more children, mostly boys, coming to the streets, it's not unreasonable to wonder what could possibly be done to prevent the breakdown of so many families. Occasionally, we find it's only a lack of money for school fees. Without the structure of school, active boys plummet into dreary idleness. In time, they seek the freedom and adventure of the street. Sometimes parents are absent from the home. They leave older children to act as parents to younger siblings. Others flee to the streets when they rebel against beatings given in the name of discipline.

Brian, like many street boys, described his first day on the street as a nightmare and bears the physical scars to prove it. He had no one to protect him. This is how he described his first day on the street.

> "It was my first time to go to the streets, and I'd just found a boy of my age who taught me how to live in the streets. The boy showed me how to get food from dustbins. He found leftovers of bread and fish. It was very hard for me to take the leftovers, but my empty stomach forced me to pick and eat them. He taught me how to earn money, but I disliked pickpocketing. After that, he taught me to take things like *bhang* (marijuana) and cigarettes, and to sniff glue.

"The days I spent on the streets were so different from all the days I spent at home. We walked in the streets and looked for ways to get money, but wherever I went, they called me *ninja* (a common term for street boys). I was chased away and couldn't even get a single coin to hold in my pocket.

"The boy who told me how to survive ran away from me and left me wondering how and where to sleep. When darkness fell, I wondered how to get bedding and have a nice sleep. After finally finding a place to hold my body, which was dead tired, I tried to sleep, but the dreams would not come. The night arrived with wide, angry eyes ready to swallow me up. And I shivered in the cold, wet weather.

"As I thought about what to do, I saw three boys in the distance walking towards me. I assumed they were coming with my brother, but as they got nearer I saw they carried ragged clothes. When they reached me, I recognized one of the boys as the one who showed me how to do the things that I needed for survival. The boy held a bucket with sewage inside. They told me to remove my shoes and clothes. When I hesitated, they said they had a knife and if I refused they would stab me with it.

"After giving them all the clothes and my shoes, they gave me the rags to put on, poured the sewage on me, and ran away. By the time morning finally arrived, I was sure I slept in another world.

"The sun rising in the east meant the beginning of a new day. I knew I had to step away from where I slept, turning to an unknown place. My hair was uncombed and my face unwashed. With the sewage all over my ragged clothes and full of fleas and lice, I started my walk to look for a cup of tea to hold in my stomach. I found nothing, so I decided to go to the lakeside and wash my body.

"Finally I decided to walk back home and apologize to my

mother for what I did. It took me one month on the streets to dry up enough to look like a stick. I am sure my character changed. My hands were too feeble to work, because I couldn't do without the crushed leaves and glue.

"My mother accepted me back, but soon afterwards I stole her money and bought glue. She asked me to tell her how I had gotten the glue. I tried to defend myself, but I wasn't able to because I reeked with the smell of glue and she had seen the bottle.

"She closed the door, and I knew I was in a jam because in her hands she held the pipe she used to cane us. She whipped me once. It didn't matter to her if I was hurt or not, so she whipped a second time. She gave me a third whip, but I ran to the door, opened it, and ran away. Eventually, I ended up on the streets permanently.

"In 1996, I met a man [Lebaus] who told me about Jesus and how He loves me. The man introduced himself and asked me questions. After that, he took me to a shop where he bought me some food. A week later, I saw him on his way to church with many other boys. They were all doing very well. The next time he came again, I asked to go with him.

"When we reached Agape Children's Home, two missionaries from Canada – Diane Kineshenko and Coby van Dam – welcomed me. I saw some bigger boys and thought they might be bullies, but they were actually nice. I took a bath and was given clean clothes and food. Although I spent the night well, I still worried about going to the streets. After breakfast the next morning, I hid myself and then passed through the fence. On the street, I wasn't comforted and had no one to play with … only the sniffing of glue.

"I decided to go back to Agape. Later, I started learning and understanding English. The next year, I was taken to Christ Church School, where I could strive for excellence every day.

I grew in my studies until one day I ranked number one. It amazed the teachers and also my fellow students, because I was known as the street boy who could not do anything. When I began at the school, I found English to be very hard. The next year, it was the easiest subject, and it is now my favorite. Now I know I can learn."

During one of my visits, I gave Brian a journal and asked him to fill it up with his thoughts and stories. I promised that when the journal was full, I would bring him another.

Six months later, Brian astonished me when I returned. He handed me a notebook full of beautifully expressed sentiments, psalms, and devotions. I was surprised at the depth of thought and the use of vocabulary. Brian obviously had a gift for writing. He shyly confided in me that he kept a dictionary open so he could look up word meanings and use just the right words. Here is one of my favorite poems:

The Water Jar

The sun
bakes the earth
like a pot of clay
in a kiln.
Lord,
in the heat
of these long, still days,
fire me.
Rid me of
my imperfections
so that I may be
the sturdy vessel in which
the cool water
of your love
can be stored.

CHAPTER 32

Soccer and Character

Tim moved to the streets after his mother's death. He was eight years old and had a hard time finding a place to sleep. Sometimes the night guards let him sleep in security near them. Other times, he was forced to sleep in an open park or shop doorway. He washed and swept cars or ran errands for people to earn a little money for food. When he couldn't find work, he resorted to begging or stealing.

Tim was one of the fortunate ones. In 1993, he was one of the first to be invited to join us when we opened Agape Children's Home. In the beginning, he remained moody and angry. But as he learned more about the Lord, he adjusted to life with his new family.

With time, he became an enthusiastic student and a good big brother to the smaller boys. Yet his real love was soccer. It turned out that a few broken windows in our rental home were worth the hassle. Tim developed his athletic talent over the next several years at Agape. Those skills advanced to the point that a German scout chose him to play in an international soccer tournament.

During school holidays, we encouraged the boys to visit their homes in the villages they came from. Tim's trip was a five-hour bus ride to visit his adult cousin in Nairobi. The change in Tim's character and his insistence that they pray before meals and bedtime amazed his cousin.

As a result, he accompanied Tim back to Agape to see what was responsible for the difference.

Tim's cousin talked to the houseparent and explained how he had never prayed before. He wanted to learn more about God. This led to a conversation that ended with his commitment to receive Christ. God's Word tells us, *A little child will lead them* (Isaiah 11:6).

Tim is a grown man now with a sweet wife and a family of his own. He also takes care of another family member's child. He has a good job in town at a TV store.

In a recent email, Lebaus wrote: "What keeps me going on is the success of most of the boys, seeing where they are now, and where they were. God has done wonders."

I say Amen to that.

CHAPTER 33

Benson Becomes a Chef

Benson was born out of wedlock to teenage parents. He never knew his real mother and lived with his paternal grandmother while small. Later, he joined his father and stepmother in Nairobi, but harassment and physical abuse made him feel like he didn't really fit in with the family.

At the tender age of seven, Benson couldn't take it any longer and left. With nowhere else to go, he lived in the streets of Nairobi. After a year and a half, he moved to Kisumu. That's where we met him. He survived by begging at the supermarket and movie theater entrances and selling scraps of paper. He found his meals by scrounging leftovers from kiosks and hotels. Because of his harsh lifestyle and inadequate nutrition, Benson developed chronic scabies and upper respiratory-tract problems.

In 1993, we brought him to Agape. Benson tended to be a calm, pleasant boy and highly intelligent. After he arrived at Agape, his growth rate improved remarkably. To this day, he has one of the best records of school attendance and performance at the home. He continued to grow in emotional and spiritual stability. He enjoyed sports, reading, TV, and movies.

During his graduation ceremony from grade school, his headmaster gave him special recognition and a gift.

He stood before the graduation crowd and announced, "Though Benson came from very difficult circumstances, he fit in well with the other children and is a boy to be proud of."

The audience erupted with cheers.

Over the December holidays, an uncle sent word that he wanted Benson to return to his home village. He let Benson know that his land was waiting for him – land he hadn't seen for seven years. Bensen was able to get this land and later attended a culinary arts training school and became employed as a chef.

Agape's intervention rescued another child from the streets into successful adulthood. He became a strong, handsome young man and one of Agape's first pioneers. The work in Kenya and the Modesto headquarters were worth it. The travel, fund-raising, challenges, setbacks, frustrations, and discouragements were all a small price to pay for the joy we will share in heaven with these children we love so dearly.

CHAPTER 34

Shadrack's Journey

W hen I met Shadrack, he stood tall and lanky and always had a ready smile. I figured him to be about fourteen years old at the time. He became one of the first boys at Agape, where he developed a love of music and singing.

Shadrack was the youngest in his family. His father died and left the boy with his mother. Later, she became ill, and Shadrack cared for her. He was with her when she died at the Kisumu District Hospital. After his mother passed away, he went to stay with an aunt who treated him like a hired hand. She forced him to do a lot of housework and frequently beat him if the work didn't please her. He also had an older brother who didn't want Shadrack, because it would complicate his inheritance. Shadrack told me he was sure he could make it on his own. But when he recalls that time of his life, he calls it "the years of suffering."

He left home in hopes of a better life in the streets. For the next four years, Shadrack survived in the streets of various towns such as Nakuru, Kericho, and Nairobi before he settled in Kisumu.

When Shadrack came to Kisumu, he was fortunate to be able to work in the food kiosks. He managed to stay away from sniffing glue, which is quite unusual for street kids. But he tells of a time he was sick with a bad fever and how someone helped him get medicine. Later, he learned this illness was rheumatic fever, and it would have deadly consequences on his life. This all happened before he came to Agape in 1993.

He shared this testimony one Sunday morning:

"I am Shadrack. I want to thank the Lord for bringing me from the streets where I was suffering and eating all kind of dirty things. He was kind to me and brought Mama Darla all the way from America to come and teach us His glory.

"My mother was the only breadwinner in our family. Now she was dead. Who will help me? I wondered.

"I asked, 'Why me God? Why didn't you take me instead of her? Now she is gone and will no longer be seen again. How will I get an education? How will I eat?' I thought of those things, and I had no choice but to go to the streets. I lived in the street for four years. There, life was very difficult.

"One day, as I begged everywhere for money, I was invited to go to Agape. Here, I found life very good. I can go to school now, and I know God has a plan in the future for me. Thank you for all your help. May the Lord bless you."

As part of our high school program, Shadrack demonstrated many gifts and exhibited the potential for being a future pastor, teacher, or counselor. He had a heart for the children still suffering on the street. We recognized his natural leadership ability. His gifts in music and songwriting complemented the fact that he dearly loved to perform in role-plays and skits. He easily translated from English to Kiswahili, which is quite amazing since he knew very little English when we first met. "Shaddie" became special to all who knew him.

After some time, it became apparent Shadrack was in trouble. His health declined. At the age of nineteen, he received treatment for asthma, which only provided mild relief from his wheezing and coughing.

By age twenty-four, he moved slowly and shuffled down the sidewalk like an old man. This was totally uncharacteristic of him.

When I asked how he was, he still replied with his trademark smile, but said, "Old man's tired." He lifted his pant legs to show me his swollen feet and ankles. The sight stunned me. His swollen ankles were the size of his knees.

The bags under his eyes and his sunken cheeks made him look much older, but this look was momentarily washed away by a wide grin across his handsome face. As the symptoms worsened, his doctor suggested we send Shadrack to Nairobi, the capital city of Kenya, for a complete cardiac assessment. He helped us make the necessary arrangements and a few days later Shadrack took his first ride on an airplane.

When we received the test results, the news wasn't good. "Shadrack has rheumatic heart disease, a sequela to rheumatic fever, which he contracted years ago when he lived on the street." The testing showed that his mitral valve had calcified to the point that all the blood in his body was trying to get through an opening the size of a pencil. He had chronic heart failure and serious pulmonary edema.

One doctor said, "Try to breathe through a straw, and you will know how Shadrack feels."

He needed urgent intervention and open-heart surgery for mitral valve replacement. The physicians estimated his condition had progressed to the point that his prognosis for survival was only three to six weeks.

Shadrack received this news with amazing stoicism. "If the surgery is not to be taken, I'll just have to die."

This type of surgery was extremely expensive. To make matters worse, mitral valves weren't easily obtained in Kenya. We prayed, explored options, and felt helpless for several days. Then we received wonderful news from a young woman named Jennie Mach who previously worked with us. At the time, Jennie lived in Milbank, South Dakota. Upon hearing the news, she contacted her family physician. He enlisted Dr. Paul Carpenter, a cardiac surgeon at North Central Heart Hospital in Sioux Falls, about two hours from Milbank. Before the day was over, he offered to perform the surgery at no charge. Even the hospital costs were covered. We knew we were privileged to witness this miracle designed and guided by the Lord's hand, specially created for a former street boy who was so precious in His sight.

We had to obtain a passport, a visa, and a flight we could afford, make arrangements for host families to care for him, and find someone to travel with him to the States. Over the following week, we witnessed Proverbs 3:5-6 lived out through a team of people the Lord drew together from all over the United States.

> *Trust in the LORD with all your heart and lean not on your*
> *own understanding; ... and he will make your paths straight.*
> (Proverbs 3:5-6)

Humanly speaking, this was an impossible situation. Even when Lebaus went to get Shadrack's ID card, he faced resistance.

The person in charge said, "It will take about six weeks to get it."

After he had already explained the situation to several people, Lebaus said in frustration, "I'm not leaving here until I get that ID card. You have all the information you need."

The officer threatened to put Lebaus in jail if he didn't leave.

"Okay, you wait to give him this ID for six weeks and I'll bury it in this boy's coffin with him," Lebaus said.

The official disappeared into his office where a conference took place. In the meantime, Lebaus prayed. "We need your help, Lord."

A short time later, they handed the ID to Lebaus. He went back to Agape rejoicing. The Lord clearly demonstrated how He cares for every one of us.

Shadrack made the long flight overseas on oxygen with the help of Jennie, who became his caretaker. Within three weeks of his diagnosis, Shadrack underwent surgery in South Dakota. I met them at the hospital, so Jennie and I were both present to talk with the doctors. They brought in several interns to witness the X-rays and other pre-op tests. The doctor said he wanted everyone to see them, since most likely they would never see such an advanced case in the U.S. again.

Several days after the surgery, Shadrack was recovering remarkably well. I think his secret was eating vanilla ice cream every time they offered it to him. I walked into his hospital room to find him propped up on his pillows "holding court" in a press conference with a reporter from the local newspaper, a photographer, the cardiologist, a resident physician, and the community relations coordinator at the hospital. They listened intently as he described his life as a Muslim, before he came to Agape, and what it's been like since he learned about Christ.

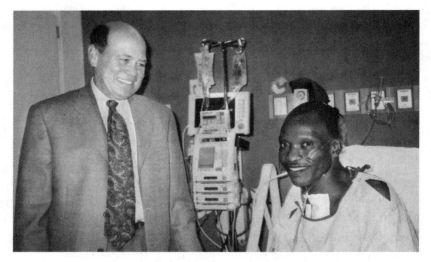

Shadrack and Dr. Reynolds

He spoke of his desire to reach boys who are still hopelessly suffering in the streets.

The hospital staff described him as a model patient, saying, "He is so cooperative."

Soon he arrived back in Kenya and not long afterwards completed his high school education.

Shadrack frequently looked down at his long scar, which he described as his "zipper," and said, "My healthy heart will always be full of gratitude."

Shadrack lived another fourteen years and married a darling young lady who gave him a healthy baby boy. It was a truly sad time for the other senior boys and Agape staff when he passed away. Many of them traveled to the rural area where he was buried. Some of the other boys and staff members offered to finish the roof on the house Shadrack and his wife were building. Several promises were made to look in on her and make sure she was able to sustain a livelihood. Those of us who knew Shadrack will never forget the miracles God did right before our eyes. We are forever grateful to all the generous people of South Dakota who played a part in his rescue. *The grace of our Lord Jesus Christ be with you all* (2 Thessalonians 3:18).

CHAPTER 35

Evans' Experience

Sing to the LORD a new song. (Isaiah 42:10)

I met Evans Kisala at the market where he sold plastic bags for produce. Even then, he was polite and smiled easily. After he came to Agape in August of 1993, Evans showed natural leadership potential. Because he had missed several years in school, we placed him in classes with younger children. That didn't always go well with older street boys, but Evans displayed an eagerness to learn and maintained a sunny disposition in spite of his placement with younger students. We weren't the only ones to notice his leadership potential. His teacher saw it too, and soon Evans led the pledge of allegiance during the school's morning assembly. It thrilled us all when he received the "most courteous student award."

At seventeen years of age, he became eligible to graduate from the eighth grade. He wrote a long poem entitled "The Importance of School," which so impressed the headmistress that she asked him to present it at an assembly for the entire student body. Here are some excerpts:

The Importance of School

Schooling, a cumbersome task.
Wake up in the morning in chilly weather,
In cold water you bathe.
Tea? No tea (meaning no breakfast).
To school you go!
Why all this?
For the betterment of tomorrow!

Schooling, a cumbersome task.
From which comes a successful life experience.
But how does it come about?
Through hard work in class,
Finding excellent character,
And putting God first.
Why all this?
Yes, for the betterment of tomorrow!

Schooling, a cumbersome task.
But without education, life in vain.
Housing? Yes, in the slums.
Bread and butter? Only at Christmas!
Bare feet cracking the ground.
Life full of sorrows and hardships.
Because of all this, I invite you to join hands with me …
For the betterment of tomorrow!

Evans' dad had left the family five years earlier, so his wife cared for the children alone. Evans remembers the day the landlord came to their house at about 6:00 p.m. He told them to leave the house because they hadn't paid the rent. They gathered their belongings and moved to another area where mud houses had barely enough plaster to keep them dry. They were just happy to find a place to rest. Evans' mother was able to get money to pay rent, and things went well for a few weeks. However, it didn't last. Again, the landlord threatened to throw them out. At this point, Evans felt helpless and he left so his mother would have one less person to feed. He described his experience in these words:

> "I found it very bad and hard to live in the streets. I started to pick things from the dirty dustbins looking for something to eat. But that was not enough for me. I decided to look for a long bag where I could store small pieces of paper. Then I took them to the hawkers who used to weigh the things I was picking. And when I made some money from this, for example, fifty shillings [about fifty cents], I couldn't forget where my mother was. And surely without wasting any time, I ran from there and took the money in order to give it to my mother to use.

> "As time went by, I decided now to live in the street as my home, sleeping beside the shops. Sometimes I found it difficult though, because sometimes other big street boys would come and kick me, pour water on me, or bring yucky mixtures of feces and urine and throw that towards me. And after all this, I found it very difficult to live.

> "I never gave up but continued staying in Kisumu. At night, the only thing was to look above to the sky and watch how the twinkling stars moved around. When the morning came, I walked around picking papers. I wasn't sniffing glue so much, but instead, I took the money and bought some things I wanted.

> "As time went on, I went to the dustbin, taking some things like small bottles and selling them to get money. As I continued living in the streets, we and other friends saw a woman coming toward us who gave us food – for example, bread, sweets, and other things.

> "For about a month, I heard my other friends telling me that

Uncle Peter wanted to see me. And I thought, *How come this man wants me?* Without wasting any time, on that day, I immediately went and found this man. Then he told me he wanted to take me someplace on his bicycle. So I jumped on the bicycle and we went to where I found a written board that said AGAPE. I felt so happy when I saw other friends who were there that I knew long before on the streets.

"I went in and was welcomed, and the next day, I saw the lady who is called Mama Darla Peters. She loved us so much and also played together with us.

"After a while, we were taught good discipline by Uncle Collins, Lebaus, Peter, and other houseparents. So I stayed there, and we were taught to read, and to sing, and do all other things. We became good and we were taken to school where we performed good and always tried to show excellent character.

"And I found it a very good and better life than I had ever met before, and I also thanked the Lord my God for helping me find a good place."

In spite of this happy time, life wasn't always easy for Evans. He knew his share of heartache. His mother still provided for the family, including his two stepsisters. After he came to Agape, he visited their rural home during school holidays and took whatever money he had to help them. We also tried to help his mother, through friends from Navigators, to set up a small business selling eggs. Things looked a little brighter. His mother even shared her love more openly.

Then, on one of our visits to Kisumu, my husband and I shared a painful time with Evans. On a beautiful Sunday morning, just before church, we received word that Evans' mother had died. Evans didn't know she had been ill. The houseparent talked quietly with him, and his happy countenance transformed into sorrow. Our hearts ached as we watched him head toward the gate.

To make matters worse, this all happened at the time of midterm exams. In order for Evans to be promoted, he needed to pass exams that week. A short three days later, Evans returned to Agape. He stayed quiet and introspective but remained determined to go to school. I admired his mental strength to be able to transition from grief to the stress of school exams. And he passed.

Evans continued in school and took several business classes. Now a mature man, Evans is married to a lovely lady he met in high school. They have an energetic little boy named Jeremy. He loves soccer and music just like his daddy. Evans has also reconnected with his father in the village and recently helped him conquer a serious health issue.

Evans also continues to develop and share his God-given talent in music. He has written several songs, is taking singing lessons, and hopes to have a future in music.

While in the process of writing this story, I received a brief but uplifting email message from Evans:

> "Just had time to visit the park today and met one of the street boys who was sniffing glue. Told him my testimony and encouraged him in God. Had to share with him something little (to eat). After you share the Word, you have to give something for the stomach."

This is a good example of holistic ministry. We must care for the whole person. Evans continues to pass on the good news he received as a child. How our hearts rejoice in this!

CHAPTER 36

Bad News, Good News

"As the heavens are higher than the earth, so are my ways higher than your ways and my thoughts than your thoughts." (Isaiah 55:9)

I'd just finished a letter to some dear friends. In it, I said, "Life can be so perplexing at times. I sometimes wonder when I'll ever learn to rest in the Lord and trust Him completely. The Bible tells us His ways are higher than our ways and He is infinitely wise. My prayer is that I'll be more aware of His grace in daily life and be less complaining about pesky annoyances. I really want to experience that kind of victory. I also have a feeling there will be plenty of opportunities ahead here in Africa."

The very next day, I received a startling message from home about Lance, my youngest son. He had a good summer job with the local school district. They were doing some re-roofing and asked Lance to toss the old sheet-metal panels to the ground. Things went well until his leather glove snagged on a panel and it took Lance down with it! He fell a full two stories, twenty feet, headfirst. The crew surrounded him immediately and called 9-1-1. When Lance looked up, he said, "I'm okay. Jesus caught me."

It was unbelievable. Lance could have been paralyzed or even killed.

But they took him to the hospital for a checkup and released him with only bruises and scrapes on the side of his face. It was truly a modern-day miracle. How else can this be explained?

If Lance had been seriously injured, I would have been on the next plane back to the U.S. I might never have worked with street children. And most likely, Agape Children's Ministry wouldn't exist. The Lord protected my son from harm. After that, I was certain I would never, ever complain again.

> *"Because he loves me," says the* LORD, *"I will rescue him; I will protect him, for he acknowledges my name."* (Psalm 91: 14).

Oh, Happy Day

In 1994, Lance graduated from college and visited me in Kenya. By then, it had been over a year since I saw him last, so of course, I was overjoyed to see him. I seriously missed my family. When he arrived, he joined right in and helped wherever possible.

A young pastor wanted to prepare a home for his future wife. He asked if our boys would like to help him build his house, and we jumped at the chance. The pastor had already built a double framework from branches stripped and bound together. He asked us to mix the mud to fill in the walls. It sounded like fun. Off we went to a location near a shallow muddy river where we found women washing their clothes.

Lance Peters helps build a house

We gave each of the twelve boys a bright-yellow five-gallon container. They joyously slipped and slid down the muddy embankment and scooped up as much water as they could carry back up. They laughed and played along the way. Boys and mud always make a great combination.

Lance and the pastor stayed behind to mix the water into clay-like soil in a rusty old wheelbarrow. It took quite a bit of effort, but it made a solid filling for the walls, which also provided insulation from the heat.

Finally, all of us packed that mud between the branches to build up the walls. We repeated the cycle over and over. The walls gradually filled in and thickened. By the end of the day, the house neared completion. Only the porch remained for other workers to finish.

Pride filled my heart for the way the boys worked together. They actually functioned as a team. Their teamwork illustrated the exact opposite of how they lived as street boys.

We returned to Agape and hosed all the boys down before dinner. Another fun mess. Then Lance and I returned to the condo to take showers and reflect on the events of the day.

I truly thank God for the opportunities to share Kisumu's unusual experiences with my sons. Otherwise, they may have thought I was "embellishing" some of my remarkable stories.

Ice Balls Popping Out of the Ground

Later that year, a freak storm hit Kisumu around 5:30 in the afternoon. I'd just visited a friend in a nearby hospital, and Lance went home with the car. Suddenly, black, angry-looking clouds rolled in, and people on foot started to scurry. I followed their lead and scuttled along faster too. Five minutes after I reached Agape, the threatening sky cut loose. Stiff winds accompanied a torrential downpour. Tree limbs cracked. Hail dropped small at first, then grew big enough to do damage.

The kids had never seen anything like it before. They asked if it was snow. I called to warn Lance not to drive. Immediately after that, the power and phone lines went dead. I watched the hail bounce and build up, and was glad everyone was safe.

The wind howled outside, and the boys in our house engaged in a candlelight contest to see how long they could stand on their heads. The cook fixed ugali on the charcoal stove and we were fine.

Meanwhile, parts of the hospital roof blew off and patients were forced to share beds – head to foot. Mud houses on the plains completely flooded and big trees toppled. We had no idea how much damage actually occurred until the following day. When I stepped outside, the extensive damage appeared to be from Kisumu's version of a hurricane. Fortunately, the town's people suffered very few injuries. We thanked God for His protection.

Years later, when I visited Agape, the topic of the storm came up in conversation. One of the boys posed the question: "Remember when those ice balls came popping up out of the ground?"

I don't know what my expression looked like to others, but his question stunned me. The hailstones came down hard and bounced on the ground when they hit, but I had no idea the kids thought they bounced up out of the ground. Needless to say, that led to a correction of the facts. And thankfully, Kisumu has never had another storm like that one.

CHAPTER 37

Daniela's First Doll

Some children leave footprints on your heart. A little Kenyan girl did just that for me. Daniela lived with her elderly grandmother in a low-lying area which often flooded during the rainy season. One of our current staff members, Mr. Charles Anyang, worked as the director of Social Services and Housing in Kisumu in 1993. His responsibilities included the social welfare of many families who lived in the outlying areas.

While on his rounds, he came to a traditional mud hut which had disintegrated over the years. During the last big rainstorm, it almost washed away. Mr. Anyang said he could "just step over the wall and be in the sitting room."

This grandmother had no protection and desperately needed help. Mr. Anyang brought Daniela to my house to stay for a few days while he arranged to have the house rebuilt.

What a treat for me. Daniela started off fearful and quiet. She had never even been in a house like mine with indoor plumbing and a bath-tub. She soon learned the warm water felt really good, especially with some bubble bath to play with.

I tried my best to make her feel comfortable. Then I remembered a little black Cabbage Patch doll tucked away in the closet. *Maybe I'd saved it for such a time as this*, I thought. But to my surprise, she withdrew and looked slightly frightened when she first saw it. Later, I learned she might have thought it was some type of voodoo doll. Her tribe feared witchcraft very much, and she had never seen, much less held, a baby doll. I cuddled it myself and showed her how to put a bonnet on it.

When she finally agreed to hold the little creature, Daniela put her legs out straight in front of her and let me lay the doll on her ankles. She stared at the doll and sat there as still as a statue. When nothing terrible happened, she let me move it to her knees. Eventually, she picked it up and held it in her arms. From that point on, she didn't put it down. She smiled and laughed. We had a good time together. She loved to ride in the car and run errands with me. So by the time her grandmother's house was built, it was really hard for me to see her go. But of course, she missed her friends and family, and it was time for Mr. Anyang to take her back.

She looked so sweet in a fresh new dress as she waved good-bye. I never saw her again, but I'll look for her in heaven someday. The Bible tells us to care for the orphans and widows. It just doesn't say how much fun it can be.

CHAPTER 38

Life Support

After Agape was born, the Lord used some key people to keep the "baby" alive. I introduced you to Dr. and Mrs. Harmeling. They invited me to that first dinner. John and Anita Henigman are another dear couple who believed in me and Agape enough to make sacrifices and take risks to further the vision. John is an army veteran. We lovingly refer to him as "the Commander." When I returned to the States for supplies and to take care of deputation, John and Anita invited me to stay in their lovely home in Fountain Valley, California.

When the time came for my return trip to Kenya, the sheer volume of items that needed to be squeezed into duffle bags overwhelmed me. By that time, sixteen boys were in our care. We needed school and medical supplies, clothing, shoes, and household goods. The prices in the States were far better, and people here were generous with their donations. John's skills saved the day when it came time to pack.

He said, "Darla girl, bring everything you want to take downstairs. I'll get it in."

I looked at the mountain of things to pack and replied, "I know you're amazing, Commander, but I can't believe even you can do that."

Lo and behold, in a couple of hours, the whole pile disappeared. He stuffed things in shoes, in corners, wrapped things together, and slid them down the sides. He had those bags packed solid. So off I went to Kenya with all the donated items tucked neatly within my duffle bags.

When newsletters needed to be sent out, John and Anita volunteered for the job. I can imagine the sheets of paper all over their counters as they organized and hand stamped every letter.

Later, when I was home between trips, my Aunt Dorothy designed our first logo. It depicted children walking toward a sun hoping for a brighter future. We didn't have enough money for colored letterhead, so I bought a bunch of yellow pencils and colored the suns. It was labor intensive, but the effect was worth the effort. We had a very humble beginning to say the least.

Then, I needed a board of directors in the U.S. to deal with the finances. John Henigman, Dr. Mark Harmeling, Roy Hamlin (a banker), and I were the members. While I ministered in Kenya, those resourceful men kept us up and running. Remember, in those days we didn't have cell phones and the Internet was sketchy at best. So they deserve a lot of credit.

Some days, it was impossible to know just how much I had left in our bank account. I believed what God said about supplying all our needs, so I'd cash a check for beans, rice, and maize. During those early days in Africa, God provided our every need. However, I don't advise that method of banking here at home. I suspect – but can't prove – that the Agape account at times dipped into the negative. I also suspect the board members made up the deficit without informing me. We used what we had and cut corners. I ate *lots* of tomato sandwiches. But we bloomed where we were planted. And those sacrifices worked together for good. I can never, *ever* thank my faithful friends enough for what they did to help Agape survive and grow. To God be the glory, great things He has done.

CHAPTER 39

Clara's Story

The most frequent question I've encountered as I've shared about Agape Children's Ministry is, "Are girls found on the street as well?" Fortunately, it's rare to find a street girl for a variety of reasons. Most importantly, a girl can seek work in another home as a servant when her home life becomes abusive or financially difficult. A young girl is even more vulnerable on the street than a boy. Even so, it does happen.

Clara was about twelve years old and disguised as a dirty street boy when I met her. A very clever girl, she wore boys' clothing as protection when she was left on her own. I would never have known she was a girl if one of the street boys hadn't tipped me off. To be truthful, I was shocked. It was like something out of a novel. Clara survived by using her wits to thread through the dangers and trials of street life.

It wasn't easy to win her trust. It took time. I spotted her in town as she watched me from a distance. Then one day, she came up beside me wearing well-worn girls' clothing. I smiled at her and tried to be friendly as we walked down the sidewalk together. A few days later, she came up again as I carried groceries to my car. She leaned over as if she wanted to help, but instead of reaching for a grocery bag, she reached for my purse. Don't ask me why I allowed that, but something, or Someone, told me to let her carry it. Then to my complete delight, she flashed a beautiful smile, stood up straighter, and walked proudly by my side. My display of trust in her was the key to our friendship.

Later, I offered her a ride to Agape. She had the opportunity to take a bath, put on some clean clothes, and have lunch with us. The boys were nice to her, but she didn't stay long. In fact, she just disappeared. But every once in a while, when she needed something, she showed up again.

Darla with Clara in her new dress

Another bath, another meal, and she would say, "I have to go."

She seemed hooked on sniffing cobbler's glue and could only be without it for a short time. In spite of that, we had some wonderful times together. And she always took charge of my purse.

Our houseparent researched her background and learned that Clara's mother was jailed for prostitution. Apparently, the police allowed Clara to visit her mother at night to keep this young girl safe. Over time, I saw her less and less ... then never again. Sadly, this does not have a story-book ending. I grieve when I think about the kind of future she faced.

What would have happened to Clara if Agape could have started out with a girls' home, like the one we had for boys? How would she have responded to the well-trained counseling staff Agape developed later? Could we have helped Clara go to school? Could we have assisted her mother to find a better way of life?

CHAPTER 40

Malachi

The next addition to our family proved why those rescues were so important. Malachi, a bright, intelligent boy thought homeschool was such a privilege that he wanted to work right through recess. His story is a sad one. When his mother died, he went to live with his grandparents. His father brought Malachi back home to cook and clean for him.

Unfortunately, his father drank heavily and beat Malachi continually. He often startled his son awake in the early morning hours when he stumbled home drunk. Finally, Malachi ran away to the street. The police caught him and put him in jail for vagrancy. Upon his release, he managed to get on a bus for Kisumu where he lived in the streets.

Our home administrator visited the grandparents to verify his situation. The ability to live at Agape was like a transition into paradise for Malachi. Perhaps someday he will go back to his village equipped to be the leader we pray for him to become.

It takes time to overcome such abusive pasts. Each new child reminded us of how much damage abuse does to the very core of a person. When the kids first came to us, they often acted like they were afraid of being beaten. They stuffed bits of food under their mattresses or in little plastic bags in case another meal didn't come. Their sudden change of environment bewildered them. They spent much of their young lives on the streets, eating from garbage, and being chased and mistreated.

Those fearful, angry children subsisted by selling scraps of paper or bits of charcoal and by stealing.

After living at Agape for a while, they allowed themselves to trust and believe God valued them and that He loved them very much.

One of our first boys, Benson, wrote this touching comment: "I would like to thank God that He has led us from the streets where we have survived with eating bad foods, bad sheltering, nowhere to sleep, no money to buy clothes. But since we came to Agape we are being cared for, our school fees are being paid, free food, beds and all this."

The transformation in those boys was a privilege to behold. We prayed that they would grow up with a sense of purpose and mission and one day be motivated to help others who might be in a similar plight. May the prophecy of Isaiah apply to them that *They will be called oaks of righteousness, a planting of the* LORD *for the display of his splendor* (Isaiah 61:3).

CHAPTER 41

There's a Doctor in the House

I had finally adjusted to being single again. My life held meaning and purpose. I had friends in Kenya and my loving, supportive family in the States. The only thing I lacked was the money to continue to expand our project. At that time, there were five hundred street children in Kisumu, and they all deserved to know they were valued and loved. So I planned a trip back to the States for fundraising in August 1994.

Since many of my supporters were from Hume Lake Christian Camps, I decided that would be a good place to start. My fun-loving friend Peggy Cross invited me to stay with her and her family in their on-site cabin. I accepted gratefully.

Every Friday night, they held a big barbecue on the Meadow Ranch lawn, and I really looked forward to it. I reminisced about standing in line shaking ketchup on my hamburger when Peggy interrupted my thoughts. "Darla, that doctor who came up to see your slides is nice looking, isn't he?"

I was stunned. "What doctor? Where?" I sputtered. "And why would anyone drive all this way just to see *my* slides?"

Peggy calmly replied, "You met him before you left for Kenya. Don't you remember when Clint and Maxine introduced you to him in Modesto?"

Clint and Maxine Ray were like another set of parents to me. They were in their seventies and used to run the camp grocery store. They both had the God-given gift of hospitality and warmly invited me to stay at their home in Modesto while doing my deputation. One morning, they suggested I visit their former dermatologist who now served as the CEO of Medical Ambassadors International. They thought it would be good for me to talk to someone else experienced in community development. I agreed. So they made an appointment, and we were on our way.

I estimate the meeting with Dr. Paul Calhoun lasted about fifteen minutes. He was kind enough to explain the mission basics, such as how Medical Ambassadors learned over the years that "prevention was better than cure." As a result, staff member Stan Rowland developed a very effective strategy to help nationals reach out to their own people and take ownership of their community needs. At the time, they had successful projects in fifty-six countries. I was duly impressed and bought their book, which explained the Community Health Evangelism strategy. We left the office, and a few months later, I headed for Kenya.

I assumed "that doctor" came to Hume Lake for business reasons. We greeted each other, and he mentioned looking forward to the meeting the next night. I was clueless.

Saturday evening about fifty people gathered in a lovely cabin on a hill overlooking tall pine trees interspersed with other picturesque cabins. The comfortable, informal setting included people sitting on the floor. I shared my story illustrated with slides and then talked with friends and answered questions. Toward the end of the evening, Dr. Calhoun approached me and asked if there would be time when we could meet the following day.

I replied, "I'm sorry. I've already made commitments for Sunday." Thinking he wanted to talk about our work, I asked if perhaps he was staying until Monday.

Paul has a somewhat different take on the evening. I will share his plans in his own words:

> "I'd been looking forward to seeing Darla again for a
> number of months, ever since I heard from Maxine Ray
> that she was coming back to the States. I accepted the

kind invitation of Clint and Maxine to travel with them to Hume Lake and stay as a guest in their cabin on the same weekend Darla was scheduled to be there.

"On the night of her program, the guests crammed the lovely hosts' home to the point that I ended up sitting on the crowded floor, nearly at Darla's feet as she towered over me sharing her Agape experiences. I craned my neck upward to look at her, then back and forth to the slide screen.

"As the program closed, I was disconcerted by the crowd of people waiting to speak with her. After lingering for forty-five minutes, small-talking with others at the party, the Rays indicated their desire to head back to the cabin. Infringing on their hospitality, I stalled. During that time, a couple of protective Agape board members encountered me. They were interested in knowing my reasons for coming. At last, the group around Darla thinned to only two elderly women, and I stepped up with considerable trepidation.

"Gratefully, the others melted away and we spoke. After a moment, I drew a deep breath and with a trembling voice asked if she would be able to find some time the following day (Sunday) that we might take a walk on one of her favorite trails. Without batting an eye and with no hint of remorse, she stated that it would be impossible, for her day was filled with board meetings and programs. I saw months of planning coming to nothing, believing we would never cross paths again. I hung at one of those life-changing *Y*s in the road, when a small spark of desperation urged me to say, 'Well, perhaps I could delay my return to Modesto and we could talk Monday morning?'

"She gave me a patronizing smile and suggested that if we don't meet too early she might be available. How encouraging."

Meanwhile, the twinkle in Peggy's eyes should have given me a heads-up. She asked about my little chat with Dr. Calhoun and mentioned something about what a godly man he was. It was then I learned he was available and that he had actually come to see *me*! I grabbed the arms of the rocking chair I had been relaxing in. "No way," I said.

Peggy pursued the topic. "Darla, I can just see the grates of a strong gate clamping down in your heart. You are trying so hard to keep painful things out, but what if God wants to let something good in?"

I tried to explain how I was committed to helping the street children and couldn't imagine giving them hope, just to abandon them back to the street. It simply wasn't possible. And as a last resort, I blurted out, "And besides, I'm fifty-two and he's way too young for me."

Paul stood about five feet ten inches tall and had blonde hair and blue eyes, thanks to his Swedish mother. He loved biking and hiking and, as a result, was physically fit and strong. I tried to maintain a healthy body, but my hair was gray and, after all the traveling I had done, I definitely felt my age.

Monday morning, while I washed my hair, someone knocked on the bathroom door. "Yes?"

It was Peggy. "Oh Darla, it's a beautiful morning. The birds are singing, the flowers are blooming, and he's fifty-six."

I grabbed a towel, opened the door, and said, "What! Come into my office."

So Peggy and I had a girl chat in the bathroom about how she found out, and I wondered why I felt a strange surge of interest in her news. Maxine had been in the gift store looking at greeting cards – the kind that tell you what happened the year you were born. Since Paul just happened to be there too, she took the opportunity to comment on the cards and cleverly asked him what year he was born. News travels fast, and there we were like two young college girls.

When Paul came to the door at 9:30 a.m. he said, "Tell you what. Why don't you pick your favorite path and we'll take a walk around the lake." That sounded natural enough, so I agreed and caught a glimpse of Peggy grinning as we walked out the door.

We had an easy talk about the beauty of the area, my time as a nurse at the Hume Lake Camps, and general things about Medical Ambassadors. Then we stopped at a big boulder and sat down. I waved to several passersby as we continued our conversation. Then Paul shared more personal things about his life. He'd passed through a very difficult time in his marriage, which sadly ended in divorce. I felt his pain and easily empathized. He had three children. The boys were fourteen and thirteen, and his daughter was eleven years old. Then I shared about my three sons and where they were in college. The conversation rambled on from there.

It must have been around one o'clock when we headed back. Paul asked what my plans were for lunch, and frankly, I hadn't planned on having any. He suggested we go visit Clint and Maxine since they would be leaving soon. He thought they might be disappointed if I didn't say good-bye. That struck me as a little odd since they never minded *before* if I said good-bye or not on the day they left. But I had nothing else planned and agreed to go. When we arrived, a wonderful aroma greeted us. A big pot of taco soup simmered on the stove. We arrived just in time for lunch.

The table was quickly set. Clint and Maxine sat on either end and Paul sat across from me. The question came, "So when do you think you might be coming back through Modesto?"

I truthfully had no plans to do that during my current fundraising trip and tried to say so in a tactful way.

But Paul persisted and added, "Well, if you do ever find a window in your schedule and could come back, I'd like to take you to dinner in San Francisco." Gulp! That sounded a little too much like a date.

I responded with all the dignity of a thirteen-year-old, exclaiming, "In San Francisco! That's a long way from Modesto." Paul looked a little taken aback and said quietly, "It's not so far."

Lunch was over, our good-byes said, and we headed back to Ken and Peggy's cabin. Paul asked if we could perhaps be prayer partners, and I couldn't think of any way to refuse. He said he would call me every Monday at 9:00 p.m., and that way we could stay in touch.

As I climbed out of the car, I heard myself say the words, "Well, if I ever do come to Modesto, I think I would like to go out for dinner."

And about three steps later as I reached the porch, I thought, *What have I done?* A note on the door caught my attention, so I didn't have much time to ponder what just happened.

The note said, "Dear Darla, I heard you were taking a walk around the lake. But how many times did you walk around it? Call me." Then I walked into the kitchen and found two more notes on the table. "Dear Darla, I've been looking for you all day. Did you go back to Africa?" And "Hi Darla, who was that cute guy I saw you with today?" I laughed to myself and thought, *Oh brother, Peggy must not lock her door.*

That was it until the next Monday night, when the phone rang at exactly nine o'clock. I tried not to get excited about the interest Paul showed, because I planned to go back to Kenya right after Thanksgiving and had a lot to do before then. Besides which, Paul traveled too, and every Monday night we ended up in different time zones. I clearly remember the night I stayed with dear friends in Texas. I excused myself to go to the bedroom just in time for his phone call. But nine o'clock came and went. Then it was ten o'clock. I tried to shrug it off and tell myself I really didn't mind. So I got ready for bed, read for a while, and drifted off to sleep.

At eleven o'clock, I was awakened by a cheerful, "Hello." I soon realized Paul lost track of the time difference and thought he called right on time. So I rallied and tried to sound bright and wide awake. That night he told me all about the book he was reading on Abraham Lincoln. It turned out that our phone calls taught us how to listen to each other. Not a bad dating strategy.

By October, I was in Colorado with the McKnight family. While in the States, I sent money to Kenya each month to keep Agape going. I sincerely missed the boys. But I also had some rather serious talks with my longtime friend Joan McKnight at her kitchen table. Joan was also the mother of three boys nearly the same ages as mine. Our families shared many happy memories when the boys were young. She knew my situation and was the perfect person with whom to share my growing but uncertain feelings.

To my surprise, she was very positive about my new friend, Paul. She even made sure I looked my best when I flew from Denver back to

San Francisco to meet him for dinner. Joan has always been a lady who knows how to bring out the best in life. She effortlessly makes an ordinary day special. She knew I was going to wear a lovely off-white dress I borrowed from another close friend in California. As a surprise, she arranged for a facial (the first and only I've ever had) and a manicure to help me feel ready for the first date I'd had since my divorce nine years prior. I will never forget her kindness.

Things went well in San Francisco. Paul drove across the Golden Gate Bridge, into Sausalito, and to the charming Spinnaker Restaurant, which was nothing if not romantic. The long, narrow restaurant, encased in floor-to-ceiling glass, extended on a wharf into the San Francisco Bay. The lights of Tiburon, Berkeley, Oakland, and San Francisco flickered to life all around the bay as the sun disappeared behind the Golden Gate Bridge.

We felt comfortable together. How far removed this white linen covered table and its shining settings seemed from the Agape Children's Center. We chatted at the prized corner table, surrounded by glass through which the stars sparkled, until the restaurant closed.

Then Paul flew to Haiti. I didn't see him again until November when he flew into Los Angeles and stopped by to meet my family. By now, even though winter approached fast, a feeling of spring was in the air. Things were under control at Agape, so I extended my stay in the States until January 1. That turned out to be a good decision. I was absolutely thrilled when Paul invited me to spend Christmas with his family in Modesto. Some of my fears were being alleviated, since Paul had spent considerable time in East Africa for Medical Ambassadors before I ever thought of moving there. He understood my crazy lifestyle and supported all I was doing. He wasn't ready to remarry and we could continue to be friends. That suited me just fine ... for a while.

CHAPTER 42

Return to Kenya

Back in Kenya, I realized that the sixteen boys and six staff members of Agape didn't think I was going to return. That explained the sad-looking faces in the photos I took before I left. By that time, they'd settled into the dorm with good windows and screens to protect them from mosquitoes. Our faithful houseparents did a great job and the boys looked healthy and energetic.

People in the States, whom I visited during my whirlwind deputation tour, were generous and caring. We reached a point financially where we could afford to invite a few more boys in from the street.

One of the things we did right in those early years happened because of necessity. We could only afford to take in one boy at a time. When a group of boys had been there for a little while, it helped a single new boy integrate into a group of peers. Had we brought several boys from the street at once, their influence could have been disastrous.

I'd like to share a little story about a nine-year-old boy named Bryson. I believe God allowed us to save his life. When we found Bryson, he sat on a rock in front of the Coca Cola plant in Kisumu. His body burned with fever caused by malaria. A dirty cloth partly covered an open sore on his hand and parasitic worms called jiggers infested his feet. In other words, he was in bad shape. I had no choice but to take him home.

The other boys welcomed Bryson warmly, and took him for a bath.

They shared their clothes with him and gave him food. We administered the needed medical care, then the houseparent took him out back with a sharp tool and some kerosene to remove the little white worms from his feet. Bryson bravely held up his legs. The jiggers fell onto a big leaf which was immediately burned. Then kerosene was poured over the wounds. As I watched this, I found out how long I could hold my breath. They certainly didn't teach us about jiggers and kerosene in nursing school. But it worked, and it wasn't long before Bryson greeted me with a radiant smile. He pointed to the soft pair of canvas shoes on his feet. Bryson found God's comfort and safety at Agape, and he grew up to be a strong, healthy young man.

The months wore on and I read the book *Hinds Feet on High Places*. In this allegory, the character, Much-Afraid, tries to find her way. I found far too many times when I related with her fears, and I longed to give the Lord my very best 100-percent effort. But I thought about Paul and wondered if our time during the holidays together would be the end. After all, Kenya was halfway around the world from California. I knew he dated and I wondered if he had found someone else. I hadn't received a letter for quite a long time.

About the middle of March, I stopped singing the song "God will make a way, where there seems to be no way," and decided to deal with my feelings once and for all. As I finished the book where Much-Afraid commits herself completely to the Good Shepherd, I felt the need to do the same. Not that I hadn't done it before, but this time I wanted the freedom to throw myself completely into the work God called me there to do. I didn't want to be distracted by loneliness and longing. So I got down on my knees on Sunday, March 19, and prayed. "Lord, please take Paul completely out of my mind this time. I don't know why you brought him into my life in the first place, but I'm no longer going to question that. My life belongs to you and I want to be wholly yours." Then I added for emphasis, "I mean it, Lord. No lamb in the thicket like there was for Isaac. Just help me move on." I wonder if that was the surrender God desired from me, because, unbeknownst to me, that very day Paul got on an airplane.

I had friends from Uganda staying with me over the weekend. We planned a return trip to Uganda together on Tuesday, March 21. I looked forward to seeing the kids from the African Children's Choir and had my hair done so I would look my best. While I was in the salon, my friend brought bad news. The car we were supposed to make the trip in developed some problems. It would be in the shop for a couple of days.

"Oh no." I said. "At least we weren't on the road when it broke down. You can just stay at my house."

I returned to Agape and spent the rest of the day there. I left in time to get home to see the sunset over Lake Victoria. Even after all those years, I still thought of it as God's signature on each day. The sun gradually moved across the horizon and painted the sky with unique and beautiful hues. My bedroom had a great view of the lake, and that peaceful time of day became a respite from the hopelessness and despair of the surrounding poverty.

A white van drove ahead of me as I maneuvered down the lane. As it neared the gate, the guard stopped it and asked the driver a couple of questions before allowing it to enter. My neighbors sat along the cement walkway amiably chatting, and my Ugandan friends were also there. When the white van stopped in front of my flat, a man with blonde hair much like Paul's stepped out. When he reached in to grab the brown leather briefcase that was always attached to his arm, I exclaimed to myself, "That *is* Paul! How could he be here?"

I forgot the talk I'd had with the Lord just the day before, and greeted him with warm enthusiasm. After initial introductions, and because I wasn't prepared to cook for a group, we went out for dinner. When we returned home, we all played Scrabble until the person sleeping on the sofa bed turned in.

As I headed up the stairs to show Paul his room, I ventured, "I'm surprised you didn't let me know you were coming, but I'm really glad you found us here."

Paul didn't say anything until we reached his room. I was ready to say good-night, when he hesitated. "Wouldn't you like to know why I'm really here?" he asked cautiously.

"Sure." I tried to be casual, yet polite. So we entered the room and sat down to talk a little more.

I have no idea what we talked about up to the point when he turned slightly to look at me directly and asked softly, "So, would you be willing to spend the rest of your life with me?"

I opened my mouth to say something, but all that came out was an incredulous, "Oh … Oh … Um, oh." I think at some point I finally said, "Are you serious?" Then he reached into his left pants' pocket and managed to pull out a little blue box.

I don't know how my heart kept beating. I felt suspended in animation. This couldn't really be happening. Then he smiled and asked, "Was that a yes?"

I said, "Oh, I thought that was a rhetorical question. Yes!"

He opened the box slowly to display an exquisitely beautiful solitaire. I drew back and told him, "I can't take that ring."

A hint of disappointment washed across his face. "Well, we can exchange it if you don't like it."

I assured him that wasn't the problem. It was just *too* nice. It looked like the moon against that blue velvet box. He slipped the ring on my finger and there I sat … engaged to be married to Dr. Paul Calhoun.

He finally explained the reason he hadn't informed me about his trip to Kenya. "I was afraid I would spoil the surprise," he said. He certainly succeeded in surprising me. And now in spite of jet lag and very little sleep in the last forty-eight hours, he accomplished his mission.

We called to tell our families. Paul's dad knew about the ring and had expressed concern that the surprise element could turn out badly. So we called Paul's parents first. By that time, it was between one and two in the morning, but because of the ten-hour time difference, it was the perfect time to call the States. My parents were as thrilled as Paul's and confided they had been praying it would happen someday. With all the excitement, we had a very short night. But I know I fell asleep with a smile on my face.

He *can* make a way.

CHAPTER 43

Wedding and Transition Time

We had a beautiful, chapel wedding and reception with friends and family in Southern California on June 18, 1995. After a brief honeymoon along the coast, we returned to Modesto and shared our joy with friends at a second reception.

Although the excitement and busyness of our new life together filled our lives, I really missed the children in Kenya. I tried to stay connected as much as possible to make sure things ran smoothly. One time, I made a phone call to catch up with Lebaus. Then I asked to talk to the boys. That's still one of my best phone memories ever. I pictured them as they stood in a single-file line and waited for their turn. To talk on the phone was a big event for them. And to talk to America was something else altogether.

The first boy took the phone and said, "Hallo Mama, is that really you? This is Sammy. When are you coming back?"

I chatted with each of them for about thirty seconds, then the phone was passed to the next boy.

"We got pigeons and built a good house!"

"Wonderful!"

"Mama, our soccer ball is finished."

"What happened?"

"It got a punctcha."

"Oh poly sana (very sorry). We'll have to find another one."

"Mama, do you know my name?"

"Is this Evans?"

"Yes, Mama, you rememba me!"

And on it went. My eyes glistened as I felt their love come through the telephone lines.

I knew they were being well cared for. Two Canadian ladies came to serve as project coordinators during my absence. Diane Kineshanko and Colby van Dam were very capable and loved the children. Colby kept the books in perfect order. While Diane filled in as a devoted mother figure and kept things running smoothly. They even rid our new storage room of displaced field mice and then organizing a fresh closet with shelves for good, used clothes for the boys.

All of their hard work gave me the ability to spend more time in the States, get used to being married again with a new extended family, and share Agape Children's Ministry with anyone who would listen. I used that time to write monthly newsletters and speak at multiple fundraising events around the country. Paul supported my efforts and even gave up the den in our home to function as my office.

At that time, I began to make visits to Agape two or three times per year and spend three or four weeks at a time. How I loved to see the children and watch their progress. I missed them when I was away, but Kisumu became my second home.

CHAPTER 44

Benard

I will take hold of your hand. (Isaiah 42:6).

Admitted in the fall of 1997, six-year-old Benard became a ward of the court after he witnessed his mother's murder. As a police case, custody of Benard fell to the Children's Department as they investigated the situation. I visited the provincial children's officer. They gave me a handwritten note that allowed us to retrieve Benard from the Juvenile Remand Home.

Benard's face beamed when he saw our houseparent Uncle Lebaus. A staff member there shared with Lebaus that Benard told everyone his uncle would come for him. We were so thankful his faith was rewarded.

Benard came to us with such a sweet spirit that it was hard to imagine the trauma he experienced in his young life. The records showed he was unconscious when authorities took him to the hospital after his alcoholic father beat him. We showered Benard with love, and now he had a special place with a new family.

With Benard's custody secured, it became necessary to visit town officials in order to keep the lines of communication open. Among other officials, this included the Ministry of Education, the Department of Social Services and Housing, the land commissioner, and the deputy mayor.

Finally, Agape became his legal guardian "until further notice." We were delighted to have him. Benard proved to be a winsome and playful little character with facial expressions that delighted us all.

Benard

After four months at Agape, we enrolled Benard in one of the best primary schools in the area. His desire to learn was evident from the beginning.

The headmistress reported, "Benard is a very intelligent, active boy who always wants to achieve more."

On the surface, he appeared to be doing well, but something troubled us. Benard told the most incredible stories and convinced people they were absolutely true.

One day, he went to his teacher and said, "I have a real nice home. My mother is so good and she is very fat [a sign of prosperity]. Teacher, you must come to my house for tea."

The teacher mentioned this to the headmistress, who fortunately was a wise, understanding woman. She recognized that Benard wasn't just telling lies; those were his dreams. The deepest desires of his heart were to have a nice home and a loving, caring mother.

The headmistress explained, "By listening to him, we are leading him to a path of normalization."

She believed Agape provided an excellent atmosphere of love and care. We met Benard's physical needs, and the school provided an environment for him to express himself. Benard's stories gradually decreased. Through God's provision of loving houseparents and insightful teachers, he became increasingly well adjusted.

Another endearing characteristic was how responsible he tried to be. One of his Agape brothers, little Tavi, struggled to keep track of his school supplies.

One day Tavi's teacher went to the office and said, "Tavi can't write anything because he lost his pencil and sharpener."

The headmistress gave Tavi replacements, with a stern admonition to take better care of them. She also called Benard and asked him to look after Tavi so he wouldn't lose his new things.

The very next day, Tavi's frustrated teacher took him to the office with the very same problem. The surprised headmistress asked him what happened. Tavi was too shy to respond. So they called Benard to see if he knew anything about the missing pencil and sharpener. To their amusement, Benard took his job so seriously that he kept Tavi's supplies in his own custody, even though the boys were in different classes. Our prayer is that all the Agape boys will stand by each other and reach out to other street boys with this kind of brotherly love.

I will indulge here for a moment and tell a side story which involves Benard. While I was in the States, I drove from Seattle, Washington, to Modesto, California, after I had thoroughly enjoyed a visit with my sons and their families. Even with an overcast sky, I reveled in my "grandma status" having been present for the birth of our fifth grandchild, Amy Renee Peters.

As I returned home on Interstate 5, rain pelted my windshield. Without warning, traffic slowed from sixty-five to twenty-five miles per hour. I hit my brakes and glanced in the rearview mirror. The car behind me had just enough room to spare. I thanked God I didn't hit the car in front of me. Suddenly, a white eighteen-wheeler thundered up the median. I barely saw it in my side mirror when the truck jackknifed. It struck the left side of my van with a powerful jolt. I sat there in shock. I couldn't believe what just happened.

My damaged door opened just enough for me to squeeze through. I hurried to check on the truck driver. He sat in his cab pale and badly shaken. The driver did what he could to avoid a disastrous collision. Without a doubt, our guardian angels protected us from harm.

When I returned to Kenya, Benard excitedly ran up to greet me and tell me the boys had "really been praying" for my safe journey.

Then he looked at me quizzically and asked, "So, Mama, what *didn't* happen?"

What an irresistible child. Yet I can only imagine what *didn't* happen that rainy afternoon on Interstate 5.

CHAPTER 45

A Little Child Shall Lead Them

He took a little child whom he placed among them. Taking the child in his arms, he said to them, "Whoever welcomes one of these little children in my name welcomes me." (Mark 9:36-37)

B enard, now fourteen, found little Jaime as he hid in the bushes to watch one of our soccer games. Terrified to be discovered by the bigger boy, Jaime picked up a stone and stood there in an attempt to look as threatening as possible while crying.

Benard looked at him and said, "Why are you crying? I haven't even beat you yet."

Jaime dropped the stone and Benard kindly took him to Lebaus, who agreed he should be admitted to Agape. The next day, we celebrated with this little boy who now smiled wide, no longer afraid. We called him our ten-year anniversary gift from the Lord.

A year later, a much more confident Jaime found another little boy just his size during the final game of a soccer tournament. Jaime brought the new little boy to greet our team of American visitors.

Tevin was the size of a six-year-old but wasn't sure of his birthday. He did have all his permanent teeth though, which indicated he was at least nine years old. He stood before us dirty and shy that day, but he flashed his sweet smile and it melted our hearts. We confirmed we had room for one more bed and took him home with us. The next day at our celebration, I asked both the boys to come forward. I explained what happened and lovingly dubbed Tevin "Our Trophy." He liked that name, so we always referred him as Tevin Trophy.

Jaime's kindness and compassion challenged us all. We asked ourselves, *If a young boy like Jaime is that concerned about the welfare of another desperate street boy, what does that say about our responsibility as adults?*

CHAPTER 46

Wilber

The number of street children in Kisumu continued to rise. Street life subjected them to harassment and frequent arrests for vagrancy (being without a fixed abode). Vagrancy was a criminal offense in Kenya with no age limit. Out of frustration, the officials occasionally ordered roundups or raids in an effort to keep the street-boy problem under control.

I cried the day I learned the details of those raids.

One of the witnesses described it, saying, "There was a large truck with policemen in the back pointing their guns at the street children sitting on the floor of the back of the truck."

They hauled the children off to the remand center where they endured days of idleness. With little furniture, they sat on cold concrete floors. I prayed with other Christians for the day when the life that those unfortunate boys were forced to live would no longer be considered a criminal offense or grounds for arrest.

Thankfully, authorities amended that law. But Kenya still has thousands of street children. I mentioned earlier that UNICEF reports that there are more than 150 million street children in the world. That's just under half the population of the United States. I can't even wrap my mind around that. Most of us haven't had a clue that a problem of this enormity even existed.

Our newly completed dorm allowed us to gradually take in additional boys. Our staff functioned like a well-oiled machine, and we had the funds to take in our twentieth boy. Lebaus told a few boys that he would meet them in the park the following day. Word spread around town. Imagine his shock and surprise the next morning when he arrived at the park and found *sixty* hopeful boys.

Faced with such a heart-wrenching decision, Lebaus did a remarkable thing. He asked the boys to choose from among themselves. What those sixty neglected boys did was even more remarkable. Instead of fighting or clamoring to the front, they came to an agreement and made a selfless decision.

They chose Wilber, saying, "Because he is the smallest, you should take him."

Wilber was somewhere between eight and nine years old, but malnutrition had stunted his growth. After his mother died, his father abandoned him. Wilber's bloated abdomen and gaunt eyes indicated he needed treatment for parasites too.

His condition came as no surprise because of how street kids rummage through the garbage for food. However, the extent of their suffering sometimes escapes us.

Wilber confided soon after he arrived, "Sometimes you get so hungry in town, you just eat dirt."

He needed so much love and encouragement. He didn't know any numbers or the alphabet, so he needed to catch up in school too. The other boys at Agape quickly welcomed him into the family as a new little brother – there was nothing more gratifying.

CHAPTER 47

Trivial Pursuits

Time is abundant in Africa, and the boys found creative ways to entertain themselves. When not in school, doing studies, or their chores, their first love was soccer. Our campus was just large enough to contain a three-quarter-size soccer pitch. The boys played in bare feet on the dirt field. It delighted them to have new official soccer balls donated by the members of the Kisumu sister-city committee in Roanoke, Virginia. Before those arrived, they kicked around balls made from tightly compressed rags and plastic bags cleverly laced with string.

Initially, the sport created considerable conflict and bickering over rules among the boys. But in time, with a lot of coaching and a big whistle, they learned to have more patience with each other. Together, the boys practiced soccer at every opportunity and actually melded into very talented teams. The first-string team frequently played other outside teams and was rarely defeated.

The second most popular competition was checkers. They took it quite seriously. Sometimes they played on a board painted onto the concrete picnic table. Dark- and light-colored bottle caps substituted for the actual checkers. The kids hunkered over the board for hours while a small gathering watched intently.

One summer, when our friend Steve Chance visited, the boys called out plays for him to make. He thought they were on his side and followed their suggestions. The boys broke into uproarious laughter when he finally realized they had tricked him. We had a lot of fun.

The boys demonstrated their ingenuity by playing pickup golf tournaments. They fashioned clubs from short sticks with a loop of wire twisted over one end. Any small ball worked. I admit, I never expected to see golf played in Africa, but it wasn't uncommon to see nationals play golf as we traveled to the airport.

One day, I came through the campus gate and found a cluster of boys gathered around the older boys. They had built their own stilts. This new piece of equipment provided much entertainment as they competed to see who could balance over the longest distance. I considered this free entertainment one of my perks as a missionary at Agape.

The boys also designed model cars from heavy wire. Their handiwork really impressed me. I complimented the boys on their creativity. The models were a couple feet long and included rubber wheels cut from the soles of worn-out flip-flops. A waist-high miniature steering wheel extended from the dashboard and actually controlled the direction of the wheels. In addition, Zack developed an advanced version. He wired two flashlight bulbs powered by a nine-volt battery to serve as headlights. It's no wonder he was the first Agape boy to get his driver's license and become a truck driver.

I found all their ingenuity quite remarkable. Then one of the security guards came to me with a mysterious problem.

He said, "I've noticed larger and larger holes in the back perimeter fence."

With no one missing, he wondered what caused them.

I knew instantly. I called out, "Boys!"

Too bad we had to put a stop to their car building, at least until we could afford to patch the fence. We bought wire, reinforced the weak spots, and put their auto manufacturing back in business with the excess wire.

Somehow, in the midst of all the chaos caused by sixteen former street boys boisterously interacting with each other, there occasionally came a soft breeze. It seemed like God tapped me on the shoulder to remind me that He was looking down and blessing our center.

One evening like that, as I watched the kids play a lively game of soccer, cool air wrapped around us as the sun melted into the horizon. It painted a beautiful sunset in its wake. The boys played well together and stayed in their team positions. They laughed at mistakes instead of becoming angry with each other like in the early days.

Even Shadrack made the comment, "Mama, the fighting has gone out of this place."

I treasured the moment in my heart like a foretaste of heaven on earth. At that moment there was no place I'd rather have been than right there with those kids.

CHAPTER 48

Video Shoot

"It was the very place for a homeless boy, who must
die in the streets unless someone helped him."
– Charles Dickens (*Oliver Twist*)

Paul and Winnie Bahn, from Big Valley Grace Community Church
in Modesto, came to shoot a video to show how Agape related to
the needs of street children. Part of the documentation included taking some footage from the streets. During the process, we experienced
many touching moments as boys with glassy eyes from sniffing glue
ran to meet us.

One night, we went to the park with our houseparent Lebaus to
illustrate where the boys sleep and how they survive. The first boy we
found slept under a petroleum truck. Then we found two little brothers.
Before long, we sat in a paper-strewn campsite surrounded by twenty-
one boys of all ages. We prayed together and grew more committed than
ever to find ways to demonstrate the love of Christ to them.

Paul Bahn reflected later:

"It always amazes me how God can take a simple idea and,
with a handful of dedicated people, accomplish so much.
What a difference between the boys at Agape and those we
spent time with on the streets. The need there in Kisumu is

as real as I've ever seen. And it's being met, as God provides, through those serving at Agape Children's Center. It's about showing these children God loves them, showing them that they matter to Him, and that there is hope; hope in Jesus.

"One of the highlights of this time in Kisumu was seeing a bright-eyed and happy Nazim. When first brought to Agape just two months previously, he reminded me of a frightened little rabbit as he came through the gate. I wish you could have seen his sudden transformation. I had to look twice to believe it myself. What a difference love makes."

I've heard numerous short-term team members say, "We just need one more day."

So I smiled as we packed up to leave and Paul said, "I just wish we had one more day."

CHAPTER 49

Golden Clay Ministries

When all the jars were full, she said to her son, "Bring me another one." But he replied, "There is not a jar left." Then the oil stopped flowing. (2 Kings 4:6)

I am frequently asked where Agape's funding comes from. We are a faith-based organization and our income varies from month to month. In 1996, when I learned our account was down to twenty dollars and I had sixteen boys to feed, I received a call from a gentleman named Steve Chance. He wanted to help by giving us two thousand dollars. At first, I was cautious and unbelieving. I wondered if someone called as a prank, but didn't think it was very funny. I let him talk a few minutes to see if he was on the level. After Steve told me he wrote a book called *Searching for Normalcy*, due to his cerebral palsy, I decided he must be serious. What a wonderful morning that turned out to be.

Later, Steve brought a team to Kenya and funded a building which held two apartments. That building was an enormous blessing to us and it has since been used for everything from living quarters, to a high school, to short-term mission team lodging. The kitchen has served more meals that anyone can count.

Ken Kemp, the chairman of the board, had this to report when he saw our project firsthand:

"As we inspected Agape's one-and-a-quarter-acre campus, we met all twenty-five of the boys. We spoke with the nine African employees – houseparents, teachers, kitchen workers, and groundskeepers – and we met some of the Christian community leaders who have taken an active role in supporting the work of ACM. The local Kisumu board includes a physician, an accountant, a private school administrator, and a banker, among others. We spent many hours with the on-site administrator, Vic Theissen, a Canadian missionary who oversees the day-to-day operation.

"In my world, we call this kind of trip 'due diligence.' I am a businessman. Our travel team consisted of three members: an educator, the director of an American Christian nonprofit organization, and myself. No questions were off limits. We probed and listened to each person from every level as they spoke about the impact of life at Agape Children's Ministry. We came away with two distinct impressions.

"1) CHALLENGE. We are much more aware of the challenges inherent in Darla's vision. Helping the street kids of Kisumu is no easy task. The effects of hunger, abuse, violence, poverty, rejection, the absence of good parenting – all this and more leave deep wounds on the heart and mind of each of these young boys. The damage is real. In some cases, severe.

"2) HOPE. We also came away with the firm conviction that ACM is a worthy effort. It is a Christ-centered, biblically based safe haven where God is doing some of His best work. Nutrition, health care, education, cleanliness, affirmation, affection, encouragement – they all matter. These boys are benefiting. At ACM, the gospel of Jesus Christ is changing lives – for good. We took a close look and were not disappointed."

CHAPTER 50

Mourice

I saw something special in Mourice. At first, it was hard to put my finger on it because of his typical street-boy appearance. A dirty, stretched-out T-shirt hung loosely off one shoulder and white patches of fungus dotted his scalp. When an adult approached him, he shied away and looked down to avoid eye contact. Yet I still saw something gentle and appealing about his manner. When he smiled, it brightened the whole day.

Later, we learned Mourice came from the western province of Kenya, an area known as Kakamega. His mother left the family when Mourice was four months old. His father didn't want to care for a baby, so the grandmother stepped in and did the best she could. However, when she passed away, life became more complicated for Mourice.

He tried to go live with his father who had since remarried. Unfortunately, the new wife's disdain for Mourice turned into abuse. So they sent him to live with another relative. As Mourice got a little older, he tried to live at his father's home once more. This time the stepmother abused him so badly that Mourice ran away for good. By the age of eleven, Mourice had never attended school. He lived on the street for two years before we rescued him. He arrived at Agape on October 5, 1997.

Once settled in, Mourice could hardly wait to go to school. It was difficult, but he worked hard to catch up with his classmates. Then in 2004, he passed his exams and qualified for high school. We all shared his joy and were delighted to see his character traits developing.

Our Kenyan staffer describes Mourice in this way:

> "Kind and cheerful with a huge, humble heart. He loved the Lord Jesus and knew God answered prayer. Among his favorite things were cake, the color blue, and cats. He especially loved to play basketball, and had the height advantage."

During our anniversary celebration in 2006, Mourice came striding in from boarding school. He looked handsome in his blue school uniform. He towered over me.

"Can I have a few words with you?" he asked.

I braced a bit, expecting a request of some kind, but said, "Sure."

To my surprise, he just wanted to thank me.

He said, "I never knew my life could be like this. My family didn't want me and chased me away. But now when they see me, they show me respect. I didn't think I could go to school, and now ...."

My eyes filled as he expressed his gratitude so humbly and beautifully.

He started again. "Now I'm president of our school's debate team." He flashed his great smile again.

While he came so far, a long journey still stood before him. He struggled to get good grades and requested prayer for confidence to do well with his studies and exams. He also requested prayer for peace among the members of his family.

Mourice did go on to become a teacher and his students adored him. Tragically, and way too soon from our human perspective, he became ill. He went home to his rural area and before he could get good medical care he passed away, possibly from appendicitis. I so look forward to the day when we will see this young man again in heaven.

CHAPTER 51

The Intrepid Tuckers

One of the most remarkable things about Agape is the quality staff the Lord has given us. Tom and Marg Tucker left their home and family in Canada in 1991 to work as evangelists in Matoso, Kenya. I met them about four years later and was impressed with their love and concern for the Luo people. By this time, we discovered that many of our older boys would not fit into the normal school system because they had missed too much. However, they had good minds and strong bodies and needed a skill to help them earn a living. We wanted to develop a vocational training center and were struggling to know how to go about it. Not only was Tom a skilled craftsman in all areas of construction, but he had already found the perfect piece of property right on the shore of Lake Victoria. It a beautiful place to build a school and bordered a Luo neighborhood fishing village. A perfect match!It took two years for the Tuckers to build their home using locally available materials and a lot of determination. They worked with a team of Kenyan laborers and managed to make over ten thousand bricks by hand. Tom is skilled in carpentry, plumbing, electrical work, farming, and truck driving. He could fix anything. His skills uniquely qualified him for mission work.

One Sunday afternoon, we traveled with a mission team in a small tour bus to Matoso, and the radiator hose blew. A plume of steam streamed from beneath the hood. There we were, stranded and surrounded by sugarcane fields in a small rural village, with no cell phones, and no mechanic in sight.

Tom Tucker demonstrating fruits of agriculture training

Dr. Wally Carroll graciously accompanied me as we hailed an African "taxi" to find the Tuckers. After an exciting ride, during which I hummed "Nearer My God to Thee," we reached our meeting place and found Tom and Marg.

Tom calmly took the situation in hand and confidently gathered the tools he needed. However, since it was Sunday, all the shops were closed, so we had no place to buy a new piece of hose for the radiator. Tom saw only one way to solve the problem. He sawed off a piece of his own vehicle's tailpipe and attached it with clamps to what remained of our radiator hose. The vehicle started right up and off we went, amazed and thankful.

Tom's work required him to do much more than rescue stranded vehicles, however. He served as a father figure to twenty-three teenage boys. Imagine! Tom often commented that while he was away from his own family members, he had many sons to call his own. He clearly wanted the best for the boys and worked daily to instill godly principles into their lives. Sometimes he ran into difficulties as he worked with these young men from troubled backgrounds. However, Tom pointed out how God never gave up on him during his wayward years, so he knew the Lord wouldn't give up on those boys.

People often commented on the dangers of life in Africa and asked, "Weren't you afraid?"

When you're in the center of God's will, nothing will happen to you that He doesn't allow for some good reason. I used the words "miracles" and "miraculous" several times as I wrote, and certainly there are times in this modern era when miracles still happen.

Tom tells a story of a miracle he experienced regarding his safety.

"It was time to load the forty ceiling boards from my carport into the truck and move them down to the lake to help build the house. So I put on my gloves and got started. One by one, I picked up each four-by-eight-foot sheet and loaded it. It was a hot day, so I wore a tee shirt, shorts, and a pair of open sandals. I got down to the thirty-eighth board and was glad to be nearly done with the job.

"When I got to the fortieth board, there, curled up under that last board, was a deadly black mamba! The sight took my breath away. It had thirty-nine chances to strike at my bare toes. Why didn't it react to the movements and noise? I could easily have died that day. But I believe the hand of God protected me and kept that snake quiet. Being in the center of God's will is the safest place to be … especially in the African bush."

Of course, it's been one of his greatest joys to see the boys do well. Recently, John Otieno, our cobbler's apprentice, stopped by the farm for a visit. Tom happened to be showing the movie *The Cross and the Switchblade* to the other boys. Then John asked if he could say something.

Marg said, "He preached to his fellow students with a God-given passion, and we both wept with joy because we realized he was one of the first fruits of our labors."

Where would those boys be without someone like Tom? Dr. James Garbarino wrote a book called *Lost Boys: Why Our Sons Turn Violent and*

How We Can Save Them. In the book he states, "Violent juvenile offenders have a crisis of meaninglessness in their lives. This lack of meaning leads to despair and plays a significant role in the lives of violent juveniles. Without a sense that their lives have some higher purpose ... these young people see no point in restraining offensive or violent behavior."

Older street boys become classic examples to illustrate that point. However, when someone intervenes and shows them a better way, miraculous transformations take place. Visitors constantly comment on the tremendous difference they see between the boys on the street and the boys at Agape. When God's agape love is shown through people like Tom and Marg, it gives the boys hope.

CHAPTER 52

A Farm in Africa

Life took on a different perspective at the vocational farm in Matoso, Kenya. On the shore of Lake Victoria, the breeze blew gently as large white egrets rode the thermals. Colorful flowers, papaya trees, and tropical birds decorated the landscape. The fish eagle checked his drift and plunged straight down to the water. It darted at an unsuspecting fish with a heavy splash.

Lush grass rolled in a gentle slope to the sandy shore where, in the morning, a long line of villagers gathered to slowly pull in a mile-long net placed during the night by seasoned fishermen paddling large fishing boats. At night, a long chain of boats was visible far out on the horizon, each one bobbed with a lantern in its bow. From the distance, it looked like a floating city. The two-hundred-mile-wide lake stretched into infinity punctuated with a distant island.

In contrast to the serenity of the setting, we went through windy, stormy times to establish the farm. Then various work teams came to shower us with the blessings of their physical labor and spiritual encouragement. Many months later, we saw the "first blooms" demonstrated through the lives of six young men who made up the first group of vocational trainees.

As we completed the arduous trip from Kisumu and drove into the compound, the boys ran down the hill as soon as they saw our van.

What a joy. The boys looked strong and healthy and appeared to be thriving in the beautiful environment. They eagerly showed us around their dorms and classrooms. From the time they arrived at the farm, they demonstrated a desire to rise to the challenge and become more independent in preparation for life on their own.

Two Kenyan instructors made sure the on-site carpentry shop ran efficiently. They taught students to saw, plane boards smoothly, and fit joints to create impressively sturdy furniture. The curriculum also included how to bid for jobs, keep accounting records, and maintain business relationships. Other trades included brick masonry, auto mechanics, fish farming, and agriculture.

Days began early with morning devotions and regular Bible studies. Students also participated in church services on Sundays. During their free time, the boys and staff joined forces for lively games of volleyball and soccer. Of course, swimming in the lake was also one of their favorite pastimes.

CHAPTER 53

Waving the Flag

We've experienced some discouraging roadblocks along the way. Young men with such troubled pasts don't always make healthy decisions for their futures. They are enslaved by the past, and the temporary comfort of sniffing glue makes the pain go away.

However, the vast majority of boys at Agape have made remarkable progress. Barnett is one of the success stories. He came through our vocational training center overseen by Tom and Marg Tucker. Barnett caught my attention one summer with his knowledge of how an engine works. He explained the process so thoroughly it even impressed his Kenyan instructor. Barnett was one of the first to pass his National Grade 3 Vocational Skills Test.

Our director, Blake Gibbs, visited Barnett at Sony where he was "on attachment" as an apprentice (in the U.S. this would be considered an internship). Blake reported, "Every floor supervisor in the maintenance shop, the boss of the heavy equipment department, his boss, and the boss in charge of all maintenance at Sony told us what a great young man Barnett is. They raved about how much he knows and how glad they are that he is there."

Of course, that makes us very proud of him, and the younger boys say, "Barnett is waving the flag of Agape in the community."

At this writing, Barnett has worked for several years as a mechanic with the Sony Sugar Company.

CHAPTER 54

Rabbits Galore

J acob provides a great example of an Agape boy. When we rescued him in 2000, he displayed shy and withdrawn behavior. He hardly ever made eye contact with adults and recoiled in their presence. We later learned that both his stepmother and father beat him. Jacob ran from his home to the streets.

In spite of his background, Jacob emerged a caring and talented young man with an eye to the future. Even with a late start in school, he excelled in the seventh grade. He found healing as he cared for animals, particularly rabbits and guinea pigs.

On one of my Kenyan visits, Jacob pulled on my arm and said, "Mama, come see the children. You have to see them."

I followed Jacob and a few other boys around the buildings to a dorm room. To my surprise, the "children" were a brand-new litter of tiny baby rabbits.

In an effort to protect the kits, he took them out of their rudimentary rabbit hutch and placed them in a cardboard box. He padded it with clumps of the mother rabbit's soft fur. The box remained safely tucked under his bunk bed. The other boys explained how at feeding times, they brought the mother rabbit into the dorm, placed her on the bed, and "plugged the babies in" to nurse.

Oh my! Fortunately, our veterinarian friend Dr. Diane D'Orazio accompanied us on that trip. She patiently explained to the boys how they could build a better rabbit hutch and ways they could improve the rabbits' care. Jacob listened to every word and put her advice into practice. Caring for those helpless little creatures gave his life a sense of purpose. It wasn't long before we put him in charge of all the rabbits, pigeons, and guinea pigs. When Diane returned with our team the following summer, she found the boys had followed her advice and it had paid off.

Jacob studied his little animals carefully and predicted with amazing accuracy when new litters would be born. It came as no surprise that his rabbits won awards at the Kisumu Agriculture Show. Rabbits held a special place in his heart, and God used them in Jacob's healing.

I'll always remember the time he presented me with a lovely hyacinth paper card. It was addressed to my six-year-old granddaughter, Shaelyn. I had shared with him that for her birthday, she received a pet rabbit with tan and white markings just like some of his bunnies. That simple information built a bridge between them, and in addition to the card, Jacob enclosed a little soapstone necklace he made. She was thrilled.

During our team visit the following summer, we met his instructor and saw where Jacob made the special hyacinth paper. The process was a wonderful use of locally available materials. Otherwise, the large hyacinth leaves created a serious problem for fishermen on Lake Victoria. We climbed several flights of stairs and finally reached the flat rooftop where the equipment was set up. After a thorough demonstration, they allowed us to try our hand at it. Papermaking turned out to be more difficult than we expected.

That day, Jacob wore a bright blue hat he made of tightly woven plastic bags commonly found in the market, another skill he taught himself. As we prepared to come back to the U.S., he gave Dr. D'Orazio a special gift in appreciation for all she had done for him. He wove a sturdy handbag from green plastic bags. His thoughtful note expressed appreciation for the way she helped his life to be recycled. Jacob proved himself a promising young man with many interests. He even became one of our Boy Scouts who eventually competed on the national level.

Later, Jacob became one of the first boys in our reintegration project.

He was a perfect candidate to return to his home. Armed with a basic education, he helped his mother provide for the family.

He now stands tall and handsome. To see him today, someone might wonder if he could possibly be the same person. His contagious enthusiasm for life and confident smile helped him become a great salesman. He continues to thrive and now has a job doing custodial work in Nairobi. Along with all this, he recently opened his own business on the side where he sells a variety of his own arts and crafts including jewelry, cards, and beautiful artwork. It's a dream come true.

CHAPTER 55

Little Calbert Had TB

W e discovered Calbert in the streets at the tender age of seven. He lived on the streets for several months after his relatives abandoned him. Calbert's parents and one of his four brothers were tragically killed when a robber attacked them in their rural home. After that terrible event, Calbert and his remaining brothers went to live with their grandmother. The grandmother was unable to provide for his needs. Calbert left for the streets because of neglect and idleness.

When he arrived in Kisumu, Calbert hung around the bus station where he begged for food from passengers and looked for scraps at adjacent hotels. His health deteriorated. When our houseparent found him, he had a serious case of tuberculosis and lived in a pathetic physical and emotional state. One of his lungs had collapsed from the tuberculosis, and he breathed with constant pain. The pain forced him to walk hunched over.

After plenty of good food, loving care, and medical attention, Calbert slowly morphed into a very active, happy boy. He quickly responded to gospel stories, embraced the Lord, and demonstrated a passionate, forgiving heart. Calbert loved to sing at the top of his rejuvenated lungs and lived to play soccer. He also gravitated to adults and soaked up the love he'd missed out on at home.

Calbert learned that the future held hope. One day, as he helped his teacher carry school materials from the classroom, he spotted some of his favorite workbooks. "I love those books. When I grow up, I want to be a teacher."

One of his favorite quotes is from David Livingstone: "God had an only Son and He made Him a missionary."

Thank God for Calbert and the role He allowed us to play in his young life.

CHAPTER 56

Remarkable Dr. Ruby

Agape board member, doctor to hundreds, and faithful friend, Dr. Ruby Sokwala, is a remarkable lady. Committed to equality and social justice for the people in her community, she has lived in Kenya for thirty-two years now, but her home still maintains the flavor and fragrances of India. We shared many meals around her family's dining table, eating chapattis with sikuma wiki, curried chicken, and Basmati rice with our fingers. Ruby often displayed her care by delivering dishes of delicious food to her patients when they were too ill to cook.

I met Dr. Ruby at the Fellowship Bible Church in Kisumu shortly after I arrived in town. The congregation was a closely knit group of Kenyans, East Indians, and missionaries from America and various European countries. After reading her Bible, Ruby made a firm commitment to follow Jesus. However, she paid dearly for her decision. It resulted in painful exile from the rest of her family. She held fast to her beliefs and maintained a gentle spirit with unwavering love for her family. As a result, her husband, son, and daughter all became united as believers in Jesus Christ.

When we needed advisors for our fledgling organization, Ruby was one of the first people I asked for help. She willingly offered to treat our street boys at no cost as often as possible. What a gift that was, since we had so little money and the boys usually arrived with health issues including malaria, scabies, lice, infected wounds, etc. Ruby never minced words and gave her patients wise and thoughtful counsel. In spite of this, God allowed her to endure a frightening experience.

It was a typical Friday afternoon with people crowded together on rickety brown benches in the waiting room. A Kenyan receptionist sat at a small desk at the end of the narrow room. Ruby called for the next patient. Two male "patients" entered her office and closed the door behind them. It instantly became apparent that the men weren't ill. They intended to rob Ruby's cash box.

Unfortunately for the robbers, Ruby already deposited the week's earnings at the bank during her lunch break. She had very little in the cash box. When she tried to explain, the young men, whom she recognized from the street, became infuriated. They threw the cash box down and knocked her to the cement floor. With mounting rage, one of them grabbed Ruby tightly around the neck and began to strangle her. Finally, the receptionist opened the door and they fled.

A shaken Ruby reported later how she never saw a more evil expression than in that man's cruel eyes. She came to church Sunday with red and purple bruises around her neck. When I asked how she was dealing with the trauma, she replied, "As I lay on the ground struggling to breathe, I thought, *If these men had only known a place like Agape, they would never have done this to me.*"

Her answer stunned me. I pondered what she said and wondered if I could think about the welfare of a person while they were trying to end *my* life. Ruby remains one of the pillars of Agape's foundation and will always have my highest admiration.

In the Boat

I personally experienced Dr. Ruby's direct and loving care when a team from Taylor University visited Agape. The team came well prepared and tried hard to engage the boys in drama and sports. They even performed amazingly fast-paced tricks with drinking cups. Everyone loved them. So we hosted an appreciation meal of chicken and pineapple at the home of our missionaries Rick and Audrey McAninch. We intended to barbeque the chickens, but none of the students felt comfortable cutting them up. They were small so there were several to cut up. Being the "mother," I took up the challenge.

As I cut up one of the hens, the sharp knifepoint went through the chicken skin and punctured the inside of my right index finger. It didn't bleed much, and I washed it carefully under the faucet. I pretty much forgot about it and didn't dwell on the fact that the tap water came from the lake … until the next morning. I woke up and exclaimed, "Ow!" I checked my hand to see why it hurt. Oh, my goodness. My angry red and swollen index finger led to a three-inch red trail on the top of my hand. I knew that wasn't good, but it was Sunday morning. I decided to show it to Ruby at church.

During the sermon, I felt woozy. I sat in the center of the row and tried to remain conscious. The pastor continued his sermon. I looked at my watch. The service usually ended at noon. I had to hang on for fourteen more minutes. I earnestly prayed, "Please, Lord, keep me upright for fourteen more minutes." I took a deep breath and tried really hard to concentrate for what felt like a full hour. Finally, we closed in prayer. What a relief.

I showed my hand to Dr. Ruby. She told me to go to the chemist (pharmacy) for some amoxicillin. At that time, you just went in and asked for the drug you needed. It seemed like as long as you could pronounce it, the pharmacist gave it to you. Unfortunately, they had no amoxicillin available that day. The pharmacist asked if I wanted some ampicillin instead. I knew I needed an antibiotic, and since we didn't know whether it was a strep or staph infection, I decided it wouldn't hurt to try. The pills came in tiny paper packets with the handwritten dosage on the outside.

I took the medication, but the next day, my index finger was even more swollen and had turned a scary bluish color. The streak now climbed up my arm.

Our missionary Audrey said, "I'm taking you to the hospital." I couldn't argue. We went to the Nightingale Hospital where a kindly doctor took a look and called for an IV. Concerned about AIDS, I mustered the nerve to ask about the needle. They assured me it had never been used before. So that took care of it. They administered IV antibiotics.

The next evening, Ruby stopped by to check on me. She took one look at my swollen hand and blue finger with two streaks now, and said sternly, "How long do you want this thing to go on looking like that? Get in the car."

I sheepishly grabbed my bag and followed her out the door. In the meantime, other people made comments about my condition and said things like, "Back home you'd be admitted to the hospital." But we had a team of students who came all the way from Indiana to work with the street kids, and I was the leader. Besides, it reminded me of the time Jesus told His disciples to get into the boat in Matthew 14:22. *Immediately Jesus made the disciples get into the boat and go on ahead of him to the other side, while he dismissed the crowd.*

They did just what He asked, but they encountered a big, very scary, windy storm. They obeyed, yet found themselves in a life-threatening situation. Then Jesus rescued them. I told everyone, "I know I'm supposed to be here in Kenya. I'm figuratively in the boat, and I'm not worried. I know Jesus will take care of this."

We went to Ruby's office in downtown Kisumu. She gave me a "jab" with what felt like a bigger needle than we use in the U.S. There was no charge, and I was grateful for her firm but loving care. Now, all the forces of several antibiotics ran through my system, and we thought that should take care of it. However, the next day held more of the same. By that point, I realized I could lose my finger if it kept up. I like to play the piano, so I didn't really want that to happen. People at home prayed. Audrey took me back to the hospital. This time one of the Taylor team chaperones, Lori Holtzman, kept me company while Audrey ran errands.

The soft-spoken Kenyan doctor approached and shook his head. That's never a good sign. Then he said, "Well, I'm going to send you upstairs to someone who's not as nice as I am." I felt trapped and wished I really was in a boat. I climbed the narrow stairwell with Lori. Eventually, the dingy cream-colored paint gave way to a brighter room.

"Sit here," a Kenyan nurse said. Then an intimidating surgical tray appeared. I quickly scanned the iodine, scalpel, and gauze. No anesthetic in sight. A large muscular doctor with green scrubs and a mask came over and ordered me to give him my hand. Lori stood in back of me with her hands on my shoulders. Then it started. The doctor brushed my painful finger with iodine, then grabbed the scalpel, and cut into it while I held my breath. I stared at the ground, balled my other hand into a fist, and curled my toes. The color drained from Lori's face, and she moved to brace herself against the back wall. At last, the doctor called for the nurse to wrap it up. Relieved, Lori and I tottered down the staircase into the fresh air.

I'm happy to report I still have my right index finger. It works just fine. I don't know what made the difference. It could have been the combination of antibiotics, the lancing, or the prayers. But God took care of it, and the storm blew over. We had an exceptionally wonderful time with the Taylor team. Our grown-up boys still remember them. Things don't always go smoothly in ministry, but it gives our faith a chance to grow, and the rewards that follow make it truly worth it all.

CHAPTER 57

A Day at the Park

Contributed by missionary Dan Schmelzer

Wednesday became known throughout the community of the street boys in Kisumu as the day for the park. It provided a respite from a life of striving just to survive. We met there around ten o'clock. More than fifty boys gathered from all directions. Their *walimus* (teachers) met them for a soccer match, a time of sharing, and the only good meal they would get that week.

As the boys arrived, a picture of filthy clothes and open sores, glazed eyes and empty stares, and the early signs of malnutrition presented itself. However, as the day got underway, that picture was transformed to encouraging smiles and laughter, gleeful shouts of play, hand-holding, and hugs. We shared a simple meal of porridge, maize, and beans. Those were the true images of a day with the boys.

We walked to an open field and raised two sticks for the goal. With teams chosen, the game began. For a few hours, the power structure of the street broke down. The game gave the boys a respite from the loneliness of street life. For a moment, they were a team that cared for and encouraged one another. As I observed, I saw the wisdom of it all. It wasn't just a game, it was a way to provide hope and affirm their value.

After the game, they gathered in the shade under a nearby sumac tree. The escape from reality ended. They pulled their glue bottles out and I watched their clear eyes glaze over once again.

Then I witnessed a touching moment as Lebaus talked of a Father in heaven.

He shared with the boys that their Savior God is always there. "He does not die, He does not abandon, He does not abuse." Lebaus talked about the love and hope beyond the trash heap and unhealed sores.

I studied their faces and wondered, *Why are they so receptive? Don't they struggle with their situation and the truth that God loves them? Can it be that the power of Jesus' love is greater than overwhelming poverty?* A lump formed in my throat as Lebaus prayed with all heads bowed. Willingly, with heartfelt devotion, each boy in threadbare clothes lowered his head and raised his heart to the throne of God. What an awesome thing faith is. It truly humbled me.

Lebaus and I walked from the field and headed for a local restaurant with fifty street boys in tow. We stepped across a two-foot-wide open sewage ditch and entered a tin-roofed shack. Into this little room, smaller than a typical child's bedroom, they gathered twenty-five at a time. The boys devoured porridge served in bowls made from gourds cut in half, along with a dish of maize and beans. The rest of the boys waited patiently outside without fighting. All knew they'd be fed.

One boy offered me some of his maize and beans. I tried to refuse politely, but didn't want him to think I was appalled by the conditions of this place, which he saw as lifesaving. Truthfully, I have to say it was difficult to hide my feelings. I wondered if he noticed.

Those boys hadn't enjoyed the blessings of Agape. This experience fueled the rest of the week, because those boys were yet to be reached and rescued. As I laid my head to rest at the end of the day, I felt closer to the heart of God somehow. He saw our spiritual poverty and was moved to love, suffer, and even be crucified to rescue us. In that moment of compassion, there was peace. I am thankful God led me to that place. Peace in poverty. What a wonder.

CHAPTER 58

Allure of the Streets

By Andrea Dowell

An inherent emotional risk comes with working with street kids. The children are rescued off the streets and brought onto Agape's campus. The staff and missionaries listen to their stories, love on them, teach them, encourage them, disciple them, and pray with them.

Hearts are opened wide to these kids so a relationship of trust can be built. But that leaves us vulnerable to heartache. It leaves us exposed, because sometimes, the children make the decision to leave Agape. It's because the streets call to the boys from just beyond the fence. Life on the streets is powerful, alluring, and addicting.

On the streets, there is freedom. Or so the boys think.

No one makes you take a bath. No one makes you do chores. No one makes you wash your clothes. No one makes you go to school. No one makes you follow the rules, and … there is glue.

Glue is powerful. It makes you forget your problems. Forget that the nights are cold. It can make you forget you are hungry, and make you forget your mistakes. It can even make you forget the rejection at home. And there is autonomy.

Street kids find scrap metal or plastic and sell it. They load or unload luggage from *matatus* or carry heavy bags of charcoal. They ride around on the garbage truck to load and unload the city's unending refuse, or pull carts loaded down with water. They can beg or steal. They can do any of these jobs to earn enough money for a little bit of food for the day or enough money for another inch of glue. There is belonging.

These powerfully intoxicating things constantly tempt the children at Agape. They lure them to walk out the gate and return to the "good life" on the streets. They don't remember the dangers of street life. They don't remember the struggle to find their own food or the constant threat from older street boys or the police. They don't remember the abusive words thrown at them in judgment by people who walk past them. They don't remember being chased and having to run and hide to protect themselves. They don't remember being beaten. They just don't remember.

Instead, they are tempted by memories of freedom, the glue, autonomy, and a sense of belonging. So after they stay at Agape for a few days, the lure of the streets overwhelms them, and they jump the fence.

We dealt with a young boy who struggled daily to stay on campus. The streets had a tight hold on him. He wanted to go, to be free. This boy craved holding a glue bottle in his hands again and finding his street "family." He longed to make his own money and buy what he desired. He didn't want to clean his clothes or make his bed. He wasn't interested in sweeping the dining hall. He didn't even want to be on the inside of the fence.

Ted, one of the managers, sat and talked with him, hoping to encourage him to change his mind. But the determined boy wanted to leave.

Sadness filled Ted's eyes as he walked into our office to ask for help. "He really wants to go," Ted said. "He wants us to open the gate for him. I don't know what to do next."

We prayed and brainstormed. The Lord brought the same person to our minds, a staff member named Christine. As one of our counselors, she had really bonded with the boy. Perhaps she could help. We asked Christine to come and talk with the boy and she agreed.

I watched with hope as Christine walked hand in hand with the boy, out of the office and towards the counseling room.

Twenty minutes later, Christine returned with the same sadness in her eyes. "He still insists he wants to go. He misses his friends on the street. He misses getting a few shillings for working. He misses his street life."

Sadness showed on all our faces. It always hurts, because we know the "freedom" these children imagine on the streets is just a lie. They are deceived. We know the reality of the dangers that await them in the streets and how difficult street life is. We love these children and want the best for them. I saw it in Ted's and Christine's eyes. This boy had already suffered too much on the street. Wasn't there anything we could do to help him see that? Wasn't there anything we could say to change his mind?

As we continued to talk about it, we agreed that if anyone could change the boy's mind, it would be Joel, our pastor. He knew the boy well, and his gentle spirit was exactly what the children needed at times.

Joel sat with the boy and listened and encouraged him. "Tell me what you miss most about life on the streets," Joel began. The boy talked about a friend who still lived on the streets, someone he knew well and worried about.

Joel said, "We can ask our Outreach team to look for your friend and talk with him about coming to Agape."

The boy went on to talk about how he used to earn his own money to buy food. He missed that too. But Joel reminded him of the big meals he enjoyed in the dining hall. The boy nodded in agreement, but went on to talk about the street family that protected him.

Again, Joel gently reminded him of all the aunts and uncles at Agape who cared about him enough to try and talk him out of leaving. Over the course of this conversation, the tug from the streets grew weaker.

Twenty minutes later, Joel walked into our office. His eyes sparkled with joy. "The boy changed his mind. He decided to stay at Agape." Pastor Joel flashed a smile. "He says he's ready to go back to class."

Something none of us thought possible just a few minutes earlier had happened. It was answered prayer. The boy was ready to keep going.

It's so hard to know these children well, to know their family stories, the problems they've dealt with, and to know the ways they've been hurt, and then watch them run back to the street life because it's what they know. It is powerful, addictive, and alluring.

But *that* day it was a celebration. *That* boy decided to stay. He chose to go back to his teacher and ask for forgiveness for his behavior. He agreed to go back to his houseparents and ask for forgiveness for his bad attitude. And then, he walked himself back to class.

The sad fact is that the allure of the streets will still be there tomorrow. It will beckon and tempt them to return. Tomorrow's battle awaits, but our staff is prepared with a listening ear and an encouraging spirit.

We at Agape know this is a long process for many children. Tonight, some children may not be able to resist the tug of the streets and will jump the fence. And we'll have to hear the news and experience the heartache again in the morning. But even then, the outreach team will be out on the streets tomorrow morning to reconnect and continue to work with them until they are ready to come back.

The struggle to leave the streets will always be difficult. For some children, it takes a few trips around the merry-go-round until they are ready. But through it all, the staff is there. Even though the bond with these children can often lead to heartache, the staff is there with an open heart and wants the best for them all.

CHAPTER 59

Listen with Your Heart

A father to the fatherless, a defender of widows, is God in his holy dwelling. God sets the lonely in families, ... but the rebellious live in a sun-scorched land. (Psalm 68:5-6)

During the early years of 2000, as many as one hundred Agape boys lived on our main campus in Kisumu, with another twenty or so at our vocational training center in Matoso.

Each of those boys had emotional issues to deal with. We found the Christian Green Bag method of counseling to be very effective in helping them. We showed various pictures and asked the children to identify with the one that most closely resembled how they felt about themselves. In one of those sessions, a boy chose a picture of a child alone. When asked to explain, he said that he felt like he was all alone in the middle of the forest with only the animals.

Another boy in the transition class chose a picture of a girl petting a dog. Why?

He said, "I can see love between them."

A third boy raised in a Legio Maria cult, when presented with the gospel, exclaimed, "I never knew God loved me. Can you tell me how I can know Him?"

Clearly, these boys longed for something. This just proved to me that we ALL need love, and our Creator is the One who loves us most.

CHAPTER 60

Loaves, Fishes, or Peanuts

"See that you do not despise one of these little ones. For I tell you that their angels in heaven always see the face of my Father in heaven." (Matthew 18:10)

Agape continued to grow. However, the number of street children also increased and the need seemed overwhelming. We knew Agape couldn't reach every street child, but we reached out to those the Lord put in front of us.

A visiting team had just enjoyed a nice farewell dinner at the local Chinese restaurant. Yes, in Kisumu, we had Chinese food and also Irish potatoes. That always amused me. As usual, we were served more food than we needed. So, because we knew two boys saw us come in, we asked the waiter to pack our leftovers in two separate plastic bags. By the time we stepped out of the restaurant, darkness had settled over the town. Street boys huddled together in groups and prepared to sleep on the sidewalk.

We gave our bags of leftover food to the two boys who waited for us to come out of the restaurant. I think they knew we'd bring them something warm and nourishing to eat. However, as we approached our vehicle, several other boys spotted us and darted across the street. I took a deep breath and rummaged in my purse for the peanuts I usually carried for such emergencies. My fingers scrambled inside my purse but only came up with two small packets. When I looked up, six little guys stood in front of us with hopeful eyes. They all stood about the same height, and I wondered how I would feel if my grandson were among them.

The security guard stationed in front of the shops came toward us with his baton raised.

"Please don't hit them. It's okay. Please don't hit them," I begged.

He stepped back and looked a bit perplexed. Then I asked the boys to each hold out one hand. Clearly, there weren't enough peanuts for all of the boys. But for an instant, the account of Jesus feeding over five thousand people with five loaves and two fish came to mind.

I poured the nuts into the boys' hands. Just as I approached the fifth boy with a nearly empty bag, I looked up to see a man holding a round basket of … more peanuts! Amazing. This was highly unusual in the evening hours. All the shops were closed and very few people walked around town. *Where did he come from?* He stopped in front of us.

"How did you know we needed these?" I asked in disbelief.

He smiled and replied simply, "I'm a businessman."

I'm quite sure we had an encounter with an angel.

I still can't quite get over that night.

The boys went back across the street to spend another night on the cold pavement. They waved their arms and yelled, "Thank you!" We returned to the hotel with the wonderment of a miracle in our hearts.

CHAPTER 61

Jairo's Long Road Home

The morning of May 13 was bright and sunny as I arrived at Agape to meet with our project manager, Lebaus Onyango. A soft knock came at the door as we discussed future plans.

"Come in," Lebaus called from behind his paper-laden desk. His face brightened as a sixteen-year-old boy cautiously entered the room.

"Eeey bwana! Now I'm a happy man!" Lebaus's expression and tone communicated both joy and relief. Lebaus stood and repeated his words as he reached out to give the young man a high five. "I'm a happy man now, bwana!"

I felt the love and concern Lebaus had for the boy. They exchanged a few more words in Kiswahili. Then the boy flashed a smile, shook my hand, and left the room. Lebaus drew a big breath and let out a long sigh as he sat back in his chair.

Lebaus explained that he'd grown concerned. "Jairo didn't return to Agape with the other boys who visited their homes during the school holidays in April."

While there were plausible reasons he might have been delayed a few days, no one had seen or heard from him for a week. So Lebaus and our houseparent John Mwalo drove out to the village to look for him.

Jairo's family lived in a remote area. It required a long, dusty journey off the main road. But the men persevered and asked villagers for directions along the way.

Lebaus continued. "When we finally found Jairo, he stood in front of a poorly maintained mud hut with his two little sisters, ages seven and nine." At that point, Lebaus hesitated in his narrative and interjected, "The Lord kept Jairo's heart in spite of his discouraging situation. He didn't give up on life and clearly still holds his goals for the future."

When Jairo saw John and Lebaus approach, he laughed in surprise and asked, "How did you ever find my place?" Then he ran to look for chairs so they could sit and rest.

Jairo's history illustrates two major reasons so many children live in the street. They are victims of poverty and the resulting disintegration of the family. Jairo's father, an alcoholic, deserted his wife and family. He left them with no financial resources and barely enough food for five growing children. Money for school fees or other necessities wasn't even in the picture. Jairo came to Kisumu in search of something better. Like many who turn to the streets, he had no idea how harsh street life would be. He was a dirty, scruffy, and hungry little nine-year-old street boy when Lebaus found him.

Thankfully, things changed the day we admitted Jairo to Agape. He finally felt safe, had good food to eat, new friends, and clean clothes to wear to the beginner's class in our school. He also learned how Jesus loved him enough to die in his place and forgive his sins. Jairo's life gradually took on new purpose and meaning. He worked hard to catch up in school.

I learned Jairo's mother hadn't been well for eighteen months. She had developed a cough and experienced chest pains. After her husband died of AIDS the previous year, she moved with her children back to her former home. Sadly, she wasn't welcomed there, perhaps because she too had become a victim of the deadly virus that claimed her husband.

When Jairo went home for his visit in April, he found his mother in a desperate situation. With no bed, she lay on the ground on a torn piece of sheet too weak to get up and walk. The rainy season had started.

Lebaus said, "They could look up and see the sky through gaping holes in the thatched roof." This obviously provided little protection from the wind and rain.

Jairo's nine-year-old sister cooked for the family, but they had very little to eat. It was a wonder they even survived.

The situation forced Jairo into the role of family breadwinner. He walked a long distance with enough money to buy a tin of maize (corn meal). That was only enough to feed the family for two days. Then he earned more money and made the trek again. Sometimes the boiled corn meal, known as *ugali* (a thick, corn meal mush), was all they had for the entire day. But Jairo searched for a plant the Kenyans called *sikuma wiki* (which means "stretch to the end of the week"). Cooked sikuma leaves are similar to turnip greens and added flavor and nutrients to the ugali. Unfortunately, their neighbor showed little concern for Jairo's family, probably due to fear.

Children orphaned when both parents die of HIV/AIDS are often considered cursed. The cause of AIDS still isn't clearly understood in some of the rural areas. Witch doctors make the situation worse by attributing deaths to evil spirits. In addition to all this, other villagers struggled to feed their own families and had little to share or give away.

To hear Lebaus tell how this courageous teenager dealt with such serious problems and walked long distances for so little food touched me deeply.

Lebaus added, "But Jairo realizes he is privileged to be the one person in his family to have an education. And he is grateful his mother became a Christian and knew she had a heavenly home waiting for her."

By that point, I understood why Lebaus reacted the way he did when Jairo entered the room. Jairo now had someone in his life who truly cared about him.

CHAPTER 62

Getting a Kick Out of Soccer

Our visiting team members from America sensed the excitement as we drove through the Agape gates on Saturday morning. Little ones greeted us with smiles and loving hugs as we stepped from the van. An impressive blue-and-white-striped canopy raised on bright blue poles and gleaming in the sunlight prepared to shade 150 visitors. Staff members moved with purpose as they set up the sound system and puppet stage. Older boys lined up to receive their brand-new polo shirts for the occasion. The entire compound prepared for a five-hour program. It included music, drama, puppet shows, original rap songs by the older boys, the presentation of faculty gifts, and speeches.

The Agape staff presented a beautifully choreographed traditional song which became a highlight of the program.

One of the many things I admire about our Kenyan staff is their willingness to relate to the children as if they were members of their own families. As a result, the boys know their "aunties and uncles" really love them.

Another family tradition that became part of our yearly celebration is the lively soccer match between the boys and the staff. It's exciting to watch the enthusiasm build throughout the week before the game. In preparation for the game, adults stretch their muscles while the big boys carry smaller boys on their shoulders and run up and down stairs to build endurance. What a kick. Finally, the players don their colorful soccer jerseys. The ref walks onto the field ceremoniously holding up the soccer ball and the whistle blows.

This year some of the older boys played on the faculty team to help them out in lieu of last year's drubbing. The faculty won handily and made their sore muscles the next day worth it all. The match held at the sports ground in the center of town attracted many onlookers. What a wonderful way to share the spirit of camaraderie we have at Agape.

The same week featured several lively events. Our boys participated in both basketball and soccer tournaments. However, it was the first time Tom, one of our senior boys, had been so instrumental in organizing a community-wide soccer tournament. It was dubbed the "Agape Open Tournament," complete with trophies and certificates of award.

Our Agape team won the semifinals. But by the final game, the teams were so well matched that no one scored in the entire game. It went into overtime with a round of penalty kicks. Each team missed one, so the score remained tied. Then the goalies were pitted against each other. Both made their goals. In the meantime, storm clouds blew in over Lake Victoria and the wind picked up. The crowd didn't seem to notice. Tension mounted. The goalies tried again. Our player made a beautiful corner kick. I held my breath as our opponent took up the challenge. He kicked the ball high, it bounced off of the top bar, and Agape won the game!

Shouts of "Olay, olay!" rang out as the boys formed a human train and danced around the field. A few minutes later, I presented the trophies and awards. It was a great day to be Mama Darla.

Winning soccer team

CHAPTER 63

God Works Behind the Scenes

It's always amazing when we have the privilege of seeing the way God works behind the scenes to orchestrate His plans for our lives. This story of Moses Otieno and our staff members Mr. Charles Anyang and Nicholas Kimatu is an example of events which can't be chalked up to mere coincidence or chance. It demonstrates the Lord's faithful love and care for each one of us.

Moses came to Agape in 1999 when he was about ten years old. At first, school excited him, but it gradually became apparent that he suffered from a learning disability. To provide him with practical life skills, we sent him to our vocational training center in Matoso. There, he met Mr. Anyang, the project director.

Years earlier, Mr. Anyang had taken a job with the local government in Kisumu. He replaced an employee who was required by Kenyan standards to retire at the age of fifty-five. Mr. Anyang received his orientation from the gentleman, and the two formed a lasting friendship. Mr. Anyang served in his position as a city official for thirty-six years before retiring.

During his time in office, Mr. Anyang played a significant role in Agape's history. He helped us obtain our Self-Help Community Project registration in 1993. Without his assistance, Agape might not exist today.

Later, a young staff member, Nicholas Kimatu, and I were privileged to pray with Mr. Anyang to receive Christ. We were overjoyed, and I told Nicholas I hoped someday Mr. Anyang would come to work for Agape. He had proven to be a kind and caring man with a wealth of experience. We had to wait several years, but in 2005, the Lord gave us that opportunity. Mr. Anyang joined our staff. With the pieces now in place, the stage was set for a drama to unfold.

During a school break, Moses went to visit his auntie's house. Our staff members frequently made home visits during those vacation days to see if the boys could be reintegrated with their families. Mr. Anyang and Nicholas were on such a mission for Moses; however, they couldn't find the auntie's house. Very few street signs existed in the rural areas and dirt roads quickly deteriorated into footpaths. The driver stopped by the roadside and Nicholas asked a villager for directions.

Suddenly, a familiar voice called, "Mwalimu!" (teacher) through the driver's open window.

It startled Mr. Anyang and Nicholas to see Moses standing there. How did he happen to be at that place just at that moment? Moses led them to the house. When they arrived, they found the auntie and Moses' mother as well.

After traditional greetings, they began an interview. Nicholas later commented about how Mr. Anyang applied his skill in digging out the details surrounding Moses' story.

His mother shared a few of the details about how Moses ended up on the street. She said, "We had been separated for seven years when Baba Moses [father of Moses] came and took away my son and went with him to Kisumu. I cried all night. I did not see Moses again." She continued with an expression of passion for her only child. "I later learned the father of my son had forsaken the child. Agape rescued him from the streets. Bless Agape."

When her husband died, his family disowned her. They forbade her to put up a house at her matrimonial home. She went on to explain how her surviving brother-in-law also threatened to keep Moses away and deprive him of his inheritance after her death.

Nicholas and Mr. Anyang pursued the matter of Moses' inheritance. They traveled another forty minutes to an even more remote area where they found the family *shamba* (homestead). A woman greeted them and explained that her husband was unwell and resting in his second wife's house. Nicholas feared the man might ask them to leave and not come back. That could have happened. Nicholas was in for a surprise.

When the elderly gentleman limped into the poorly lit house, Nicholas and Mr. Anyang rose to greet him. Upon shaking hands, a moment of recognition passed between them.

"It's you!" Mr. Anyang said as if greeting a long-lost friend.

The two of them embraced. Mr. Anyang recognized the man as the retiring officer of thirty years prior. The elderly man had since served on the city council, but he and Mr. Anyang hadn't seen each other for the past fifteen years.

The visit took on a new dimension.

The old man struggled not to shed tears as he said, "Thank you for saving my grandson. He's the only one left to remind me of my son." When asked about settling the boy and his mother back at the homestead, the patriarch said, "It can be as soon as tomorrow." To confirm he was serious, the elderly man even took them out to see Moses' exact portion of land.

As Nicholas shared the story, he said, "When it came time to leave we stood to pray; there was so much joy I would have declared the man healed. The sullen, dull, and tired face I first saw was lit with gladness and hope. All the details required for Moses' ID card were provided, and he assured us that Moses was at the right place, accepted with love, and at home. The end of the visit was such a blessing. We were refreshed as we retired from work."

CHAPTER 64

Here is Your Lastborn

"**M**ama, here is your lastborn." Soon after arriving in Kisumu, a group of boys ran up to me with those words. That's the Kenyan way of saying, "Mama, here is your youngest child."

In the center of the group stood a timid little boy named Donny, who looked to be four or five years old. At any rate, he was far too young to be fending for himself on the streets. When he arrived at Agape, his bigger "brothers" took pride in introducing him.

Adorable little Donny enjoyed all the attention. As the days went by, many of us noticed he often wanted to be held and cuddled while he sucked his thumb. Other times, he turned into a fierce little warrior ready to fight with much larger older boys. The older boys tolerated this tough-guy behavior and usually ignored it, because he was so small.

Thankfully, one of our visiting friends, child psychologist Dr. Emma Girard, recognized this as classic behavior for a traumatized child. In a series of meetings with our houseparents, she explained how trauma is something a child cannot prepare for or prevent. And it's something he can't protect himself from. She concluded, "Obviously, his young life has seen a lot trauma."

At Agape, he felt safe. He desired the warmth and security that came with being loved and protected. Yet at the same time, he feared showing weakness (even against overwhelming odds), because that illusion of control helped him survive life in the streets. How do you guide a young boy who has been forced to take on adult responsibilities back into the realm of a child? Our Kenyan staff and missionaries faced this challenge every day at Agape.

Yet because of God's healing power, we see amazing changes in the lives of many of our boys. Through prayer and the efforts of our national staff, Donny now has a chance to become a well-adjusted, carefree child.

CHAPTER 65

Make Good Choices

In his book *He Still Moves Stones*, Max Lucado states, "Faith is the belief that God is real and that God is good ... It is a choice to believe that the One who made it all hasn't left it all ... God's help is near and always available but it is only given to those who seek it."

Years ago, I met a talented young African man who regularly came to Agape as a volunteer to play the keyboard and teach Sunday school to our former street boys, as well as several little neighborhood children who eagerly waited for him by the gate. Morris was a soft-spoken man with a cheerful countenance, a warm smile, and who walked with a slight limp.

Morris never looked for a place in the limelight, but he constantly demonstrated his love and compassion for boys who struggled with their past. We were all blessed by his faithful service and the way he supported our work as a fledgling ministry.

One day during an Agape worship service, Morris shared his life story. He talked about the importance of the choices we make and how they can affect the rest of our lives. "I had polio as a young boy and couldn't walk," he said. "My father brought me a wheelchair, thinking it would help me cope with my handicap." Morris went on to explain that he had a different idea. "I wanted to walk again." So his father brought him a pole. Morris used the pole to wrap his flaccid leg around it as he attempted to support himself. "At first it didn't work too well," Morris admitted, "but I prayed and kept trying."

The boys listened intently as Morris talked about falling down more times than he could count. "The day came when I actually took my first step. I was ten years old." Later, he managed to take two steps before falling. But he stayed with it. He fell down many, many times. It was frustrating and didn't feel good. But every time he fell, he got up again. Today, he attributes his success to the choice he made.

This man of faith and perseverance became Agape's chaplain. What a wonderful example he is to our former street boys who have felt so hopeless and helpless in their situations. They still have choices to make. And what a wonderful example Morris is to all of us as we persevere through life's difficulties. The Lord must be so proud of him.

CHAPTER 66

Courage in the Face of Calamity

Our veteran staff missionaries who work with the children still on the streets of Kisumu are Steve and Dianne Warn. Before they came to Agape, they served for ten years in Costa Rica with their four children in a prison ministry. They have endured their share of personal struggles over the years, but the faithfulness of God shines through their lives and is captured in their letters.

Dianne wrote:

> "It was a Sunday morning as we made our way to the park where we hold our meeting with the street boys. As we picked our way through the crowded bus stop, it was all I could do to keep from getting hit or knocked down. But there in front of me was a sight I still picture in my mind. In the midst of all the confusion was Lebaus with a small boy under each arm, holding them close, guiding them. We were taking them to Agape. A great joy welled up in me, His joy, the joy of the Shepherd who left the ninety-nine to find the one lost sheep."

In the same way your Father in heaven is not willing that any of these little ones should perish. (Matthew 18:14)

I pictured the scene so clearly. Nothing makes us happier than to reclaim a little child from the street.

Dianne continued. She told the story of an older boy named Eddie who came to Agape in January. Four years ago, Eddie fell into a vat of boiling sugar cane syrup. It left him with one arm amputated and the other severely deformed. And there he was trying to survive in the street. Eddie attended our street kids' church every Sunday and had lots of questions. Steve and Dianne answered his questions through the Scriptures.

Dianne said, "You could see understanding light up his face. In the end, he prayed a precious prayer, finishing with, 'Lord, let me be your messenger.'"

We believe God did just that. Eddie became a leader among the older street boys and continues to demonstrate his great desire to help his friends.

Steve and Dianne Warn with Lebaus Onyango

CHAPTER 67

Wilson's World

"To the world, you may just be one person. But to one person, you might just be the world." – Anonymous

Dianne Warn offered another story which I believe illustrates the above quote perfectly.

"It was pouring down rain, and we had just finished our usual time of Bible teaching and feeding the boys on Sunday. The boys huddled under a small shop covered with a piece of plastic that barely kept the water from pouring down on them. The wind gusted hard and Wilson's thin shirt provided little warmth. He was new to the street and had a lost look on his face. It was heartbreaking to have to leave him there that day."

Dianne explained how, a few weeks later, we brought Wilson home to Agape. Our houseparent visited his grandmother and learned both parents had died from an illness (probably HIV/AIDS). Since that time, he had been badly mistreated. Many times villagers considered orphaned children cursed and didn't want them around. So Wilson, who was approximately eleven years old at the time, was forced to make his way in the streets.

When Wilson felt comfortable at Agape, he attended our orientation class where he made progress in some areas. But his teacher, Christine Onyango, felt he also showed signs of withdrawal. He displayed a short attention span and hardly ever made eye contact. This behavior led "Auntie Christine" to begin a counseling program with him referred to as the "Green Bag."

She asked Wilson to share things that happened in his life. As he struggled to explain, Christine pulled pictures out of the bag that depicted various emotions. She encouraged him to choose the ones that best expressed his own. He chose pictures of sadness, anger, and trauma. Those emotions came as no surprise from someone who lost both of his parents and experienced a lack of food and frequent beatings.

This Green Bag is a wonderful tool. It allows children who don't have the vocabulary or emotional strength to identify their pain. In this case, it gave Wilson a starting point and gave Christine something to build on.

Later, when asked what he could compare himself to, Wilson said, "I feel like a monkey because I ate bananas and guavas from other people's gardens."

Then Christine showed Wilson how Jesus wants the children to come to Him. She told him a story to help him understand. Wilson's countenance changed as he felt God's comfort and acceptance.

The next time she asked him to describe himself, he said he felt "like God's child, asleep in His big hands."

Wilson actually carried a small card with that picture on it in his pocket. On one of my visits, he came up beside me and said, "Mama, I have something to show you." He pulled a card with crinkled edges out of his pocket and grinned. "That's me."

"How wonderful is that." I gave him a mama bear hug.

Wilson had already made remarkable progress, but another amazing thing happened a few hours later.

Christine stood at the gate ready to leave for the night when something made her turn around. From across the school ground, Wilson saw her. When their eyes met, he flew across the yard and into her arms. He told her he couldn't let her leave before he said good-bye.

That brief but loving exchange meant Wilson was still able to form attachments.

Our good friend and psychologist, Dr. Emma Girard, commented, "It's also good he didn't get angry at her for leaving. That can be a problem when a traumatized child begins forming a relationship and then feels the threat of abandonment each time they are separated."

Wilson let her go and trusted her to return. There is no doubt Christine became "the world" to this young boy. What a privilege to help heal a heart.

CHAPTER 68

A Day on the Street

Dianne shared from another of her letters that shines a light on life in the streets:

"Today at 7:00 a.m. we were on the street with the boys. Several of them, fortunate enough to own gunny sacks, were just sleepily crawling out, already dressed in their grimy clothes of the past months. I was making a mental check of each boy, seeing if I could recall his name. They came over one by one, greeting us with a hearty handshake and a smile.

"Soon, more boys joined us and we moved over to our usual place in the parking lot. Steve drew the Bible lesson for the day with a piece of chalk. The boys talked among themselves while they tried to guess what he was drawing. They cocked their heads, laughed, and looked at the picture from every angle as they enjoyed the novelty of some crazy muzungu wasting perfectly good chalk.

"I wrote their names in big letters one by one next to Steve's drawing. They smiled extra big when I remembered their names. Finally, we began, and for the next half-hour, we entered another world. Their faces were fixed on listening to the Word of God. And for a few moments, the hunger, sadness, and feelings of abandonment faded from their faces as they experienced the love of God.

"By this time, a crowd had formed above us on the sidewalk. About twenty to thirty bystanders joined our group of fifty-plus street boys. We must have made a curious site as we closed, singing together, 'Into my heart, into my heart, come into my heart, Lord Jesus. *Kwa roho yangu, Kwa roho yangu, kuja kwan roho yangu, Yesu.'*"

That was the first service of the morning. At the close of it, several of the boys gathered around to show Steve and Dianne their wounds. The long list included hands and arms infected with scabies and impetigo. When those things were cleaned and treated, the Warns headed for the bus park to repeat the same service with an even larger, tougher group of boys.

After each Sunday service and Wednesday soccer game, our Kenyan administrator, Lebaus, and the Warns took the boys for traditional hot meals in the nearby kiosks. This presented challenges at times, because there were so many boys. It proved that through consistency, disheartened street boys learned to trust again and accept our love.

Occasionally, one of the children turned out to be a little girl dressed in boys clothing for protection. It highlighted the great need for a street children's ministry for girls.

CHAPTER 69

Elvin and Jean Valjean

O ne of my favorite musicals is *Les Misérables*. The story, written by Victor Hugo, takes place in France in 1815. It opens with the account of Jean Valjean, a prisoner released on parole after nineteen years on the chain gang. However, instead of finding freedom, Valjean soon realizes he is condemned as an outcast. Only one person, the bishop of Digne, shows him compassion. He offers Valjean food and a place to spend the night. But Jean Valjean, who has been embittered by years of hardship, repays the Bishop's hospitality by stealing some silver.

When Valjean is caught by the police, he is returned to the priest. Everyone is astonished when the wizened old priest covers for Valjean and says the silver was a gift. Then he proceeds to give Valjean two more silver candlesticks and suggests he forgot to take them when he left. The police have no option but to release Valjean. This generous act of kindness is the turning point in Valjean's life, and he decides to start his life anew. This Christlike example always touches my heart. It's a powerful story.

I was struck by the parallel of an incident involving one of Kisumu's older street boys. We called him Elvin. Word came to our missionaries Steve and Dianne Warn at Agape's drop-in center, that Elvin was very seriously ill. He lay motionless under a tree at the back of the dump. The other street boys were sure he was dying of malaria. So Steve, Dianne, and a fellow missionary drove over to the dump and found him. They carried him to the van and transported him to the drop-in center for care. Even with medication, he remained on the cot in his room and hardly moved for two weeks. The staff prayed fervently for his healing.

Dianne said, "He has so many sores in his mouth that he can't eat." They forced him to drink some porridge once a day just to keep him alive. After those two weeks, to their delight, he showed signs of interest in things happening around him. As he gained strength, Steve took him on errands and gradually involved Elvin in some of the small jobs around the center.

On the day of Elvin's departure, Dianne sat in the office. One of the staff members, Habib, had used her cell phone and placed it on her desk. Before Dianne put it away, someone interrupted with a situation involving another boy. She hurried from the room and forgot about her phone. Since no one was in the office, it shouldn't have been a problem. While Dianne counseled the troubled boy, Elvin translated for her. At one point, Elvin ran into the office to get a Bible. He shared a verse when he returned. After the boy left, Dianne went back to the office and discovered her phone missing.

No one else could have taken it. When confronted, Elvin denied it and tried to shift the blame. When he left, Dianne and Habib prayed together asking the Lord for a breakthrough. Then it happened. Elvin and a staff member came back with the phone but without its SIM card. The card contained all their local phone numbers and was the only number the boys in the village had to communicate with Agape when they were home. Elvin stubbornly stuck to his story. He insisted he saw another guy hide the stolen phone outside.

Dianne said, "We knew it was a lie, but it is next to impossible to get street boys to admit they stole something. Then the Holy Spirit led me to put my hand on Elvin's shoulder and look him in the eye. I found myself almost crying as I said to him, 'Elvin, Jesus loves you and we love you. And I just want you to know you are so much more important than a phone and a SIM card. Telling the truth is to help *you*. We want to help you. Telling the truth is to help *you*.'"

He broke into tears. He said, "Please help me. Pray for me because there are two Elvins; one who wants to follow Jesus…." He swallowed hard. "But the old Elvin who is so used to hurting people…." He reached into his pocket and pulled out the SIM card.

As Dianne remembers that day she says, "Even today, when I shake his hand, there is a special love and understanding between us."

I am so proud of the way our missionaries go the extra mile for the street boys who are literally the castoffs of society. *If anyone forces you to go one mile, go with them two miles* (Matthew 5:41). Dianne made the same point with Elvin that the bishop made with Jean Valjean. Your life has value and by God's grace you are forgiven. And it had the same impact. A life was transformed.

Our staff members Steve and Dianne work on the street with the boys who are not fortunate enough to come to the Agape center. They feed 130 boys each Wednesday afternoon. It's a growing ministry which produces incredible results.

CHAPTER 70

Giving to Those in Need

It was 8:00 a.m., which is early for me, when the guard knocked at the door. I answered. He quickly said, "Mama, someone is at the gate who wants to talk to you."

I'd been in Kenya long enough to know this usually meant trouble. With so many needs, it became overwhelming at times. I tried to give everything I had to the street children, but now someone else needed help. I sucked in a deep breath and let out a long sigh, "Okay, I'll come out to talk to him."

A sad-looking man with a dingy off-white shirt and khaki trousers fidgeted as I approached. He greeted me with, "Oh, morning Mama. Can you help me?" Desperation hung on every word. "I've come from the Burnt Forest. It's terrible there!" His brow wrinkled with tension. He added, "My elder brother was shot through the stomach by a bow and arrow." He pointed to his own stomach. "Now there's no one to care for the children." He hesitated, looked at the ground, then with pleading eyes, he asked, "Please, Mama, can you help me with some little food?"

I had read about the fighting in the newspaper. Many people lost their lives in the tribal clash. I wondered what I could do and remembered James 2:16. The Bible says that if we just talk about God, but don't act on our faith, what good is it?

Suppose a brother or a sister is without clothes and daily food.

If one of you says to them, "Go in peace; keep warm and well fed," but does nothing about their physical needs, what good is it? (James 2:15-16)

I'd also been conned enough times to become cautious, but this poor man's story and his body language made me believe him. I went back to the house for some cardboard packets of milk which didn't have to be refrigerated. I also had some fresh loaves of bread to share. It didn't seem like much, but at least it was something.

My missionary friend Dianne Warn also experienced similar situations. Here she shares some of her own experiences:

"Beyond our usual ministry load, we struggle with what to do when someone comes to our gate or into our lives who doesn't fall under the category of the ones we are *supposed* to help. Like the handicapped boy from the slum, or the cerebral palsy boy at the juvenile hall who has been there for years just because he has nowhere else to go, or the desperate mother of five young children suffering from HIV/AIDS.

"The first time one of our staff members approached this mother's home, she had only one request: 'I'm going to die. Choose one of my boys and take him, please.'

"She lay on a makeshift bed in her little mud hut with a leaky tin roof. It was half-filled with water from the heavy rain the previous night. The woman was eight and a half months pregnant with no food and no hope. She was truly desperate. At that point she relied on her eight-year-old son to hunt for food and firewood, cook the meals, and take care of her."

Thankfully, Agape stepped in and helped with medicine for her infections. They provided better food and a big dose of hope. She no longer had to battle her problems alone. The challenge before Dianne was to help the woman realize she could do things to support herself and her boys when she was on her feet again. Three months later, she was much improved.

Dianne talked with her about the trauma in her life and how God saw her in light of her deep hurt. She used the same counseling program we used for the children called the "Green Bag." It had a series of pictures that showed traumatized children, to help us identify problems. The pictures had corresponding Bible stories to help us encourage and comfort the children. But would it be appropriate for an adult?

Later, Dianne said, "She was riveted to the pictures with tears in her eyes. In the end, with shining eyes and a broad smile she picked up the Bible and exclaimed with excitement, 'This Book knows me.' At that moment, I could hardly see her for my own tears. She has come a long way but still has a long way to go."

Being a missionary can truly be a daunting task. We must be content with what we can do and not dwell on the enormity of the problems we can't solve. It's enough to reach one person at a time, just like the little boy's example in the much-loved starfish story:

> Once upon a time, there was an old man who used to go to the ocean to do his writing. He had the habit of walking on the beach every morning before he began his work. Early one morning, he walked along the shore after a big storm and found the vast beach littered with starfish as far as the eye could see, stretching in both directions.
>
> Off in the distance, the old man noticed a small boy approaching. As the boy walked, he paused every so often. As he grew closer, the man saw that he occasionally bent down to pick up an object and throw it into the sea. The boy came closer still, and the man called out, "Good morning. May I ask what it is that you are doing?"
>
> The young boy paused, looked up, and replied, "Throwing starfish into the ocean. The tide washed them up onto the beach and they can't return to the sea by themselves. When the sun gets high, they'll die unless I throw them back into the water."
>
> The old man replied, "But there must be tens of thousands of starfish on this beach. I'm afraid you won't really be able to make much of a difference."
>
> The boy bent down, picked up yet another starfish, and threw it as far as he could into the ocean. Then he turned, smiled, and said, "It made a difference to that one."
> (Adapted from *The Star Thrower*, by Loren Eiseley (1907 – 1977))

CHAPTER 71

Baby Edna

Another of our American staff couples, Mike and Karen Herskowitz, shared this story of baby Edna.

They had only been back in Kisumu a few days from their furlough when, in the middle of the night, they were awakened by their night watchman. Mbeta explained that he heard a small baby crying outside the compound fence. When he investigated, he found an abandoned baby girl about five months old dressed in a hooded sleeper and wrapped in a blanket. Instead of being cold from the night air, her face perspired from crying and her skin felt hot with fever.

Mike called our friends from the New Life Baby Home. They took the little one in immediately. After such an emotional experience, Karen found it difficult to go back to sleep. Instead, she prayed through her tears. She thanked God they were back in Kisumu and that Mbeta was there to rescue the baby. She prayed for the baby's family and wondered what desperation drove a mother to leave her helpless baby at the gate.

Lab tests showed the baby had a high white-cell count and was extremely dehydrated. The doctor put her on IV fluids for two days and gave her antibiotics for the fever. They notified the Children's Department, which granted New Life custody of the baby. If no one claimed her after six months, she would be eligible for adoption in Kenya. They named her Edna Penda. *Penda* is the Swahili word for "love."

Karen wrote:

> "I have been going to New Life every few days to see Edna
> and check on her progress. I am happy to say that today she
> smiled at me and reached out to touch my face. Last week
> it was so heartbreaking to see this little baby staring back
> into my eyes, searching for her mommy or someone she
> knew. We will always consider her *our* baby and we pray
> for her to fulfill the purposes the Lord has for her."

In a beautiful twist to this story, the night watchman who initially found her, Mbeta, and his kindly wife, adopted and are raising Edna.

CHAPTER 72

Delton Develops

Delton is a strapping sixteen-year-old who loves to borrow my camera and take "snaps" of his friends. He has lived at Agape since 2000 and has written over time about the changes in his life. I share this short piece from his writing to offer a firsthand account from a street boy's point of view:

> "Five years ago my life was very dangerous. But God used Agape to change my life. I learned it is good to pray. And we do pray every day before we sleep, after waking up, and before we do anything. When God is there, everything is good. Now I know Jesus came to save the sinner. God sent His only begotten Son. Remember the verse of John 3:16.

> "I love Jesus as my Savior who saved me from big sins. I encourage others to continue to pray and God will answer your prayer, because what God can do nobody else can do. I love God and am now enjoying my life."

CHAPTER 73

Something to Contribute

Eventually, I could only visit Kenya twice a year. By this point, it became quite a challenge to know all 115 boys at Agape. But the quality time I spent with individual boys was a special part of every trip. In the month of May, two of our staff members accompanied me to visit one of our young men named Constance Liyahi at his boarding school. He was in his first year there and obviously happy to see us. He introduced us to his teacher and classmates and then gave us a tour of the campus compound.

At first, Constance and I walked around the campus comfortably chatting about things in general, but the conversation quickly turned more meaningful. Constance humbly shared a deep concern. "I am not a soccer player or an artist like some of the other boys. I am not even a Boy Scout. All I know how to do is write songs – rap songs."

It was becoming clear that Constance harbored the sense that he had little to contribute to society. I said, "I would love to hear some of your music. And can you write the words down for me so they could be shared with others?"

His eyes brightened.

Over the years, we learned that writing down life experiences and feelings has been a healing tool for the boys. It provided a healthy outlet to express the trauma and stress they endured while living in the streets.

Constance was born into a loving family. Tragically, he lost both of his parents to HIV/AIDS. In spite of finding himself on the street at a very young age, he grew up to be a sensitive and caring young man. He did well in school and aspired to be an accountant.

Constance turned out to have a God-given talent for writing. The first song expressed the confidence he had in God and the Scriptures. The second song related his love for his parents. The touching words tell of the frustration and loneliness he felt in losing his parents to AIDS. After reading the lyrics, I think you'll agree Constance has not a little – but much – to contribute.

Never Give Up
by Constance Liyahi

I'm still mad about what's happening in my life.

The path is difficult

But I have to sail through

'Cause when I take a moment of silence and reflect back,

God said He'll never leave nor forsake me.

He's the horn of salvation. He knows when I'm down.

And though struck down, I cannot be destroyed,

Because He once suffered and knows what it takes.

Hold on, don't cry,

'Cause your faith is being strengthened.

He'll carry you up some day from deep valleys of death

And take you far beyond the sky.

Get Scriptures on your mind,

And tell the Enemy that you can't live by bread alone,

Never give up, just pray.

AIDS Took Them Away
by Constance Liyahi

No more time to breathe.
How could you take away our only Mom?
Now we are lonely with swallowed-up dreams,
Crying and wondering how this can be.
We cannot stop wiping our tears
When we hear the eulogy at home.
She was good.
She thought of others
And sacrificed for the welfare of her family.
But now we can only see an image
That reflects her deeds and cannot fade away.
Nobody knows the pains felt deep within.
The whole of life is crushing in.
All has become meaningless.
Failing to understand why we couldn't see our parents
Who carried us for nine months.
My dear Mom left me
Neither will I see my Dad.
Can't even trace his image.
I could have loved them.
That's what I regret.

To close this chapter, I must sadly inform you that Constance also passed away. He left us way too soon, but it's a comfort to know he is in heaven with those who love him. He has no more pain, either physical or emotional. And he can write joyful rap songs for all eternity.

CHAPTER 74

Stretching Equals More than Exercise

Shelly Heida Walker brought her considerable talents and gifts to Agape as part of our staff. She came on as a young woman who directed a sponsorship program. She traveled to Kenya a number of times to interview the boys and help update their files. She wrote an account which may impact your heart as it still does mine. I've asked her permission to share it with you and I think you'll appreciate the honest, transparent way she described her experience. She learned that being *willing* to be stretched out of her comfort zone didn't make it any easier when that stretching actually took place.

Here's a peek into her journal dated May 25, 2005:

> "It was a very interesting day, let me tell you. We arrived at the park and immediately met some of the street boys. Lebaus was leading us around different areas of town where the street boys hang out. It was incredible watching him with the boys. It is clear he knows and loves each one.

> "We stopped to watch a group of boys who were gambling with kernels of corn; their glue bottles tucked safely in their sleeves where no one could snatch them. I was impressed with the creativity. They didn't have dice, so they used what they had.

> "So there we were walking down a really busy street, and this wall of stench greeted us. Oh, my goodness, it smelled

so bad. I looked up ahead and saw a huge pile of rotting trash at the end of the road. We walked towards it. I almost panicked with nausea rising in my throat, because it smelled so bad. We reached the beginning of the pile and Lebaus walked on top of it. I was horrified.

"I looked at Blake and asked, 'Are we walking on this?' And sure enough we followed.

"I held my breath and gingerly stepped through the pile. All that separated my delicate American feet from this pile of stinking garbage were my cheap little flip-flops. I was kicking myself for forgetting to change into my tennis shoes. Regret soon changed to irritation. I thought, *Um, hello. I'm an American …. This is too much*, and other very selfish and horrible things. That is when I realized the reason for taking the safari through the filth. Lying in the midst of the rubbish was a street boy, sleeping in it! He had malaria.

"My eyes filled with tears and I forgot about my churning stomach. I felt so ashamed of how spoiled I am for thinking because I'm an American or any other thing that I don't deserve to walk on this pile when this poor street boy collapsed there because he was so sick. We walked the boy to the hospital where Lebaus paid to have him treated. My heart is forever changed because of this experience.

"After leaving the hospital, we sat and watched the street boys play a soccer game. Following the game, we walked with the boys to a little shack so they could have a meal. Today is Wednesday. Lebaus will come to the street again on Sunday and the boys can have a meal that day too. I can't imagine this life. They are only guaranteed a meal twice a week. Twice a week!

"I cannot fathom living this way, not just because of their meal situation, but because of everything they have to face.

The other night we drove through the darkness of Kisumu, and I saw a group of street boys huddled in their torn clothing around the fire, trying to stay warm. We passed back through the same place about half an hour later and the fire was still blazing, but the boys were gone. I wondered where they were. Did they go to hide somewhere? What made them leave? I thought about how scared those boys must be.

"Some of the boys at Agape shared with me that they tried very hard not to sleep at night when they lived on the street for fear of what might wake them up – other street boys coming to steal anything they might have, police brutality forcing them to go someplace else, or who knows…. I shudder to think of what else they might be afraid of. Paul, an Agape boy, still has a scar on his face from being poked by a fire-hot metal rod while he was sleeping in the street.

"For as horrible as my experience was today, I am thankful for it. A small part of me wishes I didn't see what I saw – that I could pretend I don't know about little boys who sleep in piles of trash and sniff on bottles of glue to get high and avoid the pain of their life. But a bigger part of me is thankful to know and to be able to do something about it.

"I am thankful that today I forgot to change into my tennis shoes. I needed to have the experience, the whole cycle of emotions from near resentment to utter shame. I am thankful that today I saw where our boys at Agape came from – the lives they used to live – and how far they have come. The problem of street children is completely overwhelming. The work of Agape can seem like just a drop in the ocean, but I know the ocean is forever changed because it is missing that one drop."

"Whoever welcomes one of these little children in my name welcomes me." (Mark 9:37)

CHAPTER 75

Double Blessing

It was June 27, and we held another farewell luncheon at our favorite Chinese restaurant in Kisumu. As we entered the building, a street boy who smelled of glue greeted us with a hopeful smile. He told us he was hungry, but I think he already knew he would soon be eating a sampling of assorted Chinese entrées, left over from lunch. He sat down to wait.

It was fun to leave things on the serving plates, because we knew they would bless a child who never saw the inside of a restaurant. When we reached the sidewalk, two boys waited for us and another ran toward us from across the street. The two new boys talked together. It was evident they weren't only friends, but were also twins.

Audrey, our on-site missionary, and I looked at each other. We wished we hadn't eaten so much. We divided the food among them, then she asked the boys some questions. They said they wanted to go to Agape. Their situation seemed quite desperate. One of the twins had open sores on his legs and scabies all over his hands and arms.

Audrey told them to wait for her. "I'll be back later," she told them.

To our surprise, the security guard nodded his head in approval to the boys. It was refreshing to see his compassion.

I went to Audrey's home and finished packing. I was eager to hear what happened next.

When she came in, she beamed. "Get this. Remember Felix, the little six-year-old we took in last Saturday? Well, those were his twin brothers. They lost touch with each other and didn't know Felix was at Agape. He was so surprised and happy to see them. It was a big reunion."

The good news blessed my heart, but there was more. She explained that when it was time to give them a bath and some new clothes, the twin with the scabies begged her not to burn his dirty, tattered Levi jacket. He said, "Please wash it, Mama. I want to give it to my friend in town. He doesn't have one."

She had it washed. It's hard to even write about this without feeling a catch in my throat. These children, in such desperate condition, still look out for each other.

CHAPTER 76

Never Too Young

Can you imagine a four-year-old being sent to juvenile hall and detained as a felon for an entire year? As incredible as that may sound, it actually happened to Collins. He reportedly tried to steal a camera and was turned over to the authorities. They took him to the remand center and treated him like a criminal. Each time court dates were set and his accusers failed to appear, Collins was returned to the remand center.

Lebaus has a weekly ministry there. When he saw such a young boy detained month after month, it tugged at his heart. We discussed the situation with our African staff and approached the authorities. We earnestly prayed that Collins would be released into our care. And the Lord answered our prayer.

We praised God when Collins walked through our gate to meet his new family. He quickly won everyone's heart with his vivacious personality and he didn't stop smiling. We shared the message of salvation with him, and it didn't take long for him to understand he had a heavenly Father who created him and loved him dearly. Then we saw something even more special in Collins.

For example, one Sunday after lunch, he walked back to the remand center to see his old friends. He said, "I want them to know about Jesus."

Audrey admitted that Collins dumbfounded the staff as he preached to other Agape boys. He showed unusual maturity with such statements as: "When someone wants you to work, don't tell him you are the boss." We wondered what the Lord had planned for this boy. Could he be like David the shepherd boy who grew up to lead a nation? We can hardly wait to see what lies in store for him.

CHAPTER 77

Reflection

When we host short-term mission teams, it provides us with an opportunity to get to know special people and see Agape through the eyes of a first-time visitor. One of our first-time team members, Pam Scholl, shared a small piece of her Agape experience.

"From the moment our plane touched the Kenya runway, the sights, sounds, and scents of Nairobi marked a drastic contrast to our layover in Amsterdam. As the driver wove through bumper-to-bumper traffic, many children, tattered and hungry, approached our vehicle with outstretched hands, begging. I was in tears before we ever arrived at the guesthouse.

"This is what Darla tried to prepare us for. But no amount of preparation could be enough until it became our own experience. When I laid my head on the pillow the first night, I wept for the faces I'd already seen with a sense of helplessness and even a little fear of what the next two weeks in Kisumu would hold.

"Entering the gates of Agape for the first time was another enormous contrast to what we had seen in the streets. Enthusiastic children met our van with warm smiles and glowing faces. The grounds at Agape were simple. A white building provided sleeping quarters for the boys and also included the library and two classrooms. Another building accommodated classes for grade levels one through twelve and a dining commons.

"The boys were eager to show us their garden. They're not only learning some agricultural skills but are also growing food for their daily meals, such as corn, tomatoes, and sikuma wiki (a leafy green vegetable).

"We were surprised to see on-site vocational training with the older boys finishing new dining tables and chairs. But what impressed us most was the soccer field and makeshift goalposts. This field is used daily and provides not only recreation and the sense of community but also an opportunity to refine some already highly developed soccer skills. Barefooted, the boys challenged us to a game and beat our socks off.

"During our stay at Agape, Jeff and I spent a lot of time in the classrooms, working with the Agape teachers, staff, and administrator. We observed the wholehearted commitment and dedication of the staff in the school and in the home. The ministry is ongoing as the Word of God is shared daily through devotions, individual counseling, and in the classroom. It wasn't long before my overwhelming sense of hopelessness was overshadowed by the incredible awareness that God provided a sanctuary at Agape for the street boys of Kisumu, where He is preserving a remnant in Kenya.

"Agape's program is effective and it's working. What a privilege it has been to share in the short-term mission experience in Kenya. By God's grace, we witnessed His faithfulness to the children of that nation."

CHAPTER 78

The Kenya Chicks

In 2001, three very special young ladies, Erin Kerr, Jennie Mach, and Kelly Carroll, bestowed a great blessing on Agape. While in Kenya, the three college graduates acquired the loving moniker *The Kenya Chicks*. Erin and Jennie arrived in September to serve a one-year term. Kelly was only sixteen when she first visited Agape. She returned after graduation from college for a six-month stay. All of them came to Agape to serve in a variety of ways and played a vital role in the lives of our boys. The Kenya Chicks ministered as friends, teachers, sisters, spiritual mentors, and yes, even mothers. It was such a joy to watch their individual ministries thrive.

Erin Kerr, from Sylvania, Ohio, was enthusiastic, vivacious, and loved children. Of course, they loved her back. When our team visited Kisumu in February 2002, we went into town for supplies. A few of us waited in the van while others went in to purchase groceries. Our van attracted the attention of street children. Suddenly, two boys began begging by the windows. We talked to them and asked questions about how long they'd been in town, where they slept, and how they spent their time.

One of the boys gravitated towards Erin's window and, in her friendly way, she engaged him in conversation. About twenty minutes later, when the others returned, she said through misty eyes, "Did you hear what he was saying and the way he talked? His name is Eddie. That boy doesn't belong on the street."

Her voice choked with the pain we feel when we meet new street boys. Their desperate and harsh lifestyle is so contrary to what the Lord intended for His children.

About two weeks later, she wrote this account in her February newsletter:

"There has been another new addition to Agape, and his name is Eddie. I felt a special attachment to him after my first encounter with him in town, and have enjoyed welcoming him to Agape. I was recently outside reading with George Bush when Eddie came looking for me. School was out, and he wanted to tell me all about his first day. He came and laid his head on my shoulder and just smiled up at me with the biggest smile ever. Then he told me all about what he learned that day – in full detail. He was so excited to have his new uniform and to have the chance to go to class.

"He was also very glad he decided to stay instead of going back to town with a friend. I admit I was just as glad. I realized how heartbroken I would have been if he had left. It reminded me of the chance we have to constantly remind these boys that they are loved, and that they would be missed if they left. Today Eddie found me directly after school was out. He threw his arms around me, smiled up at me, kissed my hand, and then ran off to play. No words were exchanged, but that is what made it more special. We have finally become a comfort to the boys."

Jennie Mach came from South Dakota. Her missionary heart and her compassion for the boys was unmistakable to all who knew her. On April 16, I received this encouraging message from Jennie:

"What I enjoy most is just spending time with the boys. I hardly ever have a free hand…. The boys seem to follow us everywhere. One amazing thing I've noticed about these boys is how giving and loving they can be, when they themselves have received so little. We can really see how God is transforming these boys' hearts and lives."

In those days, we prayed about how we could reach the fifteen hundred kids who still lived in the streets of Kisumu. We wanted them to know they have a heavenly Father who loves and cares for them, but we had no more room at Agape. Then a breakthrough occurred. Lebaus, our administrator, announced that the municipal government gave us permission to hold a street kids church in one of the parks. That was a big first step.

Shortly afterward, I received this enthusiastic message from Jennie:

"We are really excited about how things have gone the last two Sundays, meeting at the park with all the boys. The last couple of weeks we have had about fifty boys. Lebaus has a great vision for this ministry, and we are really hoping it will continue when we leave. The three of us *Chicks* are now supplying the bread. We have been thinking through it and wanted to suggest the idea of setting up a fund specifically for the weekly outreach for bread, first-aid needs, and whatever expense may pop up as this ministry expands. If Sunday school or Vacation Bible School kids brought twenty cents for an offering, it would buy a loaf of bread. In a few months, we may have a better idea of how many boys will be attending every Sunday, and we will know better how much money it will take to buy the bread weekly.

"Street children have so many unmet needs, not only for physical bread, but also for the Bread of Life. What a privilege we have to share *both* in this integrated ministry."

Kelly Carroll's home was in Modesto, California. She truly blessed us the six months she served before leaving Kenya to prepare for graduate school. Kelly aspired to be a nurse practitioner, and it became clear to all that she would make an excellent one. Kelly was greatly missed when it came time for her to say good-bye.

In her role as "camp nurse" she developed a process to care for minor wounds and infections. The girls organized a "medical room" and a system to keep track of boys who received the various types of treatment. In the process, another small problem arose. All the boys wanted Band-Aids. Some even scratched themselves until they bled just to get one. That is a graphic illustration of how much they yearned for attention.

We also found out several boys suffered from anemia during their physical exams performed by Kelly's father, Dr. Wally Carroll. Kelly gave out vitamins with iron to the boys who needed them. Soon those boys demonstrated more energy and their concentration in class improved.

Kelly helped each of the boys get their immunizations. That was quite an achievement. We rejoiced when one of the local hospitals agreed to immunize all the children at a very low cost. Of course, many of the boys weren't as excited about that as we were.

In fact, Erin explained how the boys behaved the next morning. "Every single one of them limped around the compound complaining about those injections." She adds, "The drama surrounding ninety children never ceases to amaze me."

CHAPTER 79

I Believe in Miracles

Alfred is a twelve-year-old walking miracle. Born out of wedlock, he was eventually sent to live with his grandparents. Unfortunately, because of their poverty and lack of school fees, Alfred found his way to Kisumu at the age of ten and lived with a gang of boys near the bus station.

Alfred's stunted growth left him small for his age, like so many other street boys who sniffed glue. On the night of February 12, 2000, he fell asleep in front of a busy gas station. A few hours later, a large country bus rounded the corner to refuel. Unfortunately, the driver of the bus didn't see Alfred lying there and turned sharply into the gas station. He ran over Alfred's lower legs and feet.

When the driver realized what happened, he left the boy for dead. Even when a passerby took Alfred to the government hospital, the medical team offered little hope for recovery. Alfred was literally helpless. He had no one to care for him or to pay his bills. Fortunately, some other street boys came to Agape for help. Lebaus heard about the situation, he rushed to the hospital to visit Alfred. He encouraged the doctors to give him the needed care and assured them we would pay the hospital expenses.

Two months later, they released Alfred into our care. The most remarkable thing is that this boy had no broken bones. There is no *earthly* explanation for that. It's a miracle of God's protection that he is able to walk. His right foot healed well but still bears obvious scars. However, part of Alfred's left heel was cut off in the accident. It took several more months to heal even with frequent applications of silver sulfadiazine. Over time, the open wound shrank in size.

Alfred faced a long road ahead. He had to learn to speak and understand English. It also took time for him to heal completely from all the emotional and mental trauma he experienced. It comforted us to know he enjoyed three good meals a day, a comfortable bed, and lots of children to play with. In addition to all this, he attended school.

One of our teenage interns, Kelly Carroll, wrote the following account about Alfred:

> "One treasure I took away was my daily time with a boy named Alfred. Ever since Alfred had his feet run over by a bus almost two years ago, one of his heels has had a huge infected wound. It never heals because he has so much scar tissue, and he can't feel it when he reinjures it over and over again. He also hasn't had it properly dressed, so it just stays infected.

> "When my physician father was here visiting, he examined Alfred and found some special ointment. Still, we needed some sort of support for his foot. Then my mother remembered that a church donated a bag of soccer cleats and, at the last minute, a lady added a pair of soft water shoes. I'm sorry to confess, at first I inwardly scoffed at that. *Soft water shoes in Kenya?* I thought it unlikely they would ever be used. But when we fished them out and tried them on Alfred – a perfect fit. God knew exactly what he needed. How can you not believe in miracles?

> "I have learned so much here about the little things that people think to do, to send, or to say that make all the difference. I am all teary writing this. Alfred was really self-conscious of that foot, and I never realized how it affected his relationship with other people too. But after a few weeks of daily dressing it and keeping it protected in the shoe, his eyes are shiny as he tells me, 'It's the wound going away.'

> "'Praise God,' I say.

> "'Amen,' he laughs."

CHAPTER 80

A Landmark Event

Anticipation charged the air as our two hundred and fifty guests arrived. No fewer than eight hundred beef sausages waited to be grilled on the barbecue by our missionaries. Our national cooks shaped triangular doughnuts, called *mandazis*, for hours. The delicacies, piled high on serving platters, were so tempting. Kenyan tea and coffee completed the menu for the grand opening of our new school.

The school, a beautiful two-story building, included eight classrooms and an administration office. It was generously funded by Mission of Mercy, headquartered in Colorado Springs, which provided sponsorship for thousands of children in developing countries. It was a great honor to partner with them and an even greater honor to have the president, Bob Houlihan, and eight other representatives of Mission of Mercy with us in Kenya to attend the ceremony. It was a very special and exciting day.

Our seventy-six boys opened the program with lively music and later executed an impressive flag ceremony. The honorable district commissioner of Kisumu presented his speech. When he finished, he unveiled the plaque and cut the ceremonial ribbon. The school was officially open.

Later, we learned that he was so impressed with the building and the number of people gathered, he sent for TV and newspaper coverage. The children were delighted to see themselves on television the next day.

Sharing the occasion with other friends from the United States made it even more memorable. A hardworking team comprised of members from California, Oregon, and Texas assisted in all the final preparations. Steve Chance, the founder of Golden Clay Ministries, and a pastoral team from Christ Church Kirkland also participated. We also hosted an eighteen-member team from Taylor University in Indiana.

I reflected on Ephesians 3:20-21. It's the theme Scripture passage for Mission of Mercy and has never been more appropriate in the life of Agape Children's Ministry.

> *Now to him who is able to do immeasurably more than all we ask or imagine, according to his power that is at work within us, to him be glory in the church and in Christ Jesus throughout all generations, for ever and ever! Amen.*

CHAPTER 81

The Taylor Team

We were privileged to share the month of January with a well-prepared group of students led by Jenny Collins and Lori Holtzman. We enjoyed time together as we worked with children who still lived in the street. The team came prepared to present puppet shows with violin and guitar music in local schools and churches. And in our free time, we watched for hippos in Lake Victoria. The students also assisted in the classrooms and were a wonderful asset to the teachers.

One of the highlights of our time together included creating drama groups where we presented skits based on the parables of Jesus, like the one about the Prodigal Son. *He longed to fill his stomach with the pods the pigs were eating* (Luke 15:16a).

The costumes they created for the son and the pigs included pink paper pig noses attached to rubber bands with curly pipe-cleaner tails. The boys laughed as they oinked and shared corn husks. Each time we needed a "commercial break," one of the boys trotted across the room with a sign bearing one of the Ten Commandments. You can imagine the fun we had.

One of the students, Sarah Hinkel, who aspired to be a journalist, wrote this touching account of her impressions:

"Tears streamed down my cheeks as the swelling voices of nearly eighty boys filled the night air. My team had been in Kenya only two days, yet I already felt the weight of unanswerable questions wrangling with the joy from my experience. Staring into the face of such immense poverty, I knew God was sovereign. But I struggled to reconcile this characteristic of the Creator with the despair of His creation. And then we came to Agape.

"Boys whose lives held more hurt and hopelessness in their tender years than I can fathom, lifted their fervent song. 'Be still and know that I am God.' Their acapella rendition of that simple phrase hit like a flaming arrow through my restless heart. Watching genuine peace settle over the young faces of the boys, their sacred song gave special veracity to the words they sang.

"My questions have not gone away, but when they threatened to crowd out my confidence in the fact that God is sovereign and, most of all, loving, I just close my eyes, hear the voices of Agape, and become still ... to know that He is God."

CHAPTER 82

Nicholas - An Essential Ingredient

Thus the saying 'One sows and another reaps' is true.
(John 4:37)

No one could have imagined how much would be accomplished by shopping for African woodcarvings. After my son Lance graduated from college in 1994, he visited me in Kisumu. What an exciting time for both of us. Lance wanted to learn all he could about Kenya. One day, he walked home from town and stopped to look at the beautiful array of animal woodcarvings, jewelry, drums, and other native handiwork displayed in the roadside stalls the Kenyans call kiosks.

While he browsed, he met a young African named Peter, who later introduced Lance to his brother, Nicholas. They talked about school life in Africa and the United States and enjoyed their time together. Lance asked if they knew where he might find a leather shield like the Maasai warriors use. They didn't know where to purchase one, but they knew how to make one. Encouraged, Lance asked if they could show him how to make one too.

The idea intrigued them, and they agreed to gather supplies. It wasn't long before I found Lance as he sat on a three-legged stool in the shade of bamboo mats. He learned how to soak the leather and stitch it to the wood. They worked side by side and enjoyed camaraderie. The Africans smiled and later confided that they weren't used to seeing a muzungu work with his hands. They believed that muzungus had a machine to do everything for them from shaving to washing the dishes.

By the time the new shield had been dried and painted, the new friends had developed a mutual respect. Lance stayed in touch with Nicholas and continued to pray for him. I took other visitors to shop at his kiosk and looked forward to seeing him. Later, I learned he graduated from the University of Nairobi. I was so proud of him.

Thankfully, the story does not end here. Instead, the plot thickens. Rick and Audrey McAninch, Agape administrators at that time, also became acquainted with Nicholas at the kiosk. One day, when their pastor from Kirkland, Washington, visited, he requested a three-legged stool for a sermon illustration. Audrey remembered that Nicholas had one and asked if they could borrow it the following Sunday. She invited Nicholas to join them for church, and to her delight, he agreed.

After the morning service, she greeted Nicholas and asked if he ever considered inviting Christ into his life.

He confessed, "I thought getting a good education would solve life's problems, but I still felt empty." He wanted to talk more, so they arranged a time to meet the next day.

Monday afternoon, Rick, Audrey, and Nicholas met at the Hotel Royale. The hotel has a lovely veranda with colorful umbrellas spread over white tables. It was a comfortable, pleasant lunch place. So there amidst the waiters and soda bottles, Rick clearly presented the gospel message. Nicholas was ready to make a decision. He bowed his head, prayed, accepted the sacrifice of Christ on the cross, and asked God to forgive his sins. There were no bells or whistles, just a sincere prayer of a man who recognized his need for God. He looked radiant. Afterward, Nicholas wanted to learn more and live for Jesus.

Nicholas spent time with Rick and Audrey at Agape. He was impressed with what he saw. Because he had lived and worked in Kisumu for several years, he knew most of the boys from when they lived in the streets. He watched them roam around and beg for shillings. He found that he truly enjoyed being with them now and felt free to share his newfound faith.

When we finished the new addition to our building, we needed another teacher. With a degree in microbiology, Nicholas was a perfect fit.

CHAPTER 83

Randy

Dressed in shabby, threadbare clothes, Randy looked like a typical street boy. Born out of wedlock, his mother died when he was only a toddler. Later, his grandmother died and a friend helped as much as she could. With no one left to care for him, he headed for the streets of Kisumu. When our missionary, Audrey McAninch, met him, Randy spoke very little English.

But with a ready smile, he eagerly approached her and said, "I am Agape" over and over. She realized he was trying to say he wanted to go to Agape. He soon became a member of our growing family.

A bright child, Randy adjusted quickly. He learned how to do puzzles and excelled in reading. Often, his voice rang above the others as he sang during morning devotions. But the biggest thrill of all was when Uncle Rick (McAninch) snuck up behind him and started the "tickle machine." Randy squealed with delight and giggled. His joy lifted the spirits of everyone around him.

Then one day after school, Randy stepped on a sharp thorn while he played in the field. Our houseparent took him to a nearby hospital for a tetanus vaccine. Along with that, Randy took antibiotics and soaked his foot in an antibacterial solution. Even with all that, he continued to hop around on one foot due to the pain. We took him to the hospital for a second tetanus booster. In spite of all this, he complained of a tight pain in his neck and chest the following morning. Audrey immediately scooped him up and took him to another doctor. She was astonished as her worst fear was confirmed. The diagnosis – tetanus.

They placed Randy in a dark, quiet room and started an IV. As a precaution, they sedated him to prevent the violent contractions which often accompany tetanus. Jonas our houseparent sat by his bedside day and night. We all prayed earnestly for his healing. But the Lord had other plans. Our dear Randy slipped away quietly on the evening of November 12.

Here in America, we know tetanus as a preventable disease, as something very rare. But in a land where electricity is rationed and inconsistent, vaccines sometimes lose their potency. And though his treatment was excellent and came from loving hands, Randy's little body wasn't able to fight the disease. We can be thankful Randy didn't die alone on the street. And we are comforted that he knew Jesus as his Savior.

Rick and Audrey wrote:

> "We are all grieving. We realize even more that each boy who roams the streets looking for food and hope is a precious treasure. I'm reminded of the man in the Bible who, when he found a treasure in the field, sold everything in order to buy not only the treasure but also the whole field (Matthew 13:44). There is a whole field full of treasures here in Kenya.

> "Jesus said that whatever we do for the least of these, we do for Him (Matthew 25:40). When Randy said the words, 'I am Agape!' we had no idea how much he would come to symbolize the reason we exist. We pray that his life will motivate us to rescue many more lost boys."

CHAPTER 84

A Tale of Two Brothers

Each boy at Agape has a unique story to tell, including two brothers named Eben and Gage.

Their father died in 1997, leaving their mother, a peasant farmer, with an income of ten dollars per month. They lived in a rural area where the river provided their main water source. Their home was a traditional hut with mud walls and a thatched roof.

With such a meager income, they didn't have enough food or the money required for school fees. As a result, the boys went to the street where they hoped to find a way to earn enough money to survive. At home, Eben and Gage were taught to be respectful and polite. So you can imagine the misery and fear they experienced in their harsh new surroundings as "street urchins."

In December 2000, Gage was eleven when he was rescued from the street and taken to Agape. His records show that upon his arrival, he just wanted to play and he felt happy to feel safe again. A year later on January 26, Eben was fifteen when he came to Agape to attend school. At that time, we had no idea he and Gage were brothers.

The boys had been separated on the street and neither knew the whereabouts of the other. I wish we could all have witnessed the reunion. It was a very special day for the two boys. Eben and Gage did well together and were even able to visit their mother during school holidays. One February, we received the sad news that she had died of a chronic illness. It made us even more thankful the Lord brought those young men into our Agape family.

Gage, at fourteen, liked reading, doing crafts, playing basketball, and being a Boy Scout. With the Scouts, he practiced for weeks on end. He assembled, disassembled, and reassembled their campsites, and studied the scouting material they would be quizzed on in competitions.

In the Lions high school, Eben caught up rapidly with his peers. It was remarkable, because he had missed a lot of time from school while on the streets. On one occasion, the teaching staff brought him forward at the school assembly, congratulated him, and acknowledged his excellent performance in science and math. When our staff member Nicholas dropped in at the school a few days later, the headmaster called Nicholas into his office and showed him appreciation as a "parent" and told him how well Eben was doing.

To give you a little more insight into the young man Eben became, here's a copy of a letter of thanks he wrote to the Rotary Club, which had contributed to the Agape education fund:

"Dear Sirs,

I hereby say a word of hello to you. This year in my academics, I am performing averagely well, and I hope for the best after the national examination in the forthcoming year.

Always remember that we are richly blessed by what you are doing back in America, and this is just a miracle from God. Sincerely, this cannot be done by any man. Surely, the hand of God is working through man. This serves as a challenge on my side, because I have to work extremely hard in school so that your work would not be in vain.

In fact, what is happening to me now was like castles in my early life before I joined Agape. I never thought of learning in a provincial school, being driven to school early in the morning, nor getting tea and bread before leaving for school, nor wearing a neatly made school uniform, and taking the best books needed in school. Surely, your work is commended by God and by us ourselves. Be blessed.

Yours faithfully,

Eben Ochieng"

CHAPTER 85

John Otieno

Each of our boys has a personal history file. The following is found in the file for one of our boys:

Name: John Otieno
Date of birth: June 1982
Date of admission: 4/17/90
Level reached at school before admission: none
Length of time on the streets: four years
John is the oldest of five siblings, although two have died. The father married another wife, who severely mistreated John and gave him heavy work duty. After that, the boy has never been the same.

Apparently, during John's early childhood he didn't receive a proper diet, which caused rickets and deformed his legs. Not only were his limbs painfully slender, but he also had red, bulging eyes. A distended stomach signaled worms, and slightly red tinged hair indicated a protein deficiency. Due to his abusive treatment, he became timid and embarrassed around other people. Because of his deformity and stunted growth, John appeared to be much younger than his age. As a street boy, John looked exhausted.

He stayed in Nairobi for one year. Police picked him up and took him to the remand center in Kisumu. Upon his release three months later, authorities dropped him off at a market to find his own way home. John never went home. Instead, he chose to try and survive in the streets. In 1996, he returned to Kisumu, where he stayed in the streets until he was admitted to Agape in April 1998. Initially, we estimated his age to be eleven years, but we were surprised. After he stayed with us for a while and regained his strength, he looked like a healthier young man. And, before we knew what happened, he was growing a mustache.

A huge transformation took place in this young man during his time at Agape. He impressed visitors with his endearing smile and desire to be helpful. John put forth a lot of effort to catch up in school, and we were very proud of him. He loved the Lord and attended the 6:30 a.m. devotions each day.

Because John was older than he first appeared to be, Audrey assigned him tasks to help him feel as if he belonged with the bigger boys. He even did some of the washing when the Taylor University students visited. You could see by his bright countenance that he clearly took pride in his work.

Then, we learned of a visiting orthopedic doctor at the Mission Hospital in Kijabe, a five-hour drive from Kisumu. Arrangements and transportation came together so quickly that we knew it was John's appointed time to have corrective surgery. He came through the first surgery on his right leg very well and recuperated in the home of Rick and Audrey under their watchful eye.

Audrey wrote that John was soon able to crutch around the compound and steadily got faster. He often sat outside with his cast propped up on a chair as he watched the activities. She wondered if he might be picturing himself riding a bicycle. She also mentioned that the other boys always made sure he had a chair to prop his leg up during meals and various meetings. Their attentiveness impressed me.

John's next surgery involved correction to his left leg. It too went well. In fact, the surgeries went so well that when he was fully recuperated, he stood two inches taller. This made him about four feet two inches tall.

When I asked John to show me his good legs, he smiled and pointed out the newly healed scars. He was so happy. Instead of his knee joints pointing to the center of his body, his legs were nice and straight. Contentment shone in his face like I had never seen before. Though still quiet and shy, he looked secure and confident.

John went to the vocational center to learn carpentry. His arms became strong, and he was a whiz at using a plane. No one could make anything smoother. But when it came to reaching things high off the ground, he was in trouble. It didn't take long for us to realize he needed a different vocation. When introduced to shoe repair, we knew he had found his niche.

After John graduated, he went to work in Migori and became a successful cobbler. People liked him personally, and he did excellent work. He liked to share his story with people as they sat together while he worked. At the local hospital, John visited people who faced surgery. He fully understood their anxious thoughts and fears. So he prayed with them and gave them verses of comfort.

People started to call him Pastor John. When we visited him in Migori, he greeted us in gray slacks, a white long-sleeved shirt, and a red striped tie.

John was recently married to a wonderful lady. They have a small house in the town of Migori where they plan to raise chickens. John is involved in his church and looks after one of the home cell groups. He loves sharing the gospel. God used Agape to spare his young man's life. What a privilege!

CHAPTER 86

Travis Overcomes a Blind Eye

Extreme poverty forced Travis to leave home at the age of eight. In spite of congenital blindness in one eye, he endured the cold, lack of food, and lack of shelter. On January 5, 2000, he met Agape missionaries who offered to bring him to our home. Today, he has grown into a man of exceptional character who loves the Lord and wants to serve Him. He learned to love and understand the Bible more than many people twice his age. He is also respected by the other boys for his teaching ability and is a gifted musician.

During a recent visit, Travis gave me a copy of his personal testimony. The following excerpts clearly demonstrate the way he applied Scripture to his daily life:

> "Sometimes I have asked myself whose sin causes me to be born the way I am; was it my own sin or my parents' sin? But I have come to know that my blindness has nothing to do with sin. I am like this so God's power might be seen at work in me (John 9:2-3). This problem or trial provides an opportunity to see how God answers prayer.

> "One important thing I've come to know is that all of God's promises are true. I can go to God in prayer. He is my helper and my friend. He hears my cries and is able to give

me His help. All He asks is that I believe. *'Everything is possible for one who believes'* (Mark 9:23)."

This explains Travis's joyful countenance. For high school, he relocated to the farm where they mentored him as a pastor and instructed him in auto mechanics.

In a letter to me, he wrote:

Hello Mum,

First of all, I would like to thank the Lord for what He has done in my life. I'm doing well in school and I still have hope to reach my dream of being a pastor. Now I am enjoying my involvement with the church programs and singing in the choir. I help lead praise and worship and teach Sunday school. The children are taught about the life of Jesus. Above all, I still love Jesus and am looking forward one day to eternal life in heaven.

I'm in mechanics class, second year, and am very happy that I can dismantle and assemble different types of engines and also drive the *lorry* (truck) we use here. I really thank the Lord for all of this and pray regularly that the will of God be evident in my life. Thank you, and may God Almighty keep you safe.

I love you, Mum,

Travis

I was not surprised to learn that this hardworking young man placed first in his vocational training exams.

CHAPTER 87

John and Prisca Ondeche

Now to him who is able to do immeasurably more than all
we ask or imagine, according to his power that is at work
within us, to him be the glory. (Ephesians 3:20-21)

When we set up our local nonprofit organization, we learned that
Kenyan law mandated all local nonprofit organizations have a
board consisting of Kenyan nationals. Because of this, Agape has two
boards, one in Kenya and the other in the United States. It was evident
from the beginning that both boards were a God-given asset, a reser-
voir of wisdom and encouragement. As a single woman and mom who
just wanted to rescue and nurture the few street boys I could handle, I
had no comprehension of the scope of the organization God intended.
To give you an idea of the caliber of people our Lord sent to make up
our Kenyan board, allow me to introduce you to John Ondeche and
his wife, Prisca.

John has a warm, loving smile, a gentle manner, and a handshake
that makes you feel like you've just met a friend. John serves as an elder
and counselor at Christ Church Kisumu. For several years, he also
worked as the finance officer of the Kenya National Bank in Kisumu.

His wife, Prisca, is a soft-spoken and gracious woman. She's the mother of four delightful children and, as a registered nurse, served as head matron of the intensive care unit at the local Aga Khan Hospital.

Both John and Prisca earned good salaries and provided well for their active family. Then God tugged on their hearts.

One day I received an email from Audrey with a subject line reading "Real Missionaries." She was quite excited. This couple seriously considered giving up their steady salaries to become missionaries to their own people, right there in Kisumu. John carried a special burden for the street children, and Prisca had a vision to help babies who struggled to survive. It would be a costly decision, not only financially but also socially. At that time, neither John nor Prisca was assured of any income. They thought of all the ways they could cut back on expenses and trusted God for their children's school fees.

John later told me that all of his colleagues and most of his friends reacted to the news with utter disbelief. Many tried to talk him out of the idea. But John and Prisca held fast to what they believed was the call of God on their lives. In October 2000, they put their faith into action. John took an early retirement as a mid-management banker. What has happened since that step of faith demonstrated how God brings people together.

The organization Mission of Mercy assisted us for a period of time with a child sponsorship program. They also looked for sponsors for the additional eighty-eight students who came to the Agape school from the surrounding neighborhood. Those additional children, both boys and girls, fell into the category of "pre-street children." They came from poor families with little or no money to invest in their children's education. They were likely candidates to end up in the street.

Mission of Mercy appointed John as the child sponsorship coordinator in Kisumu. Though he made a fraction of his former salary, John found great joy and fulfillment as he helped those needy families. His professional background, along with years of experience in church family counseling, made him well qualified for the position. Soon, he accepted the offer to become a board member of Agape.

The Lord also led Prisca to her heart's desire. She became instrumental in founding the Kisumu Rescue Center. She soon found herself surrounded by little HIV-positive and abandoned babies. It astonished me to learn that Kenya has the largest number of AIDS orphans of any country in the world. Rick and Audrey opened their home and allowed a small rescue center to be built on their compound. This center, sponsored by the New Life Home Trust, received its first three babies during one of my visits in 2001.

Very soon, the number of rescued babies at the center rose to ten, and from there the number grew even faster.

How many children can one person love? I want to find out.

Fortunate is the child who finds its way to Prisca's loving hands and the expert care she has to offer. The tender way she holds and cares for these infants tells her story. She is truly content and rejoices in the work God has given her to do. She is a model for Proverbs 31:28: *Her children arise and call her blessed; her husband also, and he praises her.*

CHAPTER 88

Charles Bentley

One afternoon, I traveled with a group from UNICEF. We drove to a garbage-strewn alley and found a cardboard home built against the back wall of a gray building. The teenagers who lived there invited me to look around. I bent down to get through the door and was surprised to see that the girls had tacked up a broken piece of mirror and a magazine picture of Princess Diana. They even accessorized with a small piece of candle in a tin can.

I didn't know what to say. I managed something like, "Wow, you've made this look real nice." Then I asked how many stayed there at night. The answer was six – if they all slept on their sides.

Later, I wondered aloud why the kids didn't clean up the garbage. Most explained it this way. "If the area is cleaned up, we will be chased away." So the garbage actually provided a measure of security for them.

However, it also meant that they put up with rats that occasionally ran over them as they slept. I shuddered at the very mention of it. Then I noticed one of the girls was pregnant. I wanted to cry. What chance would a little baby have to survive?

That morning, I talked to Lebaus and found out it was possible for a baby to survive those conditions. We had living proof in a boy named Charles Bentley. Lebaus called him in so we could become better acquainted. Charles was fourteen years old at the time. His file stated, "His mother was a street girl but the father is not known."

His mother, a young girl weighed down by her own hopeless state, left him at the age of three months. And where did she leave him? In the streets, to be raised by other street kids.

When he was three years old, someone pointed to a lady and said, "There is your mother." But she still didn't want him. So, as Charles grew up, he felt unloved and only knew the streets of Nairobi as his home.

Sometime in January of 2002, Charles managed to get on a bus to Kisumu. A few weeks later, on the evening of February 2, a car hit him and drove away. The accident left him with fractured ribs and a broken collar bone, arm, and leg. Authorities took him to a nearby government hospital and left him there. Some of the other street boys who witnessed the accident came to Agape to ask for help. This type of thing had happened before, so Lebaus knew exactly what to do. He immediately went to see the boy and made sure he received the proper care.

Charles spent two months in the hospital. They released him into our care in early April. The accident left him with a slight limp. Otherwise, he is a healthy young man. His most notable characteristic is his gentle spirit. Frankly, I didn't expect to see that quality after I heard his story. Charles made a remarkable adjustment. He thrived in our primary school. He learned how to read and write as a teenager, and especially enjoyed arts and crafts. As part of Agape's big loving family, he developed a new outlook on life.

By this time, 101 boys lived at Agape. Each one possessed a heart-wrenching story. Lebaus always tried to keep one bed open for an emergency situation. Before long, a few more beds opened up when some of our boys went to our vocational training site in Matoso. Tom and Marg Tucker, our resident missionaries there, were prepared. This turned out to be the perfect solution for a boy like Charles. He learned a trade and is able to make a living.

Charles Bentley is now an adult. He lives in Tanzania, where he puts his new skills into practice.

CHAPTER 89

Gregory

Therefore, as God's chosen people, holy and dearly loved, clothe yourselves with compassion, kindness, humility, gentleness and patience. ... Forgive as the Lord forgave you. And over all these virtues put on love, which binds them all together in perfect unity. (Colossians 3:12-14)

This is one of my favorite passages of Scripture. The words are hard to squirm out from under. The qualities the Lord wants us to develop are stated so clearly. We continually see God's agape love at work in the lives of our children in Kenya.

Last year when I visited Agape, I learned that one of the boys who met us at the gate spent the better part of the two previous days just sitting there ... waiting. As a newcomer to Agape, he heard that Mama Darla was coming. Well, I spent those same two days in airplanes and airports. I certainly didn't look my best. But Gregory didn't care what I looked like; he just wanted to be loved. When I heard about his patient vigil, I made it a point to become better acquainted with him. I was even more deeply touched when I heard his story.

Gregory was eleven years old when Dan and Patty Schmelzer met him on the street. He approached them at the market selling plastic bags for five shillings each (about three cents). As the oldest of five children, Gregory was the family's sole breadwinner. Without her husband, Gregory's mother did her best just to keep her family together. Imagine trying to feed six people by selling plastic bags at the open market for three cents each.

Though sensitive and vulnerable, Gregory behaved more like an adult than a child and seldom smiled. Dan and Patty were drawn to the boy and wondered why he carried so much weight on his shoulders. When they befriended him, Gregory told them several times that all he wanted was to go to school.

Intrigued by Gregory, Lebaus visited his home to see if there was a way to help him get into school. Gregory beamed when Lebaus arrived. When he saw Gregory's family's desperate condition, Lebaus explained that we had a home for street children with a school on our compound. Since Gregory's mother depended on him for their meager income, she had a big decision to make. But as she thought about it, love broke through her fears and she asked if Gregory could come to Agape. She knew it was the only chance for Gregory to get an education. What a touching example of a mother's unselfish love and concern for her child's future.

Gregory became part of our Agape family. Though quiet and shy at first, he soon made many friends. A highlight for me goes back to a sidewalk tournament of the card game Memory. Each time he found matching cards, he got so excited that he burst out laughing. There's nothing as sweet as the sound of a child's carefree laughter. And frankly, when it comes from a child rescued from the streets, it's even sweeter.

When it came to his schooling, Patty reported, "He has been the number-one student in his class every term since he arrived at Agape. We have never seen a child so focused on learning. We are so proud of Gregory. He really is a shining star that brightens every day with his quiet and gentle smile."

It also worked out for him to visit his mother and siblings during school breaks. He has been a big encouragement to them.

CHAPTER 90

Robert

"There are an estimated 40,000 people living in Nairobi streets" (*The Daily Nation Newspaper,* Tuesday, January 28, 2003).

After a trip to Kenya, special memories always linger. During my January-February visit, something remarkable happened. As a result of the December elections, a new administration brought a tangible sense of hope and enthusiasm to the Kenyans. Several changes in policy had already taken place. The war against corruption started and bribes were no longer an accepted practice.

For years, the number of street children in Kenya increased at a rapid pace. However, the new officials focused on the problem and started to find placement for children and older youths who lived in the streets of Nairobi, the nation's capital city.

In the past, some authorities felt the children should just be disciplined and sent back home. However, on February 4, 2003, the national newspaper reported, "Of the 2,000 [street children] in the city center, only 500 knew their homes." The article explained that the government set aside limited funds to buy blankets, food, soap, and other basic necessities while the children were being relocated in rehabilitation centers. A cabinet minister also stated that "older street children in the current rehabilitation centers will be taken to the National Youth Service for training (to become soldiers)."

The encouraging part of this account is that the government recognized that most of the children truly had no place to go, and the current officials believed "they should be removed from the streets in a very humane manner."

They organized a children's conference in Nairobi for government officials to meet with various representatives of at-risk children.

On February 17, I received an email from Dan and Patty:

> "This weekend, one of the boys will have a special honor
> bestowed on him. Robert (a member of our Boy Scouts)
> has been selected to attend a conference on the problem
> of street children in Kenya. Forty boys and girls who were
> formerly on the street will be in attendance and will speak
> to those who are striving to solve this major social issue.
> They will be invited to share their experiences and their
> views about what might be done to improve the juvenile
> justice system. Robert is very excited about this opportu-
> nity. He is a well-spoken eighth grader and will doubtless
> make an impression."

Our hearts joined them in prayer for this young man. We eagerly awaited the next update. A few days later, another message arrived from Dan and Patty:

> "Robert came by Sunday evening to tell us he was home.
> Then he added, 'I have great news, Mr. Dan.' And he did.
> He talked about how wonderful his time there was and
> how they divided the children into groups to discuss their
> experiences and what is needed from their perspective.
> Then, with a wide grin, Robert said, 'Mr. Dan, it was like I
> was someone special!'"

After his first presentation, they chose Robert as one of six young people invited to return. The others were all girls. Those young people represented thousands of other street children throughout Kenya.

"He was radiant as he shared the news." Patty added, "Doesn't it just make your heart dance? We are so proud of him."

It seemed to me that the Lord clearly prepared this young man for leadership. It was so gratifying to see a boy who once wore dirty, ragged clothes, who begged, and slept in the cold become a respected young Christian teenager. The officials of Kenya chose him to represent hundreds of other street children in Kisumu at the Undugu Children's Conference.

It's an amazing privilege to be part of an organization that makes a significant difference in the lives of children. We are humbled and thankful. It's a lot of hard work, but the rewards are eternal.

Robert attended and graduated from Moi University. Though he received a scholarship, he still struggled to get enough food and study materials to keep going on his meager funds. But he made the most of the opportunity, and his perseverance paid off.

His reward is a wonderful job in Nairobi as a team leader at Afro Energy Kenya. He is also a managing partner at Jupitaa. We wish him every success.

CHAPTER 91

Blake and Esther Gibbs

I've had some very special people in my life. Blake and Esther Gibbs are among them. I met them through my then-future husband, Paul, at a Christmas party in 1994. Esther grew up as an MK (missionary kid) in Liberia and had strong ties to Africa. Due to our common interests, we connected the first time we spoke and promised to stay in touch.

Our next encounter came as a big surprise. I stood in a long line at the Heathrow Airport in London and heard, "Darla, is that you?" I twisted around, shocked to see a familiar face as Esther smiled and waved at me. It turned out that the Gibbses and I were booked on the same plane, though headed for different locations in Africa.

After some rather animated conversation, we agreed to get together in Kisumu. I wanted them to see our little project and meet the sixteen boys who lived at Agape at the time. As the Lord planned it, Blake and Esther had twenty-four hours they could spare. A few days later, I met them at the Kisumu airport on a Sunday morning and returned them at the same time the following day. But what a difference a day makes.

Blake and Esther were so positive and affirming. They gave me some great ideas on how to organize the compound and deal with a water drainage issue. It was a big problem at that time. Several months later when Paul and I were married, Blake helped me acquire the nonprofit status for our "baby Agape."

When we needed a board of directors in the United States, Blake was pressed into service as the chairman of the board. For years, Blake and Esther worked quietly behind the scenes. They provided wise counsel in times of crisis, prayer support, encouragement, and inspiration. They also brought friends and partners into our ministry, helped write proposals, and completed the production of two videos.

Their desire to communicate what's happening on the mission fields around the world gave birth to Media 7 Ministries. Their partners, Paul and Winnie Bahn, came to Kisumu to film our first video in 1998. At the very beginning, Paul and Blake realized that, more than any other medium, video provided the means to effectively tell people our ministry story. Through video, people were instantly transported to Africa to see firsthand what's being achieved for the cause of Christ.

As our program grew, I began to feel I was in over my head for the type of administration Agape required. After much consideration, in 2005 Blake agreed to become the new Director of Agape Children's Ministry. He and Esther also made great leaders for short-term mission trips. They improved our compound and solved a serious water problem. They also pulled together a team for a building project at the farm in Matoso. Years later, they built a beautiful kitchen, dining hall, and meeting room combination in Kisumu. I thank the Lord with all my heart for bringing Blake and Esther Gibbs into my life. They are definitely among the blessings I count over and over again.

CHAPTER 92

Blake as Director

As Blake shouldered the mantle of leadership, he took on several of the pressing issues of Agape. Agape excelled at rescuing, loving, and nurturing children from the street, but two major issues needed attention. Many more children remained on the streets of Kisumu than Agape could possibly take in. But even more of a concern was the process of graduating a child from Agape after he had been raised, educated, clothed, and fed for a number of years. Agape became the child's home, and yet our founding vision was never to make the organization a retirement center.

The solution to both of those issues was to shorten the time children spent at Agape by, if at all possible, reintegrating the children back into the villages where they came from. This wasn't always possible, because some had no idea of their roots. Yet for the majority, the reintegration program proved a stunning success.

Hear the vision in Blake's own words:

> "Agape's ministry has four major elements we like to refer to as the four *R*s. The first 'R' is **Rescue.** We endeavor to rescue as many children as we can from the life-threatening environment of the streets. The second 'R' is **Redeem.** In all we do, we seek to share the transforming message of

the gospel with every child we encounter and to encourage and disciple each child in their walk with the Lord. **Rehabilitation** is the third 'R' and encompasses academic education, vocational training, counseling, and mentoring designed to equip and prepare the child to live independently as a productive, contributive member of society. The final 'R' is **Reintegration**. It is our goal, whenever possible, to reconnect and reunite each child with his family or extended family in their rural community or village.

"You may wonder why reintegration is such an important aspect of our ministry. After all, in most cases, problems in the family – whether it was poverty, neglect, or abuse – were a major factor causing the child to go to the streets in the first place.

"However, in the Kenyan culture, family and the rural village home are of utmost importance. Connection to them is essential. If you meet a Kenyan and ask where he is from, he will not tell you where he is living presently. He will tell you where his family home is, where his roots are. It's also true in the Kenyan culture that the male child will inherit at least a portion of the family's land.

"For this reason, it is very important for us to try to reconnect our children with their roots. This is often a challenging and time-consuming process, because it requires not only that we equip and prepare the child for potential reintegration, but also the family. The family may not be a traditional family unit. It may be a single mother (widowed or abandoned by an abusive husband), or perhaps a grandma, an aunt, or an uncle.

"We begin by establishing contact with the family and building a relationship with them. Over multiple visits, we endeavor to see how we can equip and prepare the family to accept the child and properly care for him. When it is safe physically, emotionally, and spiritually, we will leave the child with his family. But the process continues even after that with follow-up visits to see how the child and the family are doing, and to ensure the child continues to grow and mature in his walk with the Lord.

"One of our major efforts while we were in Kenya was to define, establish, develop, and launch a new 'Reintegration Team' – a group of staff members whose sole responsibility is to carry out the reintegration process. Prior to that time, the home visits, counseling, equipping, and preparing needed to carry out the reintegration process were conducted by various members of our Agape home staff and outreach ministry staff. Now, we have established a separate arm of the ministry with team members devoted solely to reintegration on a full-time basis.

"The reintegration team represents a significant refocusing of our efforts and involves a substantial commitment of time and resources. But we believe this is the path we should follow as we seek to do everything we can to best help the children God has placed in our hands."

This marvelous effort, which Blake spearheaded, also enables Agape to reach out to many more of Kisumu's lost children. Today, our turnover time for a child at Agape can be as little as four months as they progress through the four Rs. Seventy percent of boys and eighty percent of girls returned to their home village, with faithful follow-up, remain there. What a blessing to see them take root and be fully accepted by family and neighbors. Today, we are actively following up on over 850 children who are at home. Well over two thousand street children have been rescued from street life, glue addiction, probable incarceration as criminals, and an early and lonely death.

Reintegration as told by John Mwalo

In 2001, as the head houseparent, I approached Agape's management and asked, "Is there anything more we can do to connect these children and their families?" I felt strongly that the family unit was God ordained. With the ministry's permission, I brought children into my own home to see if they could fit into a traditional Kenyan home.

Previously, I thought street children could never be placed back into normal Kenyan society. When I realized those children were like other Kenyan children, I asked, "Why can't we try to find the homes of these children so they can be back with family?"

A huge concern was the prevalence of witchcraft in their rural homes. Poverty was another big problem. I prayed for God to give me the grace to help those kids. I requested money from missionaries to facilitate one-on-one visits with children and their families. By God's grace, we started visiting those children's homes in 2003. I was especially interested to help the children I had built a relationship with in my own home.

When I gave a report of my findings to the missionaries, we discovered our perception of the children's homes and families wasn't always accurate. Again, I asked, "What can we do to reunite those children with their families?"

Initially, we had no money or transportation to do large-scale reunification of families. I assured the missionaries, "Whatever money you give me, I will make sure to use it wisely for these children." That idea started the emphasis on reuniting children with their families during school breaks in April, August, and December.

Based upon the success we saw on a small scale, Blake asked me to develop a plan for how reintegration could best be implemented at Agape. Along with other members of our home department staff, I developed a document that explained what had been accomplished during 2004 and 2005. Blake took the information to the Agape management staff. From there, he developed a vision and plan for how reintegration could be implemented as a priority for Agape.

Initially, even the children at Agape opposed the idea. Most were very comfortable with how things operated and didn't like the idea of going home. It turned into a time of struggle. The few children who agreed to try reintegration did very well at home and are still doing well today. Some of the children in this initial reintegration group included Arthur Okembo, Ignatius Daddy, Randy, and Rashid Alidi.

In late 2008, Blake agreed this project should be established as a completely separate department. Originally, only one staff member, Ted Ouche, stepped forward to join the team. The program started with rather unclear guidelines other than the fact that we believed a child's place was at home.

We made a lot of mistakes in the beginning. As many as 75 percent of the reintegrated children came back to campus or returned to the streets. To curb runaways, Ted and I held cell meetings in the villages and shared the gospel with the families. We found that families who attended cell meetings produced children who were able to stay home. Those who refused to attend had children who went back to the streets. I shared the various challenges of the new program with Blake, and over time, adjustments were made. In order to improve the financial situation of the families, the reintegration team tried to help with microenterprise loans for small businesses. Those efforts failed.

By 2010, we realized what we were dealing with was a heart issue, not a money issue with the families. We focused on sharing the gospel with the families and saw favorable results. The large number of runaways dropped. Around this same time, the director of the remand center asked Agape to assist him with the reintegration of the children in their program.

As I've pointed out, we faced a lot of opposition to the idea of reintegration in the beginning. However, with God's guidance, over a thousand children have been successfully reintegrated during the past eight years.

Here are some examples:

Manfred: When we approached Manfred's family about reintegration, the mother and father were alive and a part of the local Legio Maria cult. The family believed their land was cursed and couldn't produce crops. They also believed Manfred was cursed and that the curse caused him to run to the streets. The reintegration team ministered weekly with the family. They prayed with the family in the *shamba* (the garden plot) and helped them plant their first crop of corn in several years. God blessed the effort with a bumper harvest. As a result, the family listened to the truth of the gospel. The whole family placed their trust in Christ and faithfully served Him. We integrated Manfred back home where he stayed all through secondary school. Manfred and his family continue to do well. The boy is now a man.

Kalil: Kalil had been separated from his family for ten years when we met them. We ministered to the father and stepmother, and something unique happened. They both accepted Christ. The father stopped drinking and got a job. Then the boy's natural mother returned, and we held cell groups at their home. Because his first wife came back, the husband asked if he should send his second wife away. We responded, "No." We continued sharing the Scriptures and were able to assist the family financially. Kalil has been stable at home since that time and is now a grown man.

Joshua: Joshua spent almost ten years at the remand center and three years at Agape. When we finally tried to track his family, I spent three days in Nakuru, about two hours away, only to find the father had passed away. Eventually, we found the place Joshua's father was buried in Ugenya. This helped us locate the family home. The local chief held a fundraiser for the family. So we left Joshua's photo with him. After a few days, the family came forward with joyful celebration because Joshua was found. Initially, he came back to Agape with us so we could prepare the family. When Joshua was fully reintegrated, we continued in ministry with the grandparents and uncles. Joshua finished classes seven and eight at home, the equivalent of junior high school, and was admitted to a national secondary school. He recently graduated.

CHAPTER 93

The Offering Story

My husband Paul's father practiced an endearing custom. He passed a dollar to each child present with him in a worship service so they had something to contribute to the offering plate. He maintained this practice even later in life. I passed the tradition on in Africa during a worship service by giving coins to our Agape boys. Our Kenyan houseparents embraced the practice and also gave the boys small amounts of money to contribute to the church offering.

Blake offered an addendum to my story:

"Several of our boys developed small garden plots on our Agape campus. Those shambas provided an opportunity for the boys to grow vegetables and fruit and were an excellent way to teach them responsibility as well as basic agriculture. It was such fun to watch the boys tend their gardens and haul buckets of water to carefully make sure their plants did well. They were very proud of their shambas and never missed an opportunity to show them to any visitors to the campus.

"One Sunday, when our boys met for Agape family church, our houseparents were delighted when one boy refused the money given to him for the offering. He came instead with three tomatoes from his garden and placed them in the offering basket. The next Sunday, another boy brought a small bunch of bananas from his garden. Needless to say, events like those melted our hearts and brought much joy as we saw the Lord work in the spirits of those little ones."

CHAPTER 94

Chadwick Made It

When Blake Gibbs became the director of Agape, I expressed concern to him about the future of some of the older boys.

Blake said, "Darla, God only asked for our obedience; the results are up to Him."

I have thought about that many times in the midst of rocky situations. To know that Agape is God's mission and that He knows the future has been very comforting.

Chadwick was one of those older boys. He had been with us for thirteen years. His time at Agape showed growth in every dimension. Physically, he grew to stand six feet five inches tall. Mentally, he was bright and showed huge potential. He transformed into a socially well-adjusted young man. And there was no question about his love for the Lord and His people. He even served as one of our worship leaders for years. However, Chadwick's walk has also been a little bumpy. He was strong-willed with definite ideas. Perhaps that was also an asset.

But in all things, the Lord saw him through. After graduating from secondary school, Chadwick desired to study music production. So Agape sent him to a college located in Nairobi. He faced lots of challenges but stuck it out, and we stuck it out with him. He completed the training and finished his apprenticeship in the coastal city of Mombasa.

Here is Blake's follow-up on Chadwick:

"A few days ago, Chadwick asked if he could meet with Mike (our missionary) and me. Based upon our history with him, we were both concerned that there was a problem. To our joy and delight, Chadwick told us that all he wanted to do was thank Agape for everything it had done for him. He told us he knows Agape's purpose was to give him opportunity and see him grow into a young man who can stand on his own independent legs. He wanted us to know he is doing that now, and he is grateful for all the Lord has done through Agape.

"We had the privilege of praying with him as he began this new chapter in his life. God has been faithful and honored all that has been poured into Chadwick's life through Agape. We are all blessed and encouraged by his success story even though at times we weren't sure we would ever see it."

CHAPTER 95

Family Visits

At times, my sons and their families visited me at Agape. Needless to say, every opportunity to see my children and grandchildren thrilled me. Often when they visited, the interaction between them and the boys left me with funny stories that still bring a smile to my face.

Sunscreen

"What are you doing?" A group of little guys stared at my daughter-in-law, Julie, as she slathered sunscreen on her children. "And why is your skin turning that pink color?"

Julie explained how the lotion prevented sunburn and asked if they ever got sunburned. Astonished at the thought, they cried out a unanimous "NO!"

Julie said, encouragingly, that God gave them the perfect kind of skin for the sun.

Next, they wanted to know if she stayed here long enough would her skin turn dark like theirs. Or if they moved to Washington, where she lived, would their skin get lighter? The following day the same boys were overheard explaining sunburn to another group. They said with assurance that where Julie comes from there is *no sun*. It's always dark and rainy.

The Magic of Making Friends

During a recent trip, my son David showed video clips on a big white sheet to all the boys, and then performed funny magic tricks. As we shared popcorn and juice later, the kids still laughed and tried to figure out how he did those tricks. What a great experience to have a "family" night like that.

At the end of the trip, we said our good-byes and got into the van. We looked back to see the boys trying to sneak my grandson Ben back into their classroom. It was truly heartwarming to see how quickly the kids had bonded with each other.

CHAPTER 96

Family Ties

F amily visits are a rare treat for missionaries overseas. My son Dave turned out to be a natural in Kenya and much loved by the staff and children alike. He entertained them with a simple magic show, played soccer with them, and fit right in buying food at the kiosks. He made friends wherever he went. His wife, Julie, was a great sport about doing their laundry in the shower. Then she spread it on clotheslines crossing their cottage living room to dry. She also made the best shepherd's pie in Kenya.

Dave and julie Peters

There are a couple of Dave's stories I just have to share.

Disgusting Grasshopper Man

On our first full day at Agape, I tried to connect with the children. A group of boys surrounded me as we exchanged volleys of questions with each other. They profoundly disapproved when they learned I enjoyed eating crab. Eeww! To them, crabs were viewed as filthy scavengers. On the other hand, I learned that they sometimes ate locusts. Out of the corner of my eye, I saw a grasshopper land nearby. I picked it up, and with just the right amount of dramatic flair, I popped it in my mouth, chewed it, and swallowed it without flinching.

The boys laughed. I thought it was because they were impressed that a muzungu ate a grasshopper. I was just trying to prove I could be like them. But they laughed because I had eaten the *wrong* kind of grasshopper. They made those disgusted faces again!

What Do I Know?

I thoroughly enjoyed my conversations with the Agape children. Our differences in perspective regarding some of the most trivial things fascinated me. One example was the children's curiosity about my various tones of skin color. We spent several hours at a pool one afternoon. When I removed my shirt, the children noticed parts of me were sunburned, others a darker tan, and other parts pale.

"Why are you so many colors?" they asked.

I tried to explain that our skin has something called pigment that gets darker when exposed to the sunlight.

One thoughtful boy asked, "Do African babies turn from light to dark when they are born and the light shines on them?"

"I don't think so," I responded.

"So how does the light get inside the mother?"

It was about then I realized I may know less than I thought about a lot of things.

Shaelyn and the Humongous Grasshopper

I don't know how many varieties of grasshopper there are in the world, but I do know Kenya has some giant ones. A boy named Wilbur hadn't been at Agape very long when Dave and his family came for a visit.

At that time, my ten-year-old granddaughter, Shaelyn, loved everything that "creeped and crawled upon the earth." Of course, the boys at Agape didn't know that and had probably never met a girl like her. So since boys will be boys, Wilbur intended to frighten her when he walked up to her with a huge grasshopper on his shirt.

He stepped closer and closer to Shaelyn and waited for a girlish scream. Other boys gathered behind him to join in the fun. When Wilbur stood directly in front of Shaelyn, she reached out and said, "Ooh, could I hold him?"

All the boys had a good laugh over that. They put the grasshopper in an empty water bottle, and we snapped a photo.

Ben Peters – Memories of Kenya
My grandson Ben, who is currently eighteen, was eleven years old when they visited. He recalled how much fun he had when he played soccer with the boys. "They were GOOD!" he exclaimed.

Ben played his clarinet for our Sunday church, which was a big treat for all of us. After he returned home, he admitted how much he missed passion fruit juice and anything black currant. He also was adventurous enough to order fish in a restaurant and eat the whole thing – including the eyeball.

The waiter surprised him later and asked how he liked the "engine," referring to the head of the fish. Ben liked the Kenyans' accent and observed that they do everything as a community. He displayed good insight for a boy his age.

Shane Calhoun
Paul's son Shane also first visited Africa at age eleven. He traveled with his dad to Tanzania, Kenya, and Uganda. With this background, Shane felt comfortable enough to travel to Kenya as a young adult. He desired to be a summer volunteer at Agape and to get to know the boys just coming off the streets. Every experience or talent a person has can be used in missions. Street children need to know they are valuable and

loved. Since Shane had an outgoing personality and previously taught gymnastics to young students in the U.S., he soon found his niche.

However, his idea presented some challenges. First, the Kenyans weren't familiar with gymnastics. Their strengths are soccer, track and field, and running like the wind. Secondly, we owned no equipment. Mats were essential. Shane used available resources. When he discovered the boys slept on vinyl-covered mattresses, he'd found the solution. So every afternoon after school, those interested took the sheets off their beds and carried their mattresses outside for practice. What great fun, and the boys learned a lot about balance and trusting each other. Thomas was one of the boys who excelled. Years later, he said it was his favorite activity at Agape.

Paul and I arrived in time for Agape's anniversary party that year. As I've shared before, that was always a special occasion. Every anniversary party was a special occasion. In fact, the boys told me it was their best day of the year. Many of the kids didn't know their actual birthdays, because record keeping in the rural villages was sketchy. They often knew what year they were born, but not always the exact date. So this anniversary party was something they really looked forward to.

After songs, skits, and speeches, it was time for the gymnastics team to demonstrate their newly found skills. Shane introduced the various events and the boys took their positions. The boys performed tumbling events, cartwheels, handstands, round-offs, and flips. For the climax of the event, they climbed on top of each other and built an impressive pyramid. The audience thoroughly enjoyed the show, and the gymnastics team showed pride in their new accomplishment.

Unfortunately, Shane hit a few rough spots that summer. But even those taught him some life lessons. He enjoyed the company of the boys at Agape and on the weekends invited them to the cottage where he stayed. It was a wonderful experience for the boys, and bonds of friendship were built. Sadly, on a few occasions, things "went missing." For Shane, this proved very disappointing, because he trusted the boys and freely opened his home to them. Because some of the locks on the closet and cupboard doors didn't work, the things left inside weren't completely safe. Shane realized, considering the boys' backgrounds, the unlocked places presented too much temptation. So while the children desperately needed to feel accepted, the situation forced Shane to exercise caution for the protection of everyone involved.

During the early years, the cottage had no television. And cell phones had not yet taken Kenya by storm. With very little to do in the evenings, in the quietness, Shane read books sometimes more than once.

Shane learned a lot that summer and came back to the States to earn a doctorate in psychology. He is now a clinician at California State University, San Bernardino.

CHAPTER 97

Disabilities Highlight God's Ability

Romans 8:28 promises us that *in all things God works for the good of those who love him, who have been called according to his purpose.* I've witnessed the truth of that verse played out in events surrounding the life of my second son, Mike.

To go back a few years will help me explain how God used Mike's life to encourage me in my work with children facing various physical challenges. His story demonstrates how the Lord works in our lives even when we don't understand His ways.

Michael Shane Peters was born February 3, 1969, five weeks before his due date. At the age of five, doctors diagnosed him with mild cerebral palsy due to a lack of oxygen at birth. The symptoms became more apparent as he grew taller because of stress on his tight heel cord. It caused him to walk on the ball of his foot, which threw him off balance. It also explained why he got so many holes in the right knees of his new school pants. His right foot didn't grow as fast as his left, and I had to buy two separate shoe sizes every time he outgrew a pair of shoes.

Mike loved to play ball – any kind of ball. He liked footballs, baseballs, soccer balls, and tennis balls. Even his favorite food was meatballs. In 1975, Mike underwent surgery to release the tension on his heel cord. A pediatric neurologist from Stanford Children's Hospital advised us to get him interested in music and crafts. Then she clarified that by adding, "because he will never be good in sports." She also warned that he might have learning disabilities as he grew older.

Somehow, I never got around to telling him that. But I did ask God why. "*Why* Lord, when Mike loves to play ball so much, have you allowed this to happen in his life? *Why* can't he have the ability to do well in sports?" And "*Why* isn't he interested in something else?" Sometimes life is hard to understand.

In spite of the doctor's dire prediction, Mike became a good left-handed pitcher in Little League and then moved on to soccer. He tried hard to be a good team player and continued to play soccer every chance he got. He even coached a team of seven-year-olds when he was still in high school. Then, after three years on junior varsity, he made the varsity team. This represented a huge milestone, but an even bigger thrill waited on the horizon.

It all transpired like something you see in the movies. The teams were down to the last play of the game with the score tied. All of a sudden, Mike sent the ball rocketing into the corner of the net and the whistle blew. The game was over. Our team won. Mike became the highest scoring player on the varsity team. I didn't even know I could yell that loud.

Afterwards, Mike said, "Well, Mom, now I have something to tell my kids." He thought that would be the highlight of his life.

Then in 1995, Mike learned the United States had a Paralympic National Soccer Team. The Paralympic games offer athletes with physical disabilities a chance to compete on an Olympic level. This event started shortly after World War II and currently takes place two weeks after the main Olympic events at the same venue.

Mike contacted the coach of the team to wish the team luck with the upcoming games in Atlanta. To his surprise, the coach asked him to submit a video of his playing. They later invited him to training camp where he became an official member of the team. That was a huge accomplishment. The biggest problem of his childhood opened a door to one of the most exciting chapters of his life. He became the captain of the team and even met Pelé during the 1996 Paralympic games in Atlanta, Georgia. Later, our U.S. team qualified for the Paralympics in Athens, Greece. I couldn't pack fast enough.

As a result of his involvement with the Paralympics, he found himself on the athlete advisory council for the U.S. Olympic Committee. Because of that position, he met his future wife, Emily deRiel. Emily is a talented lady. She won the silver medal in the Women's Modern Pentathlon during the 2000 Olympics in Sidney, Australia. Her events in this pentathlon included swimming, running, shooting, horseback riding, and fencing, all in the same day. To date, she is the only American woman ever, and the first American since 1960, to medal in that event.

Mike earned a doctorate in health communication and became a public service lawyer. He uses his skills as the chief of staff for the International Paralympic Committee based in Bonn, Germany. He is such a testimony of God's grace to us. His life also reminds us to encourage children in their abilities and desires to succeed even against the odds.

Mike Peters' visit to Agape

The Lord has a plan for each and every child. Our goal is to help them reach their God-given potential. The Lord prepared me to work with our street boys through the challenges I experienced alongside Mike.

God also gave our staff eyes to see what lies behind the vacant, hopeless expressions of a child living on the street. It's so rewarding to watch the transformation when their sense of purpose and value is restored.

The Paralympics at the Farm

My opportunity to attend the Athens 2004 Paralympic games inspired me. I thought our boys could gain a better appreciation for those athletes and a renewed sense of gratitude for their own healthy bodies if we simulated some of the events.

After we departed Greece and arrived in Kenya, we visited the farm. We had twenty-three boys in our vocational training center situated on the shore of Lake Victoria. At the time, Tom and Marg Tucker ran that arm of the ministry. The older boys who lived on-site prepared to take national exams in subjects such as carpentry, masonry, mechanics, and business. They also learned to participate in the surrounding rural community through church activities and soccer matches.

We divided into five teams and held the opening ceremonies. Each team chose a name and wore a color to represent their team. We started things out with a little parade and a hilarious water-balloon volleyball toss. Each team member tried to throw *and* catch a water balloon over the net in a beach towel. It turned out to be a great way to get things started and made us all laugh.

Other events included a beanbag toss for points, the balloon stomp (no hands), and a "blind man" leaky-bucket race. The challenge behind that game required a team member to walk in a straight line while blindfolded down to the lake with a bucket punched with holes. The teenage boys scooped up as much water as they could and then found their way back to a basin guided only by their partner's voice. Obviously, by the time they made it to the basin some of the water had leaked out. The objective – to fill the basin – required a lot of teamwork. When the whistle blew and blindfolds came off, it surprised everyone to find out who won.

After all the athletic events, we assembled. The boys and staff presented skits, songs, and speeches of gratitude for what God had given us. The closing ceremonies took place against the backdrop of a lovely sunset over the lake. We presented inexpensive shiny medallions on ribbons as rewards for each of the winning teams. By their reactions, you would have thought they were real gold and silver. The winners took on a certain swagger.

At the end of the day, we all enjoyed a delicious dinner of fresh tilapia. The day was a total success. In fact, it was such a success, the boys and staff requested we make it a yearly event.

CHAPTER 98

Scouts Surpass Expectations

In 2007, we celebrated a very special victory. Our Boy Scout troop returned from Nairobi with the first-place trophy for the National Campsite Competition. Then they went on to place second in the East Africa competition held in Uganda. That was an amazing accomplishment for a group of former street boys, but there's more to the story.

During my summer visit in 2003, the boys asked permission to form a Boy Scout troop. One of our teachers, Jairo Agalombo, agreed to lead the troop. Meanwhile, a young man in California, Torin Davey, worked on his Eagle Scout merit badge. In order to earn his badge, he helped our new troop obtain uniforms and supplies. To my surprise, the Agape boys dove right in. They assumed the name Eagle Patrol, in honor of Torin, and entered the District Campsite Competition.

For this competition, they built their own campsite, cooked their own food, and displayed their skills in first aid, knot tying, and other outdoor lore.

Erin Kerr, one of our missionary staff, reported:

"They did a phenomenal job and were so professional. They took so much pride in leading us around and showing us their creation. You should have seen the place. It reminded me of Swiss Family Robinson but without the tree. The boys thought of everything from the watchtower for their guard, to the kitchen area, and even to the placement of pit latrines. Logs and straight branches were skillfully lashed together to form furniture and appliances."

Of course, some pointed out, with tongue in cheek, that former street boys had the unfair advantage of years of outdoor living. For the district competition, they wore matching Agape T-shirts and used only the basic supplies they could gather. To everyone's surprise, they won. By the time the provincial competition took place, we had uniforms. They won again. At this point, the scoutmaster requested a uniform for himself, and rightly so, as they headed to the national competition. That year they came in third place, which was quite an accomplishment. The following year, they took top honors and brought back a beautiful shiny trophy.

Former street boys win National Scouting trophy

We built a trophy case. What a huge encouragement to all our former street boys to see a beautiful trophy in front of their school. And they weren't alone. Our overjoyed staff thanked God for His faithfulness as well. What a contrast for those boys to become winners instead of homeless children being called *chokora* (scavenger rats).

The Eagle Patrol went on to place second in the East Africa competition. Uganda came in first by a narrow margin. And Jairo was voted the best scoutmaster in East Africa. It was a great year.

The following year, 2005, wasn't so encouraging. The boys worked hard and disciplined themselves through study and rigorous practice sessions. The judges asked any questions they desired regarding the history of scouting or the campsites. The scoutmaster watched from the sidelines and wasn't allowed to participate in any way. The boys did a wonderful job and were told by observers they would surely win.

They listened with eyes full of expectation as the winners were announced, but then hope dimmed. Our troop came in fourth place. The news shocked everyone. When I asked Jairo what happened, he let out a sigh. He witnessed the judge receive a bribe. Scouting inspires good sportsmanship, so Jairo didn't protest right away. However, when he added up their points, it was clear they should have won.

Jairo issued a formal protest, which led to an investigation which took more than a year. Results of the investigation were delivered in the form of a letter from the officials. They offered a formal apology for the "mathematical error" that was made. The two judges involved in the bribe were fired, and our boys were awarded merit badges for the best school project and Scout troop in the country. The news even reached Kenyan President Moi.

The next year, we held our breath. The boys were well equipped and had confidence in their preparations. The officials rewarded them for their hard work with the first-place award in the National Campsite Competition.

In one conversation, Jairo shared with me how all the boys involved in Scouts also did well in school. He attributed this to the discipline and respect they learn through the program and said, "I would like to see more of our boys involved."

He went on to explain, "The Bible is part of their luggage. They learn what God says about respecting others, and that it's not limited to just their teachers. They also learn a good work ethic and not to expect to have things done for them."

Jairo also shared that it grew more difficult for the Eagle Patrol to win the local competitions. Three of our Scouts moved on to secondary schools and established their own troops. Now schools provided our stiffest competition. What a great problem to have.

The boys faced another challenge. They needed to create new and better ways to build their campsites, since some of their old ideas were copied by other districts, such as watchtowers and dish-drying racks. We suggested that Jairo accept this complication as a compliment and encourage his troop to continue to be creative.

Jairo assured us that Boy Scouts are viewed with much respect in the community. It might even help our future graduates obtain jobs.

I encouraged troops here in the States to get involved with our Kenyan Boy Scouts. It's a wonderful chance for boys to reach out to others their age, to broaden their worldview, and to share experiences.

CHAPTER 99

Viewpoint

One of our short-term team members, Amanda, arrived at Agape as a sixteen-year-old high school student willing to help. She graciously allowed us to use these excerpts from her journal in our newsletter. To put it into perspective, she'd never even flown before and admitted to being quite nervous about taking such a long flight. She overcame that fear by trusting in the Lord. In fact, she returned later for a second trip. We get a glimpse of the transformation she experienced from her journal.

> **January 12** (before departing): The past few days have been full of second thoughts. *What did I get myself into? Is it too late to back out? Where did all the time go?* Right now it's hard to really tell what I'm feeling. I guess I'm just trying to keep it all in so that I can trick myself into thinking that everything is going to be just fine. I hope that once I step on that plane my fears will vanish.

> **January 24-25**: I can't believe I'm actually here. The people are so beautiful … I now know the reason I stepped onto the plane. I know why I left my family to go to a land which I had only dreamed about seeing. I know now why so many people fall in love over and over again with these boys. It

is because of their spirit, their continuous joy, and their exuberant, unconditional love. They showed me Agape love … All my fears were quenched with their smiles … If only we could stop focusing on possessions, schedules, and trials, and focus on God. It would bring us so much joy and happiness. If only we would come together after supper, like the boys, and pray and sing just because we can and want to.

February 1: I realized today that I don't think these boys understand how much they mean and are truly worth … Some of these boys have been brought up in a way that can make their hearts calloused. They keep telling me that I'll forget them. I don't think that could ever happen. I don't want to leave this place.

February 7: You can see love all around here. See it while the boys interact. The older ones look after the young. The younger boys look up to the old. If one is sick, they pray. If one is happy, they pray … they pray … they pray, which is powerful enough. I never thought I'd be attached to over one hundred and twenty boys so fast. The amazing thing is that during this trip, I witnessed all the fruits of the Spirit in the lives of all those boys who were tossed aside and left unloved. I couldn't imagine going through what they have and still wearing a smile and wanting to praise God. My prayer is that everyone could at one time experience a bit of Agape love.

CHAPTER 100

Election Violence

Democratic governments are fragile entities. They depend upon the will of the people to submit to one another under the rule of law even when each constituent doesn't receive everything they wish. Kenya struggles, as do all nations, with implementing this concept so necessary to personal freedom. Therefore, each election process is approached with considerable apprehension. The 2008 elections heightened that concern. As various factions vied with each other on the political stage, ancient tribal antagonisms broke out in the streets. Chaos ruled the day.

Unfortunately, our missionaries were unwittingly caught up in the maelstrom of violence. Kisumu, the nation's third-largest city, wasn't spared. Political and ethnic violence broke out in a cycle of intensity interspersed with days of relative peace. Despite international efforts to find a peaceful political resolution to the strife tearing Kenya apart, major looting and fighting took place as the political struggle turned into ethnic, tribal hatred.

A bright light in all of the darkness was God's hand of provision and protection on Agape's children, staff, and missionaries. As many boys as possible were sent into their villages to stay with family members during the December school break, and Agape's staff stayed safely in their homes with their families during the majority of the unrest.

Later, about two-thirds of the boys returned to Agape's campus to resume school. Due to the continued violence, however, the school operated on an altered schedule in order for the staff to be able to travel to and from the school safely. The staff also asked the community children who attended Agape's school to stay home until it was safe to travel on the streets and resume their education.

Our missionaries within the country, Mike and Karen Herskowitz, Tom and Marg Tucker, and Steve and Dianne Warn, continued to work diligently with the national staff to keep the ministry moving forward. They faced huge challenges on a daily basis. Fervent prayers were continually offered for the safety of all involved. A trip across town had to be carefully planned, because at a moment's notice a group of protesters and gangs of thugs could block the street with makeshift barriers and burning tires.

Mike and Karen wrote the following during that time:

"It's very hard to put into words the emotions and experiences we have endured over the past month in Kenya. They are beyond our basic human understanding of our fellow man. Our hearts ache for the innocent, displaced people of the country. Every day we see and hear of atrocities currently taking place.

"The young men of Kenya have sought their own justice, making it worse across the nation, as politicians stand firm in their belief that they were either cheated out of the presidency or are duly elected as the president. Neighbors and friends who have worked together and lived in harmony for many years now kill each other. We have one verse that speaks to the evil raining on Kenya and why we lay our hope in Jesus. *The thief comes only to steal and kill and destroy; I have come that they may have life, and have it to the full* (John 10:10).

"Prices for virtually everything more than doubled, increasing the monthly costs of conducting ministry by six thousand dollars. The staff remained steadfastly convinced that the Lord had placed them in Kisumu for His purposes and were determined to press on as He led and guided them, moving forward with each phase of the ministry – on the streets, in the drop-in center, and at the farm.

"Finally, days of calm slowly outnumbered days of chaos, and peace returned to the land. The community of Kisumu is slowly cleaning up and rebuilding the wages of destruction. But inter-relational wounds will take much longer to heal. We continue to thank our Lord for protection of the boys, the staff, and our missionaries through this awful time."

CHAPTER 101

Leonard

I met Leonard when he was the smallest boy at Agape, but there was something different about him. His unusually shaped head looked a little too large for his small frame. His skull plates hadn't knit together as they should. Because of his deformity, his family was ashamed of him and didn't give him the proper care. He often faced ridicule and was called names like "ugly" and "stupid." As you can imagine, this rejection impacted his personality, causing him to be extremely shy. He hardly ever spoke to anyone and remained withdrawn and isolated.

But God worked a transformation in his life. He became a healthy young teenager and his growth caught up with his head size. He loved music and danced with abandon. When Agape received a donated drum set from one of our contributing churches, Leonard demonstrated an interest in the drums as the worship team played on Sunday mornings. One of our staff noticed his interest and provided an opportunity for Leonard to play the drums as therapy.

Leonard became the regular drummer for our worship team. His life has been transformed. Although he is still a little shy, he is animated. He participates and speaks with our other boys readily. In fact, he even greets our visitors. In August, a visiting team of coaches from California hosted our basketball clinic. Leonard took to basketball like a duck to water. He joined in without hesitation and developed great basketball skills. What can be more rewarding than watching this kind of progress in a child's life?

CHAPTER 102

All the Way from Romania

Gabi was a young lady from Romania. She wanted nothing more than to serve God in missions. As a student with no money, she considered herself poor. However, through an American friend, the Lord provided the funds she needed to visit Agape. Fifteen years later, she still remembers it as a personal miracle in her life. As she climbed aboard the plane in a surreal haze, she wondered if she could really be going to Africa.

Here are her thoughts upon her arrival:

"Everything was so different – people, food, weather, culture. New people came into my life. I met the boys from Agape. They were kids taken from the streets with no future, no families, kids who didn't even have what I had. Even though I came from a poor background, for the first time in my life I understood how rich I was, and that I had no reason to say I was poor.

"I learned an important lesson at that point. I was rich. It was just that I always compared my lifestyle with people in other countries. After being in Kenya for six months and seeing real poverty firsthand, God showed me how blessed

I was to be born in Romania. From that time forward, I have never dared to complain about my lifestyle again.

"It was a great opportunity for me to actually meet Mama Darla. She had such a special, kind smile. Even today, it's in my heart and inspires me to be like her. Even though we didn't spend a lot of time together, she left me with the desire to be kind like her. Kids loved her so much. I am glad to recollect images of the boys around her, just wanting to spend time with her. This is such an amazing memory for me.

"In my three months at Agape, I had great moments. I saw kids who were loved and cared for. It was such a privilege for me to share that incredible experience that changed my life and strengthened me. Through it, I learned dreams do come true. And though it's not easy, God is there, and He will take care of everything. Serving God and others is a great way to grow. But growth often comes from pain. I am so thankful for having the opportunity to serve Him and be a small part of this ministry."

Gabi is now happily married and lives in Dublin, Ireland, with her Irish husband and two adorable little girls, Holly and Jasmine.

CHAPTER 103

Dixon Mahero

Dixon

"After my mother abandoned me for a new love, all the relatives rejected me. Life became so meaningless. In fact, I wanted to run away from this world, but I didn't know where to go. I wanted to die but didn't know how to. I thought of jumping into a running train but was afraid of the pain. I wished I'd never been born, but I was alive and alone in this big world. My life was so empty and useless; my heart so dark, full of pain, and bitterness."

That was a Facebook post from Dixon Mahero, a former street boy. His life underwent a total transformation by the Lord Jesus with a little help from Agape Children's Ministry. He came to Agape as a young boy needing a place to stay and hungry for love. Dixon desired to contribute to his community. He came to me one day with a surprising request. "Mama, could we have a Scout troop?"

I never expected that from a former street boy. However, I told him we needed a sponsor. God provided in an amazing way. Dixon participated as part of our winning Eagle troop. He learned his lessons well. When Dixon went to secondary school, he helped start a new Scout troop there. His new troop became some of our toughest competition.

While he was in secondary school, Dixon started smoking. We were terribly disappointed when they asked him to leave the school and refused to let him graduate. He returned to his father's home. All of this occurred before we had a reintegration team and counselors in place. Sadly, Dixon's life took a downward spiral. We witnessed it but felt helpless to do anything about it at that point.

One day, he walked by the fence near our soccer pitch. He wanted to talk to me, and I wanted to talk to him. I asked one of our houseparents to join our conversation.

Dixon wanted to be a barber and cut hair under a tree to make a few shillings. When he acquired the basic supplies such as a razor, scissors, comb, and sterilizer, Steve Warn allowed him to cut hair at the Outreach Center. It was a win-win situation. The street boys who visited the center each week got a haircut, and Dixon earned enough shillings to have tea in his home at night.

Dixon said, "This is something I never expected to have." And now he didn't have to go to bed hungry.

As time went on, he faithfully attended Steve's Bible studies. Then the opportunity to attend Bible school presented itself. The next time I saw Dixon, he was a grown-up man in a navy-blue suit, with a white shirt, and shiny shoes. Wow! I couldn't believe my eyes. I blinked back tears of thankfulness for getting our Dixon back again.

From there, he stood on the stage and gave his public testimony to a large crowd at an outdoor evening concert organized by Stephanie Midthun. We were all so proud of him.

Currently, Dixon works with the team at Agape. They visit children on the street. Dixon writes, "I know exactly what they go through because I've been there – horrible."

He has a fantastic Facebook page which carries messages such as:

Jesus rescued me; for sure He is my Lord. Through Jesus, I see an endless hope. Endless hope or hopeless end – the choice is yours.

I want to be faithful, not famous.

If I don't make it through the night, please pass my message to the children: God is real and Jesus is the way to Him.

One of my treasured letters from Dixon states, "Mama, thank you for loving me even when I didn't deserve it." Dixon became a man any mother would be proud to claim. I understand there will be wedding bells soon, and you can be sure I'll send my most sincere congratulations.

CHAPTER 104

The Girls Home

My friend Lisa Kjeldgaard says she always wanted to go to Africa. This talented, compassionate lady, along with her husband, Erik, are the parents of eight children. They accomplished a major feat when they moved their family to Kenya for eleven months in 2012 to work with Agape. It turned into a significant experience for their family and for Agape. During that time, God drew Lisa's heart to the plight of the little girls she saw on the garbage dump as they hunted for scraps to take home to their families. This obvious need produced a call to action within Lisa's heart. So she obeyed.

After concerted prayer and research, Lisa found a house to rent and the perfect Kenyan houseparent. Lisa founded Agape Girls. What an incredible addition to the ministry. It fills a desperate need. Young girls who existed as outcasts are learning a better way to live.

Child of the One True King
by Lisa Kjeldgaard, Founder of the girl's center

How incredibly thankful I am that God's plans are always better than mine. My plans to be the next sacrificial jungle doctor held nothing to what I saw unfold before my eyes. Agape Girls opened its doors on September 5, 2012.

At first we had eight girls stay with us, some with stories so tragic that even the most stoic among you would cry and feel ill in the pit of your stomach. Girls who were discarded by family members, abused by family and strangers, and committed to children's prison without hope are now all thriving. They eagerly soaked up each lesson we taught them and many of them made professions of faith while asking hard questions about how their new faith should impact their daily decisions.

First girls' home

The girls spent their days learning to run a home, how to make Kenyan handicrafts, how to garden, and how to work diligently on their schoolwork. I couldn't be more thankful that the Lord allowed me to play a role in this exciting new work. He's blessed us with a wonderful staff of women who love Him deeply, love these hurting girls, and definitely see their jobs as a ministry.

One Saturday morning, I went to the Agape Boys campus and asked a few boys this question, "What is the worst thing you've ever been called?" The answers varied.

"Thief."

"Stupid."

"Crazy."

"Street Rat."

I wrote the words on pieces of paper and taped them to their chests. We talked about how those titles felt. Then I shared with them the beautiful truth about who they really were. We tore off those tags and replaced them with a drawn crown that declared *I am a child of the ONE TRUE KING.* It was a special and memorable moment.

Later, I went to Agape Girls. To see the beautiful faces of girls who lived in safety overwhelmed me. That God allowed me to play a role in the opening of that home is still utterly amazing to me. It was my last visit with them before coming back to the States. I flipped through my journal, and reminded them of Scriptures I shared at graduations and in some of our informal times together. I was in the process of wrapping up my random thoughts when God very clearly whispered to me to teach those girls where their identity lay.

So, as with the boys, I asked every girl to write on a piece of paper the worst thing they'd been called. The staff helped me tape the paper on each girl. I sat there stunned, surrounded by seventeen girls wearing tags that said "prostitute," "idiot," "liar," "thief," "dog," "stupid," "fool," "cursed," "rubbish," "cow," and "whore."

I boldly proclaimed that they were these things NO MORE. Those of them who had given their lives to the Lord could throw those labels away, forever. Instead, with my translator's help, I reassured them they were loved, treasured, valued, adored, and a child of the One True King. I walked to each girl, looked her in the eye, and whispered, "You are a child of the One True King."

Weight fell off the girls' shoulders. I *saw* it. As the truth washed over them, some cried, some looked away, and some whispered back, "Thank you, Mama." It was one of the most meaningful times of my entire life. I'm so incredibly thankful God allowed me to love them for Him.

Girls singing

A Girl Named Francine

by Lisa Kjeldgaard, Founder of the girl's center

"Will two thousand shillings be enough to make you go away?" I asked this of a woman who kept a shy, very ill sixteen-year-old girl as an unpaid servant. The girl had escaped and wanted to take refuge at Agape Girls.

Two days after Agape Girls opened its doors, a young girl appeared at our gate with a Kenyan friend who heard we now had a place for girls. Our friend expressed concern for the girl who had been orphaned and fending for herself in the city for a long time. The girl looked around but quickly ran off.

Three days later, she appeared at our gate, clearly afraid. We learned her name was Francine. As the staff spent time talking with Francine, we learned of the hardships she faced since she lost her parents. She endured time on the streets. Then she spent months with a bar maid where she used the only asset she had to pay her way. She ran away from that horrid situation to more time on the streets. Then she landed a "job" as a servant where she worked for food and a mat to sleep on. The sick girl needed immediate medical attention for infections that were passed on to her.

We called the woman Francine worked for and asked permission to take Francine to the doctor and for her to spend the night with us. The woman agreed, and we planned to meet the next morning. The next day, I listened for a long time to the woman defend the care she had given Francine and cringed each time she told me that Francine "belonged" to her. I couldn't take it any longer. "*Would two thousand shillings be enough to make you go away?*"

I almost couldn't believe the words that came out of my mouth. But the staff agreed that Francine needed to be saved from the situation, and my patience wore thin. The woman reluctantly agreed it would be fair compensation for the "care" she'd provided for Francine. She took the money and left, uttering just a couple threats as she went her way. Two thousand shillings was the equivalent of about twenty-three dollars.

I stood frozen as she walked out the gate. I wondered if word would get out and I'd soon have a line of people bringing me girls for pay.

Thankfully, that didn't happen. Francine quickly became a huge blessing to all of us at Agape Girls.

She took part in the first transition class we held. It was a three-week class filled with counseling sessions, life-skills classes, and much more. We tried to help the girls give up street life for lives lived to the glory of God. As I passed by that first class one day, I heard another girl ask, "If God gave us our bodies, and it's all we have, why is prostitution wrong?"

Those were the types of hard issues the social workers regularly wrestled through with the girls. I'm so thankful for each of the godly women the Lord brought my way to fill those vital roles.

When Francine finished her transition class, one of the social workers took her to find her family home. What they found was bleak. The home Francine lived in with her parents had crumbled to the ground. Her surviving grandmother lived in a shack in a village completely overtaken by witchcraft. Francine's only brother did odd jobs and had no place to live, and her only sister was believed to be in Nairobi.

By this time, Francine had watched other girls come to Agape, go through our transition class, and be happily reunited with their families. Reality hit her hard. She wouldn't have the same happy ending. We eventually located Francine's sister. After weeks of discussions, she agreed to let Francine come for a visit. Eventually, the sister agreed to offer Francine a permanent home if she had a way to earn a living.

Francine, though very bright, had missed years of school. We had been privately tutoring her, but, at sixteen, she still hadn't completed elementary school or the annual national exam necessary to attend secondary school. We encouraged Francine to choose a vocational trade, but that suggestion discouraged her. She had long envisioned becoming a nurse.

Finally, one day I sat with her. We talked about her dream to become a nurse, and I explained, "Choosing a trade now doesn't mean you can never be a nurse. You can continue your elementary school work alongside your vocational training. A trade might make it possible to work while you are in nursing school."

I laid my hand on her cheek and told her I didn't want her to leave

Agape Girls until she had a way to earn money that wasn't using her body. We both cried as she whispered, "Thank you, Mama."

Francine just completed her salon (cosmetology) training at an excellent school in Kisumu. She excelled on her exams. She has moved to Nairobi to live with her sister while she completes her attachment (internship), which will hopefully lead to employment. In her extra time, she continues to study her primary schoolwork. In November, she will return to Kisumu to take that exam. Hopefully, she will do well enough to earn a position in a secondary school. We pray for Francine as she transitions from her nine months at Agape to life with her sister.

How the Girls School Began
by Lisa Kjeldgaard, Founder of the girl's center

During the twenty-five years I spent wishing I was a missionary in Africa, not once did I picture helping open a home for street girls. My plans to adopt a bunch of darling black babies, while being the next sacrificial jungle doctor, held nothing to what I saw unfold before my eyes.

Last week a missionary found a small eight-year-old girl wandering the streets and crying. The girl told a tragic story and thankfully the missionary knew of our new home and brought her to us. Our staff loved this little girl and cared for her. The next day, when we found her home, we were excited to reunite her with the family that raised her.

Her story could have turned out very different. It's common for young lost girls to be taken into the homes of Kenyans or Asians as "house helpers." Unfortunately, the girls aren't paid or educated and are often abused. In essence, they become slaves.

If this lost little one had been fortunate enough to escape that fate, she might have ended up committed to the Remand Children's Home. One of our girls lingered in that home for two and a half years, because the staff at remand never tried to track down her family.

It turned out that the little girl we found that day ran away from home because of a petty fight with another child. She could have faced a similar situation in the Remand Children's Home. Instead, she lived safely in our care. We fed her, bathed her, braided her hair, and shared the love of Jesus before we returned her home the very next day.

God's Work at the Dump

by Lisa Kjeldgaard, Founder of the girl's center

He raises the poor from the dust and lifts the needy from the
ash heap. (Psalm 113:7)

"Scraps of bread," the outreach worker whispered. "They are look-ing for scraps of bread."

Able, Vincent, and I climbed amid the Kisumu city garbage dump one warm Saturday morning. For weeks, I passed by the dump and felt drawn to it. Early on in our time here, I told Kate that someday Agape would have a ministry on the dump. "Something is pulling me there."

We found six young girls. They all looked for bread to take home to their families so they would have something to eat that day. It painted the starkest picture I'd ever seen of the desperation that poverty triggers.

In one of those incredible ways that God works, I felt strongly that I needed to bring loaves of bread to the dump that day. The girls burst into tears when Vincent handed each of them a full loaf of bread.

Just a couple of weeks before, I boldly announced at dinner that I planned to go to the garbage dump and look for girls. The reaction from my family was predictable. My husband, Eric, stared at me with wide eyes and wondered where this wife of his had come from. My daughter Kate wanted to join me. My son Stephen immediately said, "It's the most dangerous place in Kisumu. There's no way you're going." And my son Jack started to cry, because he worried I would be hurt.

The very next morning, I received a text message telling me Able would take me to the dump on Saturday. The thing is, no one told Able of my desire. God placed it on his heart at the very same time He placed it on mine.

Able, Vincent, and Selestine, the social worker from Agape Girls, traced the homes of each of the six girls we found that day. Most of them lived with their mothers. We followed up on those moms, encouraged better protection of their daughters, and paired them with an organiza-tion in their neighborhood that would help them find ways to generate additional income for their families.

The men who spend their days scavenging on the dump insisted that the girls needed our help and shouldn't be there. We couldn't agree more.

Now, our team visits the garbage dump each week as a new component of our outreach program. We pray that the Lord will continue to show us the girls who need our help.

One of the girls we found that first day on the dump was Gracie. She lived in a horrible situation where she became a seven-year-old servant with no hope of ever attending school. Within hours, Gracie was clean, well fed, and safe at Agape Girls while we attempted to locate family members who could care for her.

Gracie gave her life to the Lord and was no longer the teary, shell-shocked girl I found that day. She became healthy and full of joy. She ran into my arms each time I walked into the Agape Girls home. God certainly rescued her.

Gracie lived with her mother and stepfather, but we searched for a more suitable home. Our social worker had Gracie hop on the back of a motorcycle, and Gracie directed them to an uncle's home. He welcomed us and turned out to be a kind man. He contacted Gracie's father who had no idea his daughter lived in such a desperate situation. Today, Gracie remains safe in her father's home.

Bursting at the Seams
by Andrea Dowell, Director of Agape Girls Center

Our staff at the Agape Girls campus learned of three children, two sisters ages eleven and six and their four-year-old little brother, who were taken to remand (juvenile hall). We knew remand was no place for those little ones, and our staff brought them to Agape Girls. The next night, one of our staff found an eleven-year-old girl wandering the streets alone, tired, dirty, and hungry. We brought all four of those children to Agape.

This presented a challenge. We only had very cramped space for sixteen beds. The four new children brought our count to nineteen.

We continue to pray the Lord will provide land and a building just down the street from our main Agape campus for a new, larger Agape Girls facility. This past month, things at Agape Girls have been eventful. Our house was bursting at the seams, and it kept us busy. Although life at Agape Girls can be a bit chaotic at times, it's always a blessing. I am challenged and encouraged daily in this role.

I had the opportunity to accompany the girls to Nyalenda, one of the slum areas in Kisumu. Once or twice a month, they walk to a home in need and participate in community service. That particular day, we travelled to the home of a very old, blind woman. She lived with a young grandson in a very poor home. The empty two-room mud home proved to be both barren and pungent. I watched the girls as they greeted the elderly blind grandmother who was in ill health. They handed her the small items we brought: bar soap for cleaning clothes, sugar, and rice.

The woman clasped each item tightly to her chest and exclaimed, "Praise Jesus! Hallelujah!" over and over and over again.

We told her, "We came to help you clean your home, your clothes, and your floors."

Silent tears rolled down her cheeks. "Praise God," she whispered. "Praise God."

Our girls got to work, without a word of complaint or a sideways glance. They washed soiled clothes and bedding. They fetched water. And some of the girls stayed and talked with the woman. The whole experience humbled me. Many of those girls came from homes much like this one. They had so little themselves, but there they were, bent over basins, walking to fetch water, and humbly serving another person in great need. What a powerful picture of the love of Jesus.

I sat in that bare room with tears in my eyes. I listened to the old lady talk and watched her raise her clasped hands in joy to God, so thankful for the answer to prayer. I was thankful too, thankful for the love of Jesus I saw poured out by Agape girls that day.

Evelyn

by Andrea Dowell, Director of Agape Girls Center

I met fourteen-year-old Evelyn my first day back at Agape Girls. She immediately stood out to me because she was about four to five months pregnant. I talked with her for a few minutes. She spoke perfect English. I continued to watch. The other girls interacted around her and I realized she was the "mother" of the girls. They always went to her for help, advice, and laughter. Evelyn served as friend and peacekeeper. But she was still only fourteen.

Events that led her to Agape Girls were filled with sadness. Evelyn persevered through many challenges with God's help. He replaced her sadness with love, peace, and hope.

At the age of two, Evelyn was separated from her parents. She wandered for a long distance before a kind woman found her. She took Evelyn in and gave her food and a place to sleep. The next day, the woman took her all around town and tried to find her family. After the search ended unsuccessfully, they reported the case to the police. The police had nowhere to house Evelyn and asked the woman to keep her while they continued to search.

Every single day, the lady and Evelyn searched for her family. She reported the case to police countless times over a period of two years. They never located her family, and the case finally went to court. The woman filed to formally adopt Evelyn, and the court accepted.

For several years, Evelyn enjoyed life with her new family. She went to school, her adoptive parents had children, and the family grew. Evelyn was a wonderful big sister. Unfortunately, the parents had marital problems and chose to separate. The mother moved back to her home area, but didn't want to move Evelyn in the middle of the school year. She asked a family friend from church if Evelyn could stay with her just until the end of the school year. The family friend agreed.

A man who lived next door to her new home came around frequently. Sadly, one night he found Evelyn alone and raped her. Evelyn told the family what happened, but they didn't believe her. It happened repeatedly and still no one believed her. Evelyn realized she must stand up for herself. So she walked to the police station and reported the case on her own. This took an unbelievable amount of courage. The police removed her from the home, took her to remand, and put the man in jail. Medical tests confirmed Evelyn was pregnant by her rapist. The news crushed Evelyn and filled her with sadness and bitterness.

We brought Evelyn to Agape Girls Center in November 2013. The staff helped her overcome the many challenges she faced in her young life. Over time, she discovered her identity in Christ. She understood that even though people in her life had abandoned, abused, and disappointed her, God would never leave her. She learned about God's everlasting love and about the difficulty and importance of forgiveness. They also taught her ways to cope with the trauma she experienced. Evelyn stayed at Agape Girls for three months. During that time, an incredible amount of change took place in her heart.

One of the most important ways Agape Girls supported Evelyn was when they stood alongside her in court as she told her story and faced her rapist. We supported her as she bravely made her voice heard. Although that difficult experience was filled with tears and deep emotion, Evelyn shared with us that her fight for justice helped her heal. Her strength blew me away.

In February 2014, the court allowed Evelyn to leave Agape Girls and move back home with her adopted parents. Evelyn and her adoptive mother cried tears of joy when they were reunited.

Together, the family kept the baby, and Evelyn returned to school. We continued to visit Evelyn's family until the baby arrived.

Evelyn continues to heal emotionally, and it will be a lifelong process. Through God's power, Evelyn was transformed into who she is today. We are blessed to know this strong and courageous girl, and blessed that God allowed the Agape Girls staff to walk alongside her.

Rebecca

by Andrea Dowell, Director of Agape Girls Center

Rebecca's sweet smile and laughter were absolutely infectious. If you looked at this beautiful girl, you would never have known the incredibly difficult life she lived. The weight of life's burdens no longer showed on her face. Rebecca experienced more in her young twelve years than anyone should. But God watched over and protected her throughout her childhood and brought her out of a terrible situation.

Rebecca arrived at Agape Girls Center right after it opened. She came to us from remand, the Kenyan juvenile detention center. Children sometimes stay at remand for years as they wait to find a way back home. That's what happened to Rebecca. When we found her in 2012 at remand, she had been there over two and a half years. That's longer than any other girl.

When we met her, hate and anger filled Rebecca's heart, and a permanent scowl etched her face.

The remand staff said, "Rebecca's been that way throughout her years here. She won't tell any of her life story."

No one knew her history before remand because she refused to share it with anyone. Through Friday Bible studies with the girls at remand, Hellen, the manager of Agape Girls, got to know Rebecca. After the Agape Girls Center opened in September 2012, we brought Rebecca to stay with us.

Hellen poured her love into Rebecca's life. She encouraged, shared, and talked with her daily. Eventually Rebecca opened up and shared some of her story. Hellen discovered Rebecca's history to be very traumatic. Both of her parents died when she was very young. After they died, a man abducted Rebecca from her home at age seven and sexually abused her. That man even changed Rebecca's second name to make it appear she was from a different tribe and area. He held Rebecca for a year until she found a chance to run away. Eventually, authorities rescued her and took her to the Kisi Remand. She spent over a year at Kisi Remand before they transferred her to the Kisumu Remand. She became very closed off and refused to tell anyone where she came from or anything about her history.

It took Hellen's love to help Rebecca open up. After she shared her story, Rebecca told Hellen that she remembered just one word from the name of her old school. Hellen believed she knew where the school was located. Together, they traveled there. After hours in a crowded van and more hours on a motorcycle, they found the school. Old women from the village were brought in to help when the school heard Rebecca's story. One of the women recognized her. They took Hellen and Rebecca to the home of Rebecca's stepsister, who still lived in the area. The stepsister couldn't care for Rebecca, but she provided directions to the area where Rebecca's father's family lived. Both of her parents were buried there.

Hellen and Rebecca traveled to the paternal home area. There, they found Rebecca's half brother. He also was unable to allow Rebecca to come and stay with him. Hellen asked about any other relatives who might let the child come live with them. No one provided help immediately, but Hellen left her phone number with the family and returned to Agape Girls with Rebecca.

Months later, the half brother called Hellen and gave her the phone number of Rebecca's biological brother. Hellen followed up immediately. Soon, other family members called, delighted to learn that Rebecca was alive. An uncle and aunt were especially excited and insisted Rebecca come and live with them.

When the uncle and aunt came to Agape to meet Rebecca, it turned out to be a very happy reunion. Rebecca now had a family, one that loved her and cared for her and wanted her to live with them. After such a long list of tragic events, Rebecca finally had some security and went to live with her aunt and uncle.

Agape staff continued to visit Rebecca once a month to check in on her family. She continued to thrive in her stable environment, and was happy to be back in school. During the Agape staff visits, the family shared how grateful they were that Agape brought them together. Even after such a traumatic beginning, Rebecca now had hope. The permanent scowl once fixed on her face was replaced with her sweet smile. God did some amazing work in Rebecca's life. Out of a hopeless situation, He brought hope.

Recently, Agape Girls held its fiftieth transition class graduation since opening in September 2012. Transition class is a curriculum developed at Agape to help street children learn more about God and about themselves.

As one of our transition teachers explained, "The curriculum was designed to smooth the rough street edges off of the children and prepare them to go back home and better handle problems they face in the future."

Through the curriculum, the children learn about God and His love for each individual. The curriculum encourages positive character traits like honesty, obedience, and respect. Each child goes through group counseling sessions designed to help them recognize ways they experienced hurt in their lives. Then they're shown how to deal with those emotions in a positive way and are encouraged to allow God to start the process of healing their hearts. The class also teaches valuable life skills such as how to avoid negative peer pressure and develop appropriate male/female relationships.

Through the three-week curriculum, we watch each child transform in amazing ways as they learn more about themselves and come to understand how much God truly loves them.

In the past twenty-two months, God blessed us with the opportunity to walk alongside 139 girls as they went through the transition class. Praise God! We are so thankful for the many lives He has forever changed at Agape Girls.

Girls study beneath photos of reintegrated girls on wall

Special Circumstances and Special Needs

by Andrea Dowell, Director of Agape Girls Center

One night, I came across a note written on a half-sheet of paper stapled to the back of a counseling report for a thirteen-year-old girl at the center. I'll call her Mary. Mary made some big mistakes in her life and hurt many of her family members deeply by her actions. She displayed disobedience and disrespect. Her actions truly hurt nearly everyone who ever reached out to try and help her. She ran away from every home that took her in with loving arms. On top of all this, she lied to, stole from, and falsely accused family members of things that never happened. Most recently, she ran away from her grandmother's house, the only family member left who hadn't given up on her yet.

Hellen saw through all of Mary's actions. She knew and understood something deeply emotional and painful was going on underneath all of this behavior. Something caused Mary to act out with so much hatred and anger.

Over time, with lots of love and counseling, Hellen built a foundation of trust. Mary opened up to Hellen and shared more and more of her story. She revealed information about her parents who died when she was little. She included memories of the life she knew when her parents were alive and how she felt so vulnerable and alone because they weren't here anymore.

Finally, she shared the root of her bitterness – the thing that filled her with rage and anger. She was born with HIV. Yes, she was very angry, and, really, I thought her anger was healthy at that point.

Hellen walked with Mary through every step. She helped her process the death of her parents, the reality of her status, and the reason she refused to take her medication (antiretroviral therapy). Together, they worked on Mary's incredible emotional issues. Slowly, she started to heal.

Finally, one Friday, our staff took Mary home to stay with her grandmother. They accompanied Mary to help her ask for forgiveness from her grandmother for her previous bad behavior and to help reconcile that relationship.

Before she left, Mary handed Hellen the note I found stapled to the back of the counseling report. Translation:

Now that I have come back to my senses, I want to go back home and these are the things I would like to do.

1. I would go back to school and learn extra hard so I can catch up with others.

2. I will obey my grandmother in everything she tells me.

3. I will be always thankful for the staff at Agape Girls.

4. I won't let Satan misuse (trick) me to run away again.

5. I will be praying and praising God every time I go to sleep.

6. I will seek advice from people who can help.

7. I will throw down all my heavy loads that I have been carrying on my head.

Mary arrived on our doorstep. Literally. She ran away from her home hours away, came to Kisumu, and found her way to our gate. I have no idea how she found out about us, but she did. She knocked on our door. And now, she was ready to go home. It's nothing short of a miracle.

We took her home and followed up with her weekly for a while to make sure things were stable, and walked with her through little missteps along the way. We continued to counsel and encourage her and her family.

That little half-sheet of paper brought me a world of blessings. That is Agape. Thank you, Mary. Stay home.

Reasons Jesus praised the two Marys in Scripture:

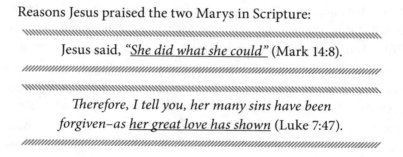

Jesus said, *"She did what she could"* (Mark 14:8).

Therefore, I tell you, her many sins have been forgiven–as her great love has shown (Luke 7:47).

A second young woman I'd like to mention is Hilda – a very sweet young woman who brought me so much joy. At fifteen, Hilda had never stepped foot into a classroom. Her circumstances robbed her of that opportunity. Instead, she wandered around the city, a very dangerous activity for an innocent, special-needs young woman. Her family was unable to keep track of her.

When she arrived at Agape, we thought she was non-communicative.

She refused to talk, sing, dance, or play. She just sat and watched. Day after day, she remained withdrawn. But God changed that. She blossomed over time. The staff saw how bright Hilda really was and looked for a chance for her to go to a school for children with special needs. She was offered the chance to join a boarding school in town. They work specifically with children with autism. It is an incredible opportunity, and we know Hilda will absolutely thrive there.

Today, Hilda talks non-stop and loves to just sing and praise God. She dances with enthusiasm and loves to laugh.

These are just two examples of some of the extra-special children Agape has been privileged to work with.

Joy

by Andrea Dowell, Director of Agape Girls Center

In July 2013, as we were in the States to raise support to return to Kisumu full time, a fourteen-year-old girl (I'll call her Joy) was brought to Agape Girls Center. On average, a girl stays on campus for about two or three months as she works through rehabilitation programs. But this case wasn't average. When we arrived in Kisumu six months later, Joy was still at Agape and far from ready for reintegration. Her background full of traumatic experiences wouldn't be fully uncovered for months.

As a painfully shy and withdrawn teen, Joy refused to open up in counseling, share her story, or socialize. She only spoke a few words each day. But over time and with the right tools, our counselors finally uncovered Joy's past wounds which still deeply affected her. Finally, she shared her story and started the process of healing. It took months, but we saw Joy start to heal after a year at Agape. For a variety of reasons, it wasn't possible to find a family member for Joy to live with.

Our head teacher, Ann, stepped forward and asked to be allowed to foster Joy. She and her husband felt God called them to be Joy's family. So, seventeen months after her arrival, Joy went home. Over the next few months, we were ecstatic to hear Joy excelled in school and thrived at home. Then around the first week of March, we received a text from Ann. Joy had run away from home early that morning and hadn't gone to school. She couldn't be found.

It left Ann terrified. "She's in danger!" she said. She knew the city wasn't a safe place for young girls to wander alone.

Jonathan quickly arranged a search party with staff members. All morning they talked with Joy's friends, teachers, and neighbors. They reported her case to the chief and police station. They searched the slums of Kisumu. They returned at lunchtime empty-handed. After lunch, Jonathan and Ann went out to search again and spent hours walking from house to house.

It broke my heart to see Ann ask everyone she could if they had seen her daughter. Worry lined her face. Nightfall came and still no sign of Joy. The danger level climbed. We reached out to friends and family in the U.S. and asked them to pray for God's hand of protection on Joy, and that He would bring her home safely. The night grew darker and darker, and our hopes fell lower and lower. We kept praying.

Finally, at 10:30 p.m. the text message came in. A woman found Joy asleep on the ground in a market. The woman returned her to Jonathan and Ann. She was home and safe. God is good and He is faithful. He hears our cries. Even when we've given up hope, He is there.

The next day Joy visited campus and asked for forgiveness for running away. Tears spilled down her cheeks as she heard about the hundreds of people she had never met who prayed for her safety. She had no idea how many people loved her even without meeting her. After she talked with counselors, the campus pastor, houseparents, and social workers, she spent the afternoon being warmly greeted, loved, and encouraged.

That's what she needed in that moment – LOVE. And, that's what she received. So why the search party for one girl? We have seventy kids on campus who need counseling, teaching, love, and support. We have new kids run away or jump the fence each week. Why pound the pavement for Joy?

Jesus' parable of the shepherd searching for one lost sheep offers a beautiful illustration. He left ninety-nine to look for one. Jesus does that for us. And this girl had been through enough. She survived more than anyone should have to. She needed to feel love. God used the experience to show her she was worth being searched for, and that she needed to be picked up and carried back home. We don't do this for many runaways.

But Joy, in that moment, needed more than most. And through it all, God protected her and then He lovingly carried her back home.

Expansion

Agape Children's Ministry started with a handful of faith and a little obedience to the Lord. We had no idea what lay ahead or if Agape would even be able to survive. In fact, like a desperate adoptive mother, I tried on several occasions to pass this project on to organizations which were well established.

But a very wise gentleman chided me for that, saying, "Darla, the Lord gave you the vision, so you must take good care of it. Don't give your vision to someone who will change it."

My friend Donna Sundblad added to that concept by saying, "We should join God in what He is blessing, not ask Him to bless what we are doing."

God made it crystal clear that He intended to bless Agape in order to free more of Kenya's children from the streets. It's mind-boggling to think there used to be close to one thousand children in the streets of Kisumu and now there are only seventy-three under the age of sixteen. Forty of them have been to Agape previously and have chosen to return to street life, meaning only thirty-three new children were found for Agape to rescue in a recent research report. This is mainly due to Agape's work with reintegration.

So now what? Agape has such an experienced and devoted staff, we can't waste this treasure. We have a practical and effective counselling program. Our reintegration team works like bloodhounds to track down families and keep the children connected to them. We have missionaries who love the children and this ministry enough to consider Kenya their home. It's like a sponge so full of water (or blessings) that it can't hold anymore. The only thing we can do is squeeze it out and let it splash onto another dry area. We are called to bless others with the blessings we've been given.

Mr. George Nyorka from SOS Children's Villages said, "Street life is dirty, violent, and short."

We know this is not God's plan. Left to the streets, these children will undoubtedly die young or grow up to be the thugs of the future. And that's why Agape intervened. Because of the success we've experience and the model we've developed, we are considering an expansion of the ministry into the city of Kitale.

Luke 12:48 says, *From everyone who has been given much, much will be required ; and from the one who has been entrusted with much, much more will be asked.*

CHAPTER 105

The Anything

I read *Kisses from Katie* by Katie Davis. What a treat. It reminded me of my own experience in Uganda in 1987 shortly after the civil war ended. Those were horrific days for Ugandan families. Thousands of children had been abducted by the National Resistance Army. So many people lost their lives that human skulls were piled in mounds in the rural areas of the Luwero Triangle. That area also came to be known as the "Killing Fields of Uganda."

As we drove by the gruesome sight, I asked why the skulls hadn't been buried.

The reply was, "No one knows who they belonged to, so local families don't know what to do." We were on our way to the children's home sponsored by an organization then known as Ambassadors of Aid. (They changed their name when so much attention was focused on HIV/AIDS. It misrepresented their work with children.)

I learned a lot in Luwero, and loved the rural setting with such faith-filled people who had suffered so much. In fact, I told the Lord I would do *anything* for those children. Many were left orphans. One downside to life there, however, was a lack of facilities. No electricity, no running water, and no bathrooms – only latrines.

I had already learned how to bathe standing in a large plastic washbasin while I poured a pitcher of water over my head. I quickly washed my hair and face and then used the water in the basin for everything else. It's quick, especially if the water is cold, and it works.

Much of what they accept as normal wouldn't even be considered in the Western world, but their ingenuity meets needs. For example, it always made me smile to see the five-gallon containers of water capped off with a green banana. You have to find one that's just the right size, but it works. The latrines were in a different category altogether. They were located out back and at a lower elevation than the rest of the buildings.

The children needed something to do and I was a novelty, so they followed me everywhere I went. The latrines were old and that made it difficult to keep them clean. The little bugs and insects enjoyed life in that dark, moist place. The latrine crawled with things like blue bottle flies, cockroaches, mosquitoes, plus more than a few spiders. The doors fell from their hinges from age and use. They just leaned against the opening.

The first time I went down to the latrines, a half-dozen curious little friends escorted me. They took a seat on the embankment and covered their mouths as they chatted with each other. Since all children laugh in the same language, I knew a "tee-hee" when I heard one.

I had a choice to make. I could either go in and cover the opening with the door so the kids couldn't watch what I was doing, or leave it open enough to see where the creepy crawlies were. Fortunately, I remembered to stuff some tissue in my pocket. I choose the latter, but while I was there, I exclaimed out loud, "Lord, *this* is the anything I said I would do."

While we stayed in Luwero, we slept on the floor of a bullet-ridden, dirty-walled room with an impure water supply, poor food, and only a few people who understood our language. It all caused me to think about what life would be like if everything I had was taken away. What if I lost family, friends, belongings, safety, and my health, just like Job? The visible suffering all around me made the concept easier to imagine.

I saw more clearly how the most important thing, the core of our existence, is our relationship with God. When everything else falls away and that's all that's left, it is enough. Second Corinthians 12:9 says, *My grace is sufficient for you.* It's our foundation. Religion is not a crutch as some people believe. Instead, all the other things we fill our lives with become the actual crutches. We prop ourselves up and believe we are secure. It becomes easier to leave God out of our lives as we value being self-sufficient. But our love for the Lord and the resulting love for one another is the only true basis for happiness. I hope I never forget that lesson.

CHAPTER 106

Se Afrique

Se Afrique ("This is Africa") became the right thing to say on multiple occasions while in Kenya. Used to our fast-paced way of life in America, we definitely encountered frustrations. Thankfully, time sifted out the memory of those frustrations and left behind a residue of good humor. Here are a few fun stories for you to enjoy.

I committed to make an airline reservation for my friend Andrea's trip from Kisumu to Nairobi. I attempted the task a second time after not getting through the first time. After numerous tries over a period of an hour, resulting only in busy signals, a man answered and told me to call a different number. I tried the new number. Also busy. I waited awhile and tried again. At that point, I learned the new number was "not going." In other words, it was out of order. I received a third number and tried it with bated breath. A man answered. He said, "We have a flight at six in the evening."

With a huge sigh of relief, I gave him the information he asked for. Then he remembered it was Wednesday. "There are no flights on Wednesdays. Sorry." Click. Just like that, the call ended. Ugh! *I didn't have to pull my hair out, because it was falling out on its own!*

Phones weren't the only frustration. Interaction with the government presented many challenges too. For instance, a decree from the government required everyone in Kenya to have a pin number in order to get car insurance. I dutifully went to an office to apply for my pin number. Everyone tried to get their pin number at the same time. This created another problem. It took about six months for mine to come from Nairobi.

In the meantime, I still had to drive around town. Fortunately, I kept my application in the glove box. Despite driving the speed limit in a residential area, a matronly policewoman flagged me down. She wore a police hat, white cotton blouse, navy-blue skirt, white bobby socks, and black walking shoes. She clutched a clipboard with a pen attached as she approached my car. Her body language let me know she took her official duty seriously. Without a word, she walked slowly around my car and looked at each sticker on the windshield. At one point, I thought I saw a faint smile on her lips. She continued her search around the back of the car. Then she came up to the window and tapped forcefully. As I rolled it down, she blurted out, "Where is your pin numba?"

I replied meekly that mine hadn't arrived yet and opened the glove box. When I pulled out the application copy and showed it to her, she studied it carefully. Then she folded it up, handed it back to me, and declared, "Well, don't let me catch you again. Next time I won't have so much mercy."

What! I pulled back onto the road scratching my head but thankful for mercy.

Another time, I delivered keys to a friend who had a guard stationed at his gate. The sun had set, and since it was raining, I planned to hand the keys over and run back to the car. However, my friend insisted I come in for a moment to get out of the rain. I accepted the invitation and stayed just long enough for a brief chat.

When I returned to my car, I noticed the passenger door slightly ajar. To my horror, my purse was missing with my driver's license, a new roll of pictures, sunglasses, and my wallet. It was about 8:00 p.m. and still raining. The only one around was the guard. He didn't see a thing. *Sigh*.

Days went by, and I received a message from the police station. Someone found my license in the mud with the photo missing. The finder turned it in, which showed kindness. When I took it to the

Kenyan DMV, they explained I needed a photo. Feeling well prepared, I produced a copy of my passport photo.

The lady informed me, "You must have it stamped."

"Okay, please go ahead and stamp it. I can pay for that."

She looked up and said, "But I don't have a stamp."

So I asked the obvious. "How do I get a stamp?"

"You have to get one in Nairobi," she stated in a matter-of-fact tone.

My mind raced. *Nairobi is a full day's drive from Kisumu and gas is expensive.* I hesitated but finally asked, "Excuse me. What will happen if I drive all the way to Nairobi without a stamped license and get stopped at a police checkpoint?"

She thought for a moment before replying. "Well, you don't have to go today." She closed the window. *Se Afrique!*

Another time, I had never seen the Indian Ocean and wanted to go to the coast in Mombasa. Sally France and I had a few days to travel, so off we went. However, Sally urgently needed to mail a letter. As soon as we reached the hotel, we stopped at a booth to buy stamps. A pretty African lady stood behind the glass case. The stamps were neatly lined up according to value. Sally confidently pointed to the stamp she needed and asked to buy it.

The lady shook her head and said, "I can't sell you that stamp."

Sally stood there with the correct change in her hand as she explained how she needed to mail her letter. She finished by asking, "Why can't you sell the stamp?"

The lady looked at her sweetly. "That's my last one. If I sell it to you, I won't have anymore."

Yes, she was serious and refused to sell the stamp. Poor Sally. Se Afrique!

People in different cultures see things through different lenses. For instance, some hardworking Maasai ladies made beaded necklaces, which were very popular with the tourists. Because they sold so quickly, the Maasai ladies stopped making that particular design. It frustrated them to spend the time and then have them disappear so quickly. So what should you say? "Se Afrique!"

Some Favorite Photos and Quotes

God has taught me much, blessed me much, and He isn't done with me yet. In closing, I'd like to leave you with some favorite thoughts and quotes which have come in handy during rocky times. Some may be thought-provoking, others are just for fun!

Boys preparing dinner

When something bad happens, you have three choices. You can either let it define you, let it destroy you, or let it strengthen you.

No better place to sleep

"To put a different spin on an old adage, Jesus knows that suffering needs company." *He Understands Me* by Tommy Walker

First buildings with help from Lions Club

Trust in the Lord and He will give you the desires of your heart. Where did those desires come from in the first place?

Cook preparing lunch in primitive kitchen

Lord, if I can't do great things, help me
do small things in a great way.

Sick street boys outside Agape clinic

Bread donations kept us going

If *Plan A* doesn't work, the alphabet
has twenty-five more letters.

Family photo at first Agape home

Boys at Agape church

Courage is not the absence of fear, but the
conquering of it through faith.

New school building

Agape teacher and her students

Kenyan staff and students

People don't care how much you know,
until they know how much you care.

Learning to ride unicycle on Agape compound

Father and son reunited

Tutoring new boys

"To work with street children, one must have the
heart of a dove, the skin of a rhino, and the patience
of a Tibetan monk." Anonymous African man

Agape boys sing at a wedding

You don't need a reason to help people.

Snack time at the Outreach Center

Mom and son reunited

Paul helping boy with sidewalk

"I built you with one central need, and that
is to be accepted and loved. And loved you
are!" *A God Thought* by Tommy Walker

Darla and Daniel at street church

"Why me? Why would God choose me to do this?
But as I think through my life, I see how blessed
and loved I have been. I think it is only normal
that God would ask, even require, me to share this
love with others who may not know it."
– Katie, in *Kisses from Katie*

Street boy in park

Now-healthy former street boys

Children all smile in the same language.

Epilogue

When We Listen by Deborah Hobbs

We are blessed to bless others.

Every individual experiences a moment in life (more than one, if we are listening) when their lives are completely and forever changed. Some call it a defining moment, some call it a turning point, and others refer to it as a wake-up call. I believe these are the times, few and far between, when we actually answer God's call instead of letting Him go to voice mail. Such a moment occurred for me when I heard Darla relate the story of how she struggled to start a ministry to street children. She wondered where she would find the available resources.

God used a young African girl to touch her heart with a simple message: "Mama, all you need is three stones and a pan." From the moment I heard Darla's story about how God provides our every need in life, my life was forever and gloriously changed.

How to Win a Street Boy's Trust

Introduce yourself. Then joke with him and smile. Ask his name in a happy mood.

Treat him like he is someone special.

Disregard his glue habit and its offensive odor.

Ask a friendly question.

When he replies, look at him like you're really interested.

Listen well.

Tell him what you heard him say in your own words.

Say encouraging words.

Trust him and accept him.

He will probably offer to shake hands. Use your alcohol sterilizer only when street children are completely out of sight. Otherwise, you send a message that makes them feel like lepers.

When you say good-bye, tell him you hope you'll see him again.

It's better not to give him something unless you are by yourself or have enough for a bunch of kids. Others might come, and not having enough becomes a fight about to happen.

Remember that saying "maybe" you'll do something sounds like a promise to him.

Give him hope. Your kind words are like a cool drink of water to a thirsty soul.

Meet the Author

Darla was eight years old when she opened her heart to Jesus at a Vacation Bible School. Six years later she received a compelling nudge from the Holy Spirit when she heard a missionary speaker at a Christian camp. From that point on, her goal was to become a medical missionary.

After twenty years of growing in life experiences, raising three sons, and working as a registered nurse, Darla had the opportunity to travel to Kisumu, Kenya, with a community development team. While learning the local tribal language, she became acquainted with many of the street boys and was touched by the tragedy of their lives. As a result, Agape Children's Ministry was founded with a leap of faith in 1993.

The ministry has grown by God's grace beyond all expectations. To date, over two thousand children have been rescued from the streets. Agape specializes in reintegrating street boys and girls with their families. Currently, more than ten thousand annual home visits are made by Agape's staff to ensure a good adjustment. This sets Agape Children's Ministry apart as a unique organization in Kenya.

Please visit www.agapechildren.org
for updates from our ministry

All proceeds from book sales are committed
to Agape Children's Ministry

Meet the Coauthor

Donna Sundblad spent her first twelve years of marriage without Christ and held various jobs while she raised her children. In the late '70s, she and her husband owned and operated a record store and developed friendships with some of their regular customers. Donna and her husband didn't own a Bible, but a customer changed that when he gave them an extra Bible he had on hand. This started their quest for truth, which took another four years.

As Donna approached age fifty, she felt the Lord ask, *When are you going to use the gift I've given you?* That gift was her ability to write, and she knew it. She'd allowed the busyness of life to push writing aside … until she had time.

So when the Lord asked her that question, it caught her attention.

What am I waiting for? she asked herself. *Am I waiting till I'm seventy?*

To obey God's call on your life is not something to put off. She responded by taking classes to refresh and hone her skills. Soon, she found herself published and working as an editor for a small publisher. Today, she is a published author, editor, and ghostwriter. Her most recent novel, *The Inheritance*, is a spiritual allegory about a young man's quest for truth and his journey through the Valley of Shadow.

At such a time as this, the Lord brought these two women of faith together to bring you this story of how Jesus is at work among the street children in Kenya.

Other Similar Titles By

"Don't waste your pain," says unlikely missionary Avis Goodhart. She didn't – and neither should you.

Despite a background of childhood abuse, dyslexia, and marital infidelity, Avis took her first international mission trip at age fifty. The church, school, and orphanage she later founded in northern Peru, all products of both her pain and her radical obedience to the Lord, have brought thousands of others out of the dust. This compelling story of an ordinary woman who serves God in extraordinary ways will challenge, inspire, and empower you to:

- Eliminate excuses from your life

- Recognize that in God's kingdom, availability matters more than ability

- Allow your pain to produce – not prevent – your obedience

- Serve the Lord with the same abandon shown by one unlikely missionary

Available where books are sold

Do you ever sell yourself short? That's what Katherine Hines did before she realized she was selling God short. After years of tragedies, Katherine learned that God could do more in her life than she ever imagined if she trusted Him and believed. She discovered that He wants to change lives through us and bless us in the process. Whoever we are, wherever we came from, God can use us to make a difference in someone's life.

Katherine's story begins with tragedies, but God touched her heart at a crusade and led her to Uganda as a missionary to the children. Leaving her prestigious job and home, she went to a land of mud huts and polluted water. In the midst of sickness and poverty, she loved and cared for the orphans of the war-torn country, as she faced witch doctors and Muslim agitators. Katherine shares her life story to help us know that we can all make a difference – if only we let God . . .

Available where books are sold

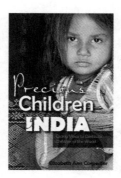

Children around the world live in dire conditions without even the basic necessities of water, food, shelter, and love. They often suffer in silence, struggling just to exist among the unexplainable and irreversible conditions in which they find themselves. Many are so young they do not know what they lack – the love of a family and the comfort of a home. Survival is their only concern as they grow up in a world of adults who seem to have forgotten them or are so busy with their own survival that they really do not have time to care.

These first person narratives are compiled from conversations with dozens of boys and girls in India. They put a voice to the suffering that they and thousands more like them endure every day. Children bravely share their stories of being caste bound, trafficked, beggars, witnesses to murder, unwanted, and of suffering great loss. Each child is a witness to his or her own story of survival. From their voices can be heard the desperate plea for someone to care, and if not for themselves, then for those even less fortunate whose voices have not been heard.

Available where books are sold